Gender and Family Issues in the Workplace

Gender and Family Issues in the Workplace

Francine D. Blau
Ronald G. Ehrenberg
editors

Russell Sage Foundation
New York

The Russell Sage Foundation

The Russell Sage Foundation, one of the oldest of America's general purpose foundations, was established in 1907 by Mrs. Margaret Olivia Sage for "the improvement of social and living conditions in the United States." The Foundation seeks to fulfill this mandate by fostering the development and dissemination of knowledge about the country's political, social, and economic problems. While the Foundation endeavors to assure the accuracy and objectivity of each book it publishes, the conclusions and interpretations in Russell Sage Foundation publications are those of the authors and not of the Foundation, its Trustees, or its staff. Publication by Russell Sage, therefore, does not imply Foundation endorsement.

Library of Congress Cataloging-in-Publication Data

Gender and family issues in the workplace/
Edited by Francine D. Blau and Ronald G. Ehrenberg.
    p.   cm.
    Papers presented at a conference held in April 1995 at the New York State School of Industrial and Labor Relations, Cornell University.
    Includes bibliographical references and index.
    ISBN 0-87154-117-3 (cloth)   ISBN 0-87154-122-X (paperback)
    1. Working mothers—Congresses.   2. Married women—Employment—Congresses.   3. Work and family—Congresses.   I. Blau, Francine D.
II. Ehrenberg, Ronald G.
HQ759.48.G47   1997
306.874'3—dc21   96-46510
                                  CIP

Text design by Suzanne Nichols.

RUSSELL SAGE FOUNDATION
112 East 64th Street, New York, New York 10021
10 9 8 7 6 5 4 3 2 1

Contents

Contents

Contributors

Francine D. Blau is Frances Perkins Professor of Industrial and Labor Relations at Cornell University and research associate of the National Bureau of Economic Research in Cambridge, Massachusetts. At Cornell University, she is also research director of the School of Industrial and Labor Relations, director of the Institute for Labor Market Policy, faculty associate of the Cornell Employment and Family Careers Institute, and affiliate of the Women's Studies Program.

Ronald G. Ehrenberg is the Irving M. Ives Professor of Industrial and Labor Relations and Economics and director of the Cornell Higher Education Research Institute. He is also research associate at the National Bureau of Economic Research and is president-elect of the Society of Labor Economists.

Barbara R. Bergmann writes on social policy issues. Her latest book is *Saving Our Children From Poverty: What the United States Can Learn from France* (Russell Sage Foundation).

Rebecca M. Blank is dean of the School of Public Policy and Henry Carter Adams Collegiate Professor of Public Policy at the University of Michigan, Ann Arbor.

Ileen A. DeVault is associate professor of labor history in the School of Industrial and Labor Relations, Cornell University.

Paula England is professor of sociology at the University of Pennsylvania. She is also research associate of the Population Studies Center and an affiliate of the Women's Studies Program.

Marianne A. Ferber is professor emerita of economics and women's studies at the University of Illinois, Urbana-Champaign.

Claudia Goldin is professor of economics at Harvard University. She is also director of the Program on the Development of the American Economy at the National Bureau of Economic Research.

Jonathan Gruber is professor of economics at the Massachusetts Institute of Technology.

Marjorie Honig is professor of economics at Hunter College and the Graduate School of the City University of New York. She is also chair of the Department of Economics at Hunter College.

Lawrence F. Katz is professor of economics at Harvard University and research associate at the National Bureau of Economic Research.

Jacob Alex Klerman is a senior economist at RAND in Santa Monica, California, and a member of the faculty of RAND Graduate School.

Renee M. Landers is deputy general counsel in the U.S. Department of Health and Human Services.

Arleen Leibowitz is professor in the Department of Policy Studies at the University of California-Los Angeles School of Public Policy and Social Research and consultant at RAND in Santa Monica, California.

Janice Fanning Madden is the Robert C. Daniels Term Professor of Urban Studies, Regional Science, Sociology, and Real Estate at the University of Pennsylvania.

Olivia S. Mitchell is the International Foundation of Employee Benefit Plans Professor of Insurance and Risk Management and executive director of the Pension Research Council at the Wharton School, University of Pennsylvania.

H. Elizabeth Peters is an associate professor in the Department of Policy Analysis and Management at Cornell University.

Solomon W. Polachek is distinguished professor of economics at the State University of New York, Binghamton. He is also dean of Harpur College of Arts and Sciences.

James B. Rebitzer is Tracy Carleton Professor of Economics at the Weatherhead School of Management, Case Western Reserve University.

Cordelia W. Reimers is professor of economics at Hunter College and the Graduate School of the City University of New York.

Donna S. Rothstein is research economist at the U.S. Bureau of Labor Statistics in the Office of Employment Research and Program Development.

Christopher J. Ruhm is Jefferson-Pilot Excellence Professor of Economics at the University of North Carolina-Greensboro. He is also research associate at the National Bureau of Economic Research.

Myra H. Strober is professor of education and affiliated professor of economics at Stanford University.

Lowell J. Taylor is professor of economics at the H. John Heinz III School of Public Policy and Management, Carnegie Mellon University.

Jackqueline L. Teague is research economist in the Center for Economics Research at Research Triangle Institute.

Jane Waldfogel is associate professor of social work and public affairs at the Columbia University School of Social Work and research associate at the Centre for Analysis of Social Exclusion at the London School of Economics.

Michael Waldman is Charles H. Dyson Professor of Management and professor of economics at the Johnson Graduate School of Management, Cornell University.

Acknowledgments

The papers in this volume are based on a conference held at Cornell University's New York State School of Industrial and Labor Relations in April 1995. We are grateful to the School's Institute for Research on Labor Market Policy and to the Russell Sage Foundation for funding this conference. We are also indebted to Richard Shore and Pat Dickerson for their extremely able staff work in organizing the conference, to Janet Marler for her help during the conference, and to Brenda Lapp for her highly efficient assistance to us in communicating with the authors and the publisher in preparing this volume.

FRANCINE D. BLAU
RONALD G. EHRENBERG

Chapter 1

Introduction

Francine D. Blau and Ronald G. Ehrenberg

One of the most striking labor market developments since World War II has been the dramatic growth in the labor force participation of women. Between 1940 and 1995, women workers increased from one quarter to nearly one half (46 percent) of the labor force. The sharp rise in married women's participation in work outside the home that has spurred the expansion in the female labor force has caused a "subtle revolution" in gender roles in the family and in the larger society. While in 1940, 86 percent of married women were full-time homemakers, by 1994, 61 percent were in the paid labor force (see Goldin 1990).[1] Initially, it was older married women (over age 35) who were drawn into the labor force. Given the fertility patterns of the time, they tended to have school-age or grown children. One of the most significant shifts over the past twenty-five years has been the substantial growth in participation among younger married women, many of them mothers of young children. At the same time, an increase in the divorce rate and in nonmarital births has resulted in a large increase in single-parent families headed by women. Single heads constitute another large segment of women workers with significant family responsibilities (Blau, Ferber, and Winkler, forthcoming; Leibowitz and Klerman 1995).

The increased involvement of women in work outside the home has focused growing attention on the status of women in the labor market. Over the past twenty-five years, women have made important progress in narrowing the gender gap in pay and reducing "occupational segregation" by sex. Occupational segregation is the tendency of men and women to work in different jobs. Figure 1.1, based on published government data, shows the trends in the male-female earnings ratio for two earnings series: weekly earnings of full-time workers and annual earnings of year-round, full-time workers. The figure indicates that after over two decades of constancy, the gender earnings ratio began to increase in the late 1970s or early 1980s. Progress was steady through the 1980s, but the ratio appears to have plateaued in the early 1990s. Nonetheless, cumulative gains have been substantial: Between 1978 and 1995 women's weekly earnings (of full-time workers) increased from 61 to 76 percent of men's earnings.

1

Figure 1.1   Female-to-Male Earnings Ratios of Full-Time Workers,
              1955–1995

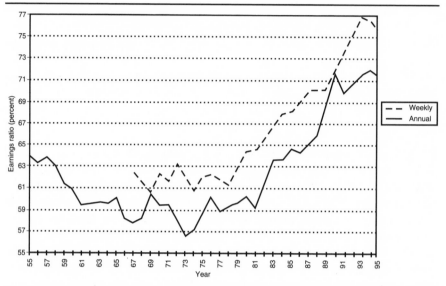

Sources: Bureau of the Census, *Population Reports,* Consumer Income Series P-60, various issues; U.S. Department of Labor, Bureau of Labor Statistics, *Employment and Earnings,* various issues.

Women have also made important progress in reducing occupational segregation. Analyzing the distribution of men and women across the hundreds of detailed occupations listed by the Bureau of the Census, researchers found high and stable levels of occupational segregation through the first half of the twentieth century. In this case, signs of progress first appeared in the 1970s as women began to enter traditionally male professions and managerial jobs in unprecedented numbers. The Index of Segregation is a useful summary measure of the difference in the male and female occupational distributions. It gives the percentage of women who would have to change jobs for the occupational distribution of men and women to be the same. This index fell from 67.7 in 1970 to 59.3 in 1980 and 52.0 in 1990 (Blau, Ferber, and Winkler, forthcoming).

Despite important recent gains, however, women continue to earn less than men and to be heavily concentrated in "female" jobs. Moreover, women in the labor market complain about a "glass ceiling," a set of subtle barriers that appear to block their attaining the highest reaches of professional success. For example, when *Fortune* magazine surveyed male and female middle and top managers among its subscribers, in September 1995, both men and women agreed that women working in corporate America face considerable obstacles. An overwhelming 91 percent of women and 75 percent of men believed that the "existence of a male-dominated corporate culture" is the single most important barrier for women. Among the other chief barriers cited by women were the existence of a glass ceiling, women's exclusion from informal networking, management's belief that women are less career-oriented, and a lack of female mentors (Worton 1996). Of course, it is difficult to assess the accuracy of such beliefs; however, it is indeed the case that, despite the enormous growth in their share of the management ranks, women constitute only 3 to 5 percent of senior managers of companies included among the Fortune 1000 Industrial and Fortune 500. There are also relatively few women in Congress or governorships and few female college presidents (see Glass Ceiling Commission 1995).

One reason for concern over persistent gender differences in labor market outcomes is based on equity or fairness. In this view, the elimination of discrimination against women in the labor market is "a matter of simple justice."[2] Equity concerns over gender pay differentials, regardless of their source, are heightened by the growth in families headed by single women, as well as the increasing dependence of married couples on the wife's earnings. A second reason for concern is based on efficiency. To the extent that the gender gap reflects discrimination, such differential treatment of otherwise equally qualified men and women is wasteful. More broadly, social welfare is maximized if we obtain the greatest possible productivity out of all our resources, including our human resources.

OVERVIEW OF THE VOLUME

Initial versions of the papers in this volume were presented at a conference held at Cornell University in April 1995. The purpose of the conference was to better understand the factors that have impeded women's progress in the labor market and to suggest what can be done to promote gender equality. The papers focused on selected topics deemed to be particularly relevant to women's success. Given the changes in women's roles within the family that potentially affect all family members, attaining greater gender equity in the labor market requires addressing the issues that arise from shifts in gender roles in the family. Chief among them is how workers of both sexes can more effectively mesh their home and work responsibilities. These are not new concerns. In her paper, Claudia Goldin chronicles this tension between career and family for college women throughout the present century. Cohorts of women graduating from college in the early 1900s faced a stark choice between career and family. Considerable progress has been made since then, but Goldin finds that surprisingly few women, even among recent cohorts of highly educated women, have been able to attain both substantial career success and a family. Further evidence of this problem is provided by Jane Waldfogel, who reports in her paper that gender differences in the effects of marital status and children on wages account for a substantial and growing portion of the gender pay gap.

Since women continue to retain primary responsibility for the household in most families, this set of issues is of particular relevance to their ability to succeed in the labor market. The appropriate policies may involve voluntary employer responses to labor market shifts in the gender composition and family responsibilities of workers, government mandates, or a combination of both. To illustrate both the problems and the potential of formulating policies to deal with these issues, we focus on one of a number of possible policy approaches: parental leave.

Parental leave policies are particularly interesting in that their potential impact on gender equality in the labor market is complex. Access to leave permits women to maintain their tie to the firm after childbirth, thus enabling them to continue to reap the gains of their investments in firm-specific training or hold on to an especially good job "match." From the broader social perspective, parental leave may facilitate parents spending more time with their children during the crucial early months.[3]

However, the policy may have negative effects, depending on how it is specified, even on women's economic outcomes. While it seems clear that relatively short leaves are likely to increase women's labor force attachment and wages, extended leaves, especially if generous benefits are also provided, may arguably do the opposite. Moreover, since leaves tend to be disproportionately taken by mothers, even when they are available to both parents, they may reinforce traditional gender roles in the family and thus help to perpetuate differences in labor market outcomes between men and women. One example, though admittedly an extreme one, is that in Germany, as of 1992, women have had available to them (for each child) fourteen weeks of fully paid maternity leave, of which two months are mandatory, as well as an additional three years of parental leave with a paid allowance. The German parental leave is paid as long as the parent taking the leave works no more than nineteen hours per week (Blau and Kahn 1996). Rather than facilitating women's attachment to work such a policy seems virtually an invitation to their retaining a traditional role within the family. Moreover, to the extent that parental benefits are costly, government mandates of employer provision may result in lower wages for women (to finance the costs of the benefit). It is also possible that employers will be reluctant to hire women who are considered likely to claim leave. More generally, some economists are concerned that mandated benefits, by interfering with the market, may take a toll on economic efficiency.

A final aspect of parental leave policy that makes it of considerable interest is that U.S. policy in this area has strongly diverged from that of other industrialized nations. Specifically, while virtually all other advanced countries have long provided such entitlements, there was no federal mandate in the United States until 1993. This suggests that we may have much to learn from international comparisons.

Three of the papers in this volume investigate particular aspects of this issue and together illustrate the fruitfulness of such a concentrated focus. First, Jacob Kerman and Arlene Leibowitz study the impact of maternity leave on women's labor force attachment by comparing the labor supply behavior of women in states that passed maternity leave laws in the 1980s with the behavior of women in states that did not. Second, Jane Waldfogel examines the impact of maternity leave on wages by comparing outcomes for women who returned to their initial employers following a birth with those who did not. Finally, Christopher Ruhm and Jackqueline Teague examine possible efficiency effects of parental leave by looking across countries to see the impact of the presence and duration of leave entitlement on various macroeconomic outcomes in an effort to ascertain whether or not mandated family leave has negative effects on economic efficiency. Taken together these papers suggest that the effects of family leave on employers, workers, and society as a whole are quite positive. The relatively modest maternity leave likely to be taken by workers in the United States appears to increase the wages of women by enabling them to retain their tie to the firm and thus increase their experience and tenure. At the same time, the cross-national results indicate that moderate amounts of leave do not adversely affect economic efficiency.

Another area where work-family conflicts may manifest themselves is in the scheduling of work. A number of dimensions of scheduling may be at issue, ranging from the total number of hours worked to their flexibility and even where they are worked, at home or at the workplace. We have chosen to focus on the first of these issues: the long hours that are often required to achieve success in management and high-level professions. Given that women so often retain disproportionate responsibility for household tasks, even when they are employed outside the home, such requirements pose an especial burden for them. They also constitute a barrier to men taking on a larger share of housework. What function do long-hour requirements serve and what are the prospects for changing them? We may think the answer to the first question is obvious. Employees are (explicitly or implicitly) required to work long hours to get more done. But in their paper Renee Landers, James Rebitzer, and Lowell Taylor suggest that the answer may not be quite so simple.

Long hours (or other types of extremely high performance standards) may be used to screen out employees who have less of some hard-to-observe trait like ambition or motivation and who cannot otherwise be identified. To the extent that the authors are correct, it may be particularly difficult to modify the environment so that workers (of either sex) with family responsibilities have an equal chance to succeed. For example, we might try to increase the ability of such workers to put in long hours by providing subsidized child care. However, if an important purpose of long-hour requirements is to screen out "less-committed" workers, employers may respond by lengthening work norms even further so that these workers will nonetheless be successfully screened out!

This finding implicitly raises a concern that was addressed frequently in the course of the conference: the importance of equalizing household responsibilities between men and women. Were these responsibilities more equally shared, women would not be disproportionately penalized by long-hour norms. Further, employers' adherence to such norms might weaken as they found themselves excluding large groups of men as well as women by such policies.

In the final paper, Donna Rothstein looks at another question that has been raised by women's increased presence in the workplace: the gender match between supervisor and worker. Do employees prefer to work with supervisors of the same sex? Do they perform better when they do? Or is it perhaps the case that both men and women prefer male supervisors? The last question is prompted by the possibility that male, and even female, employees have prejudices against women in supervisory roles. While it is likely that such prejudices have declined with the large-scale entry of women into management, as recently as 1996 a Gallup Poll found that 37 percent of men and 54 percent of women responded that they preferred male bosses.[4] On the other hand, the initial questions are prompted by a substantial literature suggesting that women benefit from the presence of other women at higher levels to serve as role models and mentors. And, as we have seen, many women believe that the absence of mentors is one of the barriers they face in the job market. Rothstein's paper makes a valuable contribution by more rigorously developing the empirical implications of alternative views of the impact of the sex of the supervisor. Her empirical results suggest, however, that testing such models may be difficult.

The volume closes with three perspectives on policy by Olivia Mitchell, Barbara Bergmann, and Elizabeth Peters. A number of interesting and important insights emerge from their consideration of these issues, some of which we discuss more fully below. However, we would like to emphasize here that no matter how helpful the research by economists and other social scientists in evaluating potential policy interventions, decisions about social policy in this area, as in any other, inextricably involve value judgments. These may relate to some very practical issues as well as to broader ones. For example, what is a family for the purposes of providing benefits and formulating other social policies? Does it include unmarried same-sex and opposite-sex couples as well as married couples and single heads? Does it include stepchildren as well as those related by blood or adoption? How do we factor in the needs of other relatives, like elderly parents, who may sometimes live in different households? Or as another example, to the extent they conflict, how do we trade off the needs of parents and children? These and many other questions cannot be answered solely by the "experts." We must all wrestle with these issues and hopefully, after careful study and debate, achieve social consensus. We now turn to a more detailed consideration of the papers in this volume.

FAMILY AND THE ECONOMIC OUTCOMES OF WOMEN

The Goldin paper sets the scene for the others through its examination of the changing role of work and family in the lives of college women over the course of the present century. Given traditional gender roles, men tend not to face the same problems as women in balancing work and family responsibilities, or tend not to face them to the same extent, since desirability as a spouse and ability to contribute economically to one's family are positively related to labor market success for men. While shifting gender roles within the family may be increasing the prevalence of family responsibilities among men, considerable gender differences remain. College women are a particularly interesting group to study because they are likely to have had an especially strong interest in pursuing a career. Goldin motivates her study of earlier cohorts by noting the frustrations of the current cohort of college women, her "cohort V," as they seek full equality in the home and the workplace. As Goldin points out, an understanding of the trade-offs made by past generations can assist us in understanding how we have arrived at the choices confronting college women today.

Goldin considers the experience of four earlier cohorts of college women. As we noted above, those women constituting cohort I, who graduated from college in the first two decades of this century, were forced to choose between marriage and family on the one hand and career on the other. As a result, more than 50 percent of them either did not marry or, if married, did not have children (compared with only 22 percent of non–college graduates). In 1940, when this cohort was between ages 45 and 54, 88 percent of never-married childless women were in the labor force compared with only 28 percent of currently married women with no children, suggesting that marriage itself, not just the presence of children, constituted a major barrier to work outside the home. Goldin characterizes this group as choosing between "family or career."

In the decades after 1940, female college graduates became demographically more similar to other women, and employment outside the home became more common for all married women. However, as Goldin points out, the tendency for women in her cohort III, who graduated between 1946 and 1965, was to sequence activities so as to enter or reenter the labor force after their children reached school age or older. She characterizes their choice as "family then job." In this we may note that they were quite similar to their non–college-educated counterparts. Moreover, the sequencing of family and work over the life cycle as well as other indicators (for example, the unequal division of housework between husbands and wives and the higher incidence of part-time work among women) suggest that while women did increasingly work outside the home, they either were not able or did not choose to pursue "careers." Hence Goldin's use of the term "job."

In recent decades, the desire to "have it all"—that is, to successfully pursue a career and to have a family—appears to have become an increasingly prevalent goal among women. While there is no way of knowing precisely how prevalent it is or has been, Goldin's results show how rarely women have been able to achieve both career and family, even among a relatively recent cohort of college women. Using data from the National Longitudinal Surveys, Goldin looks in detail at attainment of career and family by the women in cohort IV, who graduated from college between 1966 and 1979. She characterizes their choice as desiring "career then family," as many of the women in this cohort postponed marriage and child-bearing to pursue a career. Yet she finds that by the time they were between ages 37 and 47, 29 percent had not had a first birth. Moreover, while 33 to 36 percent were on what she defines as a "career track," based on their earnings by the late 1980s, only 13 to 17 percent had attained "family and career," where the former is defined in terms of having had a first birth.

Goldin's primary definition of career is having hourly earnings in the selected years exceeding that of the 25th percentile of men with sixteen years or more of schooling in the Current Population Survey (CPS). This is a relatively stringent definition by which substantial (though considerably smaller) portions of college-educated men in each year would also not have careers. What is perhaps most surprising is that when Goldin shifts to a much lower cutoff, being in the labor force in each of the three years she analyzes and generally working full time, the incidence of career and family among the women remains extremely low at 22 percent. Another way to see the apparent difficulty these women have faced in combining family and career is that, under all three definitions, approximately one half of the women with careers have not had a first birth.

Some qualifications may be raised about these findings. We do not know what proportion of the childless women were disappointed with not having children. However, Goldin does present evidence that half or more had indicated that they desired children when surveyed in their early- to mid-20s. Another qualification is that since this cohort has postponed marriage and childbearing, childlessness among them is likely to be overestimated because some have not yet completed their childbearing. At the same time, the measured career attainments of the cohort may appear especially low during the years surveyed because of the presence of young children among the women with families (increasing the proportion out of the labor force or employed in part-time, low-wage jobs, for example). Yet even these qualifications suggest that these women are making decisions and trade-offs seldom confronted by their male counterparts.

This conclusion is further reinforced by the results presented in the Waldfogel paper. She finds for young people (mean age 30) in both 1980 and 1991 that the wages of mothers were markedly lower than the wages of nonmothers and men. Over the period, women made substantial progress in narrowing the gender pay gap. Overall, the female-male pay ratio for this age group rose by fully 20 percentage points, from 64 percent in 1980 to 84 percent in 1991. However, mothers' wages rose considerably less dramatically (from 60 to 75 percent of men's wages) than nonmothers' wages (from 72 to 95 percent of men's wages). Thus, the relative disadvantage of mothers compared with the others increased. Waldfogel's analysis of the determinants of wages for men and women indicates that men receive a positive return to marriage, and children have either no effect on their earnings or a positive effect. In contrast, women receive a smaller return to being married than men, as well as a negative return to being parents. These findings of a negative effect of children on women's wages are especially striking in that Waldfogel controls for the effect of such human capital variables as age, experience, and education. Putting it somewhat differently, having children has a direct negative effect on women's wages, above and beyond whatever indirect effect it has on their experience or educational attainment.

Waldfogel finds that these gender differences in the effects of family status on wages account for a substantial and growing portion of the gender pay gap: over one third (36 percent) in 1980 and over one half (53 percent) in 1991.[5] Her results imply that effective policies to address the issues that confront parents in the labor market could have substantial beneficial effects on the gender pay gap. As noted above, we especially focus in this volume on family leave. Regardless of whether leave is for the temporary medical disability of pregnancy and childbearing or for the care of a newborn or young child, and regardless of whether it is available to men as well as women, in all countries women are disproportionately likely to take the leave.

IMPACT OF FAMILY LEAVE

Ruhm and Teague's paper provides a history of family leave legislation in Europe and North America. Virtually all industrialized countries now provide entitlements to job-protected absences from employment associated with childbirth. Often fathers as well as mothers qualify for time off work and most countries provide some income support during the leave. Until recently the United States was a major exception to this pattern. Prior to 1993, there was no federal legislation mandating parental leave and only a few states required job protection; although since the passage of the Pregnancy Discrimination Act of 1978, employers who have a medical disability program have been required to provide coverage of pregnancy and childbirth on the same basis as other medical disabilities. With the passage of the Family and Medical Leave Act, the United States now requires that those who employ fifty workers or more offer up to twelve weeks of unpaid leave to eligible employees. While this legislation is modest by international standards, as the authors note, it represents a substantial change in U.S. policy.

What are the potential effects of maternity leave on women's employment and wages? We may analyze these effects using the model developed by Klerman and Leibowitz, who make the important point that maternity leave is relevant only to labor markets where employers and workers tend to form long-term attachments. To see how this works, suppose that a woman is currently employed and that her employer offers a maternity leave of four weeks. If she becomes pregnant, she has two choices: She may remain with her current employer by taking the maternity leave and returning to work in four weeks, thus continuing to earn her current wage; but if she desires more than a four-week leave, she faces the choice of leaving her current employer and returning to work when she likes by finding a new job. How much will she earn in her new job?

Klerman and Leibowitz argue that her alternative wage elsewhere is likely to be less than her current wage for two reasons. First, workers often accumulate training on their jobs. Some of this training may be general enough to be transferable to other firms. However, some is likely to be "firm-specific," that is, useful only in the current job. Since such firm-specific skills will not be rewarded elsewhere, the wage available at other firms is likely to be less than it is at the current firm. Second, the current job may be a particularly good "match" between the worker's skills and abilities and the needs of her employer. This is especially likely to be the case if the current job was located after a considerable period of job search. If the current job represents an especially good match, then an alternative job located when the woman returns to the labor force is likely to pay less.

How will women respond to the choice between taking a leave of up to four weeks at their current wage versus a longer leave at a lower wage? There are three possible situations to consider. First, women who would in any case desire a leave of four weeks or less are not "constrained"; they will simply stay out their preferred amount of time and return within the four-week period. Second, some women who would prefer a longer leave, given their current wage, will decide that it is not worth the cost of a lower wage and will also opt for the four-week leave; however, they are "constrained" by the employer's leave policy. Finally, a third group of women who prefer a longer leave will decide to quit their current job and return to work at a later point. Their leave is prolonged by the constrained choice they face: Once they sever their ties to the firm, the opportunity cost of labor force withdrawal falls; hence, they are likely to stay out of the labor force longer than they would have at their higher preleave wage.

We can use this analysis to understand the impact of an increase in leave from, say, four to twelve weeks. Klerman and Leibowitz focus on the case where the leave duration is increased by government mandates; however, the same reasoning would apply if the employer simply extended the leave time voluntarily. In examining the labor supply consequences of leave it is useful to distinguish three labor market states: employment, leave, and work. A woman who is out on maternity leave from a specific employer is employed but not working. The behavior of the first group of women who were not constrained by the initial leave policy would be unaffected by change. The second group of women who preferred a longer leave but settled for a four-week leave would stay out longer. Using Klerman and Leibowitz's distinction between employment and work, the weeks of employment of this group would be unchanged (that is, they would remain with the employer in either case), but their weeks worked would be reduced. Finally, with respect to the last group who left their jobs rather than accept only a four-week leave, two outcomes are possible. Some of the women in this group will now choose to remain with the firm and take a leave of twelve weeks or less. Both their weeks of employment and their weeks worked are likely to increase. Others in this group may still decide to leave the firm and stay out their preferred amount of time (more than twelve weeks) in exchange for the lower wage. Their employment and weeks worked will be unchanged.

What can we conclude about the impact of an increase in the duration of maternity leave on the employment status of new mothers? This analysis suggests that their average weeks of employment should unambiguously increase. Weeks of employment of women who would have remained with the firm in any case are unchanged, while some women who would have left the firm will remain employed. If we look at employment probabilities as Klerman and Leibowitz do, we expect the probability of employment to increase. However, the expected effect of an increase in the duration of maternity leave on average weeks worked and the probability of working is ambiguous, since there are countervailing effects. On the one hand, women who would have preferred to stay out a longer period of time but made do with the four-week leave will stretch their leave time and reduce their weeks worked. On the other hand, some women who would have left the firm will remain with the firm and return to work sooner. Finally, the probability of being on leave (that is, employed but not at work) rises, since the number of women quitting their job is reduced.

What about the effect of an increase in maternity leave duration on women's wages? Here the situation looks less complex initially, but there are some hidden complexities that need to be taken into account. If we are considering leaves of relatively short duration, women's wages are very likely to be increased. This is because, at the longer leave duration, more women will choose (or be able) to remain with the firm and retain the higher wages that come from their firm-specific training or from their initial job being an especially good match. However, if the duration of the maternity leave is very long, such as is the case in some other countries, women who would otherwise have stayed out a relatively short time may be induced to extend their leave a great deal. The effect on wages is then less clear. Even remaining with their current firm, the extended time out is likely to lower the wages of these women compared with what they would have earned if their time out was shorter. Thus, maternity leaves of long duration may have an adverse effect on women's wages. This is especially the case if they are also generously paid, as they are in some industrialized countries, further tipping the scale in favor of a prolonged absence from the job.

Klerman and Leibowitz test the employment implications of this model while Waldfogel sheds light on the wage implications of maternity leave. Before turning to an examination of these findings, it is worth considering the desirability of various outcomes. If we view maternity leave from the perspective of women's labor market status, we are likely to be especially interested in its impact on wages and to regard relatively short work disruptions as good outcomes. However, as pointed out by Klerman and Leibowitz, many advocates for children supported the Family and Medical Leave Act as a measure that would allow mothers more time to develop healthy, secure relationships with their infants in the months immediately following childbirth, without forcing them to quit their job. They interpret this as meaning that a favorable outcome would be a reduction in weeks worked or in the probability of working by new mothers (that is, an increase in time spent with their newborns). However, as we have seen, maternity leave laws could simultaneously increase time spent by women at home with newborns in the first several months after birth, but increase work time after the child is older by encouraging attachment to the firm of women who otherwise would have left their jobs. Given these potentially offsetting effects, the welfare effect on children of a finding of constant or even increased work probabilities must be regarded as uncertain, even by those who would like to increase the amount of time new mothers spend with newborns. Indeed, since a primary concern of advocates of the Act was the bonding that occurs between mother and child in the first few months after the birth, this type of mixed effect might be quite consistent with their goals.

Klerman and Leibowitz use an ingenious "natural experiment" to assess the impact of increased leave availability on women's labor supply. Specifically, they compare 1980–1990 changes in the labor supply of the mothers of infants in the six relatively small "experimental" states where maternity leave statutes were passed in the late 1980s with changes in these probabilities in the "nonexperimental" states without such laws. However, it is possible that women's labor supply changes might have differed between the experimental and nonexperimental states, even in the absence of the leave legislation. To address this possibility, they also examine the differences in labor supply between the experimental and nonexperimental states for new mothers relative to the differences for a control group that would presumably not be affected by the legislation: mothers of toddlers, two and three years old. These comparisons constitute a more stringent test of the effects of the maternity leave legislation. In further analyses, Klerman and Leibowitz also explicitly control for the state unemployment rate and for the demographic characteristics of mothers. While some results are consistent with the theory, estimates from the more stringent comparison, also including demographic controls, imply that the maternity leave statutes have no statistically significant effect on employment, leave, or work.

This finding of no impact of leave statutes is surprising. Moreover, Klerman and Leibowitz also find that their results appear to be highly sensitive to specification; this constitutes an important caution for future work. However, the discussants of their paper point to a number of reasons why it may have been particularly difficult for the authors to uncover the effect of maternity leave statutes in their study. It is quite possible that more robust conclusions may emerge from future research employing this framework for analyzing the impact of changes in laws in larger states (such as California) and by the federal government.

Waldfogel examines the impact of maternity leave on wages for two cohorts of young women (with mean age thirty) from the National Longitudinal Survey of Young Women (NLS-YW) and the National Longitudinal Survey of Youth (NLSY). The NLS-YW sample consists of women who are observed working around 1980; the NLSY sample consists of women who are observed working around 1991. Explicit information on maternity leave coverage is available only in the NLSY data; however, Waldfogel is able to observe employment continuity over the period of childbirth in both data sets. A woman is classified as maintaining employment continuity over childbirth if she returned to her previous employer post-birth, regardless of whether or not this was the result of utilizing a formal maternity leave policy. Waldfogel finds that maintaining employment continuity over childbirth was associated with higher pay for both cohorts. This finding reflected in part higher starting pay among women who retained employment continuity, suggesting that they were a positively selected group. However, it also reflected their higher level of subsequent work experience and job tenure. Where it was possible to observe maternity leave coverage, Waldfogel found that women who were covered and returned to their original employer had higher subsequent wages, owing in part to pre-existing differences and in part to the higher levels of experience and tenure that they accrued after childbirth. Given that maternity leave in the United States is generally likely to be of relatively short duration and unpaid (see Mitchell's contribution in this volume), these findings are consistent with our theoretical discussion. Waldfogel's results suggest that job-protected maternity leave could be an important remedy for the pay penalties associated with motherhood.

As noted above, one issue of concern to economists is the potential impact of mandated family leave policies on economic efficiency. Ruhm and Teague investigate this question using a longitudinal cross-national data set assembled by the authors to examine the impact of leave policies on macroeconomic outcomes. As the authors note, economists' concerns about mandated leave policies stem from their assumption that workers and firms will *voluntarily* agree to the provision of family leave if the expected benefits exceed the expected costs. If costs are greater than benefits, workers will choose to forgo the leave in exchange for higher compensation. By mandating leave in all circumstances, this flexibility is eliminated, thus making employers or workers or both worse off. Proponents of mandated leave generally emphasize its desirability in terms of reducing gender inequality or protecting the welfare of children. Ruhm and Teague note, however, that for these arguments to have weight on efficiency grounds, rather than simply for equity reasons, there must be some "market failure," that is, some reason why the market left to its own devices does not produce the most efficient outcome.

Ruhm and Teague explain that family leave could provide a positive externality if young children receive better care when one parent takes time off from employment. A portion of such benefits are reaped by society as a whole—for example, in the form of lower medical costs, some of which would otherwise be paid by the government, or fewer problems in school. In such circumstances workers will undervalue the benefits of family leave from society's perspective and this would provide an efficiency rationale for government intervention. They also develop another economic justification based on asymmetric information, which refers to a situation in which the two parties to a transaction have different amounts of information. In this case, they assume that workers have greater knowledge of their probability of having children and taking time off than their employers do. In such circumstances, firms that voluntarily provide leave are likely to disproportionately attract workers with a high probability of taking it, increasing the costs of these firms. Parental leave mandated by the government eliminates this "adverse selection" problem.

Ruhm and Teague test for a negative effect of mandated family leave on efficiency by examining its impact on a number of important macro-economic outcomes, including gross domestic product, the employment-to-population ratio, the labor force participation rate, and the unemployment rate. Even if negative effects on efficiency were found for mandated family leave, such mandates could still be advocated on equity grounds—for example, for reducing gender inequalities in economic outcomes. Their results, however, provide little support for the view that moderate periods of parental leave reduce economic efficiency, and there are even some indications of modest beneficial effects, particularly when paid time off work is considered.

WORK HOURS AND GENDER EQUALITY

As discussed above, another issue of importance to women in the workplace is the long hours expected of workers seeking to succeed in high-powered professions. Landers, Rebitzer, and Taylor develop a fascinating and provocative new analysis of how work hours are determined in such settings. They argue that in many cases long work hours (or other performance measures that entail long hours) are used to screen employees for other valuable characteristics that are hard to observe, such as commitment or ambition.

The problem is again one of asymmetric information. A "short-hour" worker—that is, a worker who would like to work short hours in the long term, say after making partner in a law firm—knows who he or she is. However, the firm is not able to distinguish such short-hour (less committed) workers from their long-hour (more committed) counter-parts. Firms may respond by setting work-hour norms at extremely high levels to discourage short-hour workers from applying. In such a case, firms that individually lower their hours norm would be flooded by short-hour workers, and this adverse selection problem will deter firms from doing so. A "rat race" equilibrium will result in which firms are unwilling to offer shorter hours even if, with the increase in women in these fields and growing household responsibilities for men, a larger proportion of professionals might want them. The authors present considerable empirical evidence in support of their model, drawn principally from law firms.

This model has strong policy implications. It suggests that overly long hours represent a coordination failure in the labor market. A single firm abandoning stringent work norms will suffer adverse consequences; it will be inundated with short-hour workers. If, however, all firms simultaneously abandon their hours norm, short-hour employees will be distributed across many firms, with no one firm suffering undue costs compared with its competitors. As a consequence, policy interventions that correct this coordination failure can, in some cases, improve both equity and efficiency. However, their consideration of specific policy interventions uncovers serious potential problems with each possible candidate for social intervention. For example, one approach to the hours problem would be to reduce the cost of long hours for employees who would otherwise be likely to work short hours. This might include policies like parental leave or subsidized child and elder care services. Yet the model implies that as long as firms remain committed to screening out short-hour workers, interventions that increase the hours of short-hour workers may have the perverse result of making prevailing work norms even more stringent.

It is uncertain how widespread "rat race" equilibria are in the real world. Both discussants suggested alternative explanations for long-hour outcomes in the professions. Moreover, as we pointed out above, their disproportionate negative effects on women would be mitigated if household responsibilities were more equally shared between men and women. And such policies might appear less desirable to employers if they resulted in substantial numbers of men as well as women being screened out.

GENDER OF SUPERVISOR AND ECONOMIC OUTCOMES OF YOUNG WORKERS

In the final paper, Rothstein investigates the impact of the sex of the supervisor on male and female workers' wages and other employment outcomes. Rothstein formulates three possible models of supervisor-employee matches on labor market outcomes. First, she asks what the impact would be if male employees had prejudices against working under female supervisors. Drawing on the work of Becker (1971), Rothstein develops a model suggesting that in this case male workers will receive a wage premium for working for a female supervisor. The higher wage is necessary to induce discriminating male workers to accept jobs with this "unpleasant" working condition. Owing to the greater expense, employers will make every effort to match male workers to male supervisors. But where they cannot do so and are forced to pair male workers with female supervisors, male workers will receive a wage premium. Such male workers who are employed with female supervisors at a higher wage will feel as well off as male workers employed with male supervisors at a lower wage.

Second, Rothstein analyzes the case where the gender of the supervisor affects worker productivity, specifically where the productivity of male employees is reduced when they work for a female supervisor. This could occur, for example, if same-sex supervisors have better rapport with employees. (This case may be easily reversed to consider the possibility that women are less productive when they work for male supervisors.) In this circumstance, male workers will not receive different pay depending on whether or not they work for female supervisors. If male workers were paid less when working with female supervisors, in accordance with their lower productivity, none of them would be willing to accept such assignments. The wages of male and female workers and male and female supervisors will be set so that the cost of producing a given level of output is the same for each type of work group (that is, a same-sex or opposite-sex match between worker and supervisor).

Finally, Rothstein considers the case where male employees matched with female supervisors have higher training costs. This may occur, for example, because same-gender supervisors serve as more effective mentors. Male workers on the "training track," that is, in jobs where substantial on-the-job training is taking place, will be assigned to male supervisors to reduce training costs. This implies that male employees with male supervisors should have faster wage growth and higher promotion probabilities than male employees assigned to female supervisors. If we assume that female supervisors are more effective at training female workers, then we also expect female employees with female supervisors to have faster wage growth and higher promotion probabilities than female employees assigned to male supervisors. This model is of particular interest because it points to possible long-term effects on career development of the gender match between young workers and their supervisors.

Rothstein's empirical work is based on data from the National Longitudinal Survey of Youth. The empirical results indicate that for both young men and women there is a negative impact on current wages associated with working for a female supervisor. A female supervisor is found to have no effect on individuals' perceived likelihood of promotion and minimal positive effects on employee wage growth. Rothstein concludes that, taken together, the results do not provide clear-cut support for any of the three theories. She speculates that, in the empirical work, gender of supervisor may serve as a proxy for percentage female in the occupation, which has been found to negatively affect the wages of both women and men owing to "crowding" (Bergmann 1974). She notes that it is also possible that female supervisors are lower down in a firm's hierarchy, suggesting that the employees that they supervise would also be at lower levels on their job ladders.

IMPLICATIONS FOR POLICY

The policy implications of the papers presented at the conference and of the discussions that they stimulated are formally considered by Mitchell, Bergmann, and Peters. In her contribution, Mitchell provides a useful summary of recent trends in the availability of "family friendly" policies based on data from the Bureau of Labor Statistics' Employee Benefit Survey of employees of medium-sized and large firms. She finds that between 1988 and 1993 there was a sharp increase in the proportion of such employees who were at firms that offered unpaid maternity and paternity leaves: to 60 percent in 1993, up from 33 percent in 1988, for maternity leave; and to 53 percent in 1993, up even more dramatically from 16 percent in 1988, for paternity leave. Mitchell attributes this rapid change to the implementation of the Family and Medical Leave Act and expects coverage to rise still further since the 1993 data collection occurred partway through the Act's implementation period. The Act does not mandate paid leave, however, and Mitchell finds no upward trend in the extremely small proportion of employees at firms offering paid leaves. She also finds surprisingly little growth in child care assistance. Only 7 percent of sampled employees worked at firms that provided direct financial support to parents who needed adoption help and child care in 1993.

There were, however, some areas of rapid growth in the provision of family-friendly benefits. For example, there has been a sharp increase in the proportion of employees at firms that offer flexible benefit and/or reimbursement accounts: to 53 percent in 1993, up from 13 percent in 1988. Elder care assistance has also increased considerably, although the nature of the assistance is not specified. It is likely that many offerings are of the "resource and referral" variety, which also constitute the bulk of firm offerings in the child care area. More substantial financial assistance remains rare.

In their papers, Bergmann and Peters address some of the broader issues raised as policies evolve in this area. Bergmann examines the impact of family-friendly policies on gender equality and cautions that some policies that appear to make life easier for women, and may even be welcomed by a majority of women, could actually promote greater gender inequality. For example, policies that provide additional opportunities for part-time work or provide maternity leaves that extend significantly beyond the time necessary to recover from the disability caused by childbirth tend to reinforce the traditional division of labor within the family and may actually facilitate maintenance of traditional arrangements. In contrast, workplace policies that encourage greater participation by the male partner in family tasks or that promote the purchase of substitutes for unpaid family labor tend to promote equality. The bottom line is that the impact on gender equity of family policies needs to be carefully scrutinized.

As Peters points out, family and workplace policies are designed to address a number of goals, and these goals may potentially conflict. One potential conflict that she addresses is closely related to the points raised by Bergmann: a conflict between a concern with gender equality of opportunity and the well-being of children. Peters contrasts child care subsidies that are the primary family and work policy in the United States with maternity and paternity leave that tend to be more extensive and generously provided in other countries. Peters notes that employers are likely to value continuity of employment and short leaves of absence. While child care subsidies clearly facilitate employment, the impact of maternity leave is unclear. Were we to move in the direction of more extensive and paid maternity benefits, and if this caused more extended absences from work, employers might become more reluctant to hire or promote women of childbearing age. In terms of the well-being of children, Peters notes that an implicit motivation for an extensive leave policy is the idea that parental care is "better" than nonparental care. Yet most research has found no evidence of a negative effect of maternal employment on children over age 1. For infants, the evidence is mixed, with some studies finding negative effects and other studies finding no effects.

The policy presentations as well as many of the papers in this volume point to important links between family issues and the economic outcomes and well-being of women. Given traditional gender roles in the family, this link is perhaps inescapable. A fundamental need in addressing these issues is the development of appropriate social and employer policies to meet the needs of workers with family responsibilities. Also of great importance to women's labor market status is a more equal sharing of household responsibilities between men and women in the family. Although this outcome may be less directly amenable to policy intervention, it is nonetheless extremely important that policies be formulated to facilitate greater gender equity within the family as well as in the larger society.

NOTES

1. The 1994 figure is from U.S. Department of Labor, Bureau of Labor Statistics *1995 Handbook of Labor Statistics* (prepublication data). The term "subtle revolution" was coined by Smith (1979).

2. This was the title of the President's Task Force of Women's Rights and Responsibilities report (1970).

3. There is some evidence that nonparental care during the first year of life may have negative effects on children, but not all studies have found this to be the case. See the contribution by Elizabeth Peters for a consideration of this issue.

4. See "Bias Alive in Workplace," *St. Louis Post-Dispatch*, March 27, 1996. Since men tend to staff upper-level positions in most firms, many men and women make this assessment without having had an opportunity to compare. When workers are exposed to women bosses, pre-existing stereotypes tend to break down. Ferber, Huber, and Spitze (1979) found that both men and women who had ever had a female boss were considerably less likely to prefer a male boss.

5. These figures include the effect of gender differences in family status characteristics, but such effects are negligible: 1 percent in 1980 and 0 percent in 1991.

Chapter 2

Career and Family: College Women Look to the Past

Claudia Goldin

Recent college graduate women express frustration regarding the obstacles they will face in combining career and family. Tracing the demographic and labor force experiences of four cohorts of college women across the past century allows us to observe the decisions each made, the constraints each faced, and how the constraints loosened over time. No cohort of college graduate women in the past had a high success rate in combining family and career. Cohort I (graduating c. 1910) had a 50 percent rate of childlessness, whereas cohort III (graduating c. 1955) had a high rate of childbearing and an initially low labor force participation. Cohort IV (graduating c. 1972) provides the most immediate guide for today's college women and is close to the end of its fertility history. It is also a cohort that can be studied using the National Longitudinal Survey of Young Women. In 1991, when the group was between ages 37 and 47, 28 percent of the sample's college graduate (white) women had yet to have a first birth. The estimates for career vary from 24 to 33 percent for all college graduate women in the sample. Thus, only 13 to 17 percent of the group achieved "family and career" by the time they were about 40 years old. Among those who attained career, 50 percent were childless. Cohort IV contains a small group of women who have combined family with career, but for most the goal remains elusive.

College women today tell us they want both family and career. They have succeeded in achieving parity in numbers with their male counterparts, their educations are of about equal quality, and they are continuing in professional and graduate schools more than ever before.[1] Yet full equality—in both the home and the marketplace—still seems an elusive goal for them and they express a palpable frustration.

I describe here the demographic and economic fates of prior cohorts of college women. How did each combine family and career? Trade-offs of substantial consequence were made by all past generations of college women, compromises that the present generation appears unwilling to make. Despite shifting trade-offs and changing gender inequality in demographic and economic outcomes, each generation of female college graduates set the stage for the next. To comprehend how we have arrived at the choices faced by the current generation, we must understand change across the past hundred years.

FIVE COHORTS: A SUMMARY

I consider five cohorts of college graduates, each about twenty years in duration (see table 2.1). The differences among them and the progression of trade-offs can be summarized in the following manner. In cohort I—a group graduating about 1910 and born around 1890—college presented a stark set of alternatives between family and career. For most of these women it was one or the other, and when the selection was a career, it almost always involved teaching. Although college men in this generation married and had families at about the same rate as men without higher education, college women in this generation were set apart from their noncollege counterparts. More than 50 percent of college graduate women in this cohort either did not marry or, if they did so, did not have children.[2] College women were a small proportion of the young population, but college men were almost equally so. Although all college students were drawn disproportionately from the upper echelons of American wealth and standing, there is evidence that differences in the demographic experiences between college women and their noncollege counterparts were largely due to a "treatment effect" of college, rather than to selection bias.[3] That is, the college experience affected them.

The second cohort—graduating about 1933 and born around 1910—attained higher marriage rates than its predecessor cohort. But the proportion of the relevant population attending college for four years or more did not increase much. That is, the marriage and child-bearing rate of this cohort increased from the previous one, but the apparent selection into college did not change. Mary McCarthy's autobiographical *The Group*, which concerns the lives of eight Vassar women in the class of 1933, opens at the wedding of one in the group just six weeks after her graduation. That would not have been the opening scene for a novel about the previous cohort of college women. The members of this second cohort not only married, but they also entered the workplace just after graduation. They remained at work for several years, frequently with aspirations, rarely fulfilled, of a full career. "They were a different breed than those of the previous decade," wrote McCarthy of her group, "not one did not propose to work this coming fall." But family eventually intervened. I characterize cohort II as attaining "job then family" and view it as a bridge from I to III. The full blossoming of the movement of college women into the American mainstream came after the 1940s with cohort III. I will not go into any further detail on cohort II.

Table 2.1   Characterizations of Five Cohorts of College Graduate Women

Cohort	Year Graduated from College	Approximate Birth Year	Characterization
I	1900 to 1919	1878 to 1897	Family or career (attaining)
II	1920 to 1945	1898 to 1923	Job then family (attaining)
III	1946 to 1965	1924 to 1943	Family then job (attaining)
IV	1966 to 1979	1944 to 1957	Career then family (desiring)
V	1980 to 1995	1958 to 1973	Career and family (desiring)

College offered the women in cohort III—graduating about 1955 and born around 1933—the opportunity to have both family and paid employment. But the two were to be serially scheduled. Family came first, in terms of timing and priority, and then employment. The employment of choice was, once again, teaching, for it allowed such serial timing without a large penalty. It was a profession one could "fall back on," because teaching would always be in demand and teaching credentials generally remained valid during job interruptions. But college also afforded the women of this cohort the opportunity to marry a college-educated man.

One might ask of many of the women from cohort III whether the direct (pecuniary) returns to college justified the tuition and opportunity costs of their four years of higher education. The answer was that it generally did not, but that college allowed them to tap into the market for college-educated men. Not only did women who attended college stand a considerably higher chance of marrying a college-educated man, but they also married the higher-income-generating man from among the college-educated group as well as from among the high school–educated group. As college became more accessible to the masses and as America became swept away by the post–World War II revival of family, college women married and had children at almost the same rates as their noncollege contemporaries. Despite all appearances to the contrary, however, the college woman of the 1950s set the stage for the events of the 1970s and the resurgence of feminism.

The women of cohort IV—graduating about 1972 and born around 1950—are the first for whom a considerable proportion have considered the career path. They are currently between ages 38 and 51 and their childbirth and marital histories are nearly complete. A portion of the cohort—those who were between ages 14 and 24 in 1968—were sampled in the first National Longitudinal Survey of Young Women (NLS-YW) and are studied in detail below. I find that among those who attained the B.A. degree, 29 percent had not yet had their first birth by 1991 when the group was between ages 37 and 47.[4] Although about 26 to 33 percent were on a "career track," using a generous definition concerning their earnings in the late 1980s, only 13 to 17 percent had achieved "family and career" by that time.

College appears to be offering the women in cohort V—graduating in 1980 or later and born in 1958 or later—the opportunity for true equality with their male counterparts. College women today reject the choice of "family or career," the options of cohort I, and "family then job," that of cohort III. And they are uncomfortable with the choice of "career then family," that of many in cohort IV who just preceded them. They are unwilling to schedule events serially and thereby risk forfeiting one of them. Many of the doors that were closed to previous generations of college women are now open. Yet many of the female graduates of the past decade appear nervous, even frustrated.[5]

COLLEGE ATTENDANCE AND GRADUATION DATA
FOR MEN AND WOMEN

Before exploring the basis for the characterizations just offered, it is instructive to examine the percentages of males and females who attended and graduated from college across this century. The fewer who attended college, the more they could be a highly self-selected sample from among the entire population. Because I would like to isolate the "treatment effect" of college, it is imperative to understand the process of selection into college.

Prior to 1940, the proportions of men and women who attended college were low, but the percentages were remarkably similar by sex.[6] Among those born around 1890 (from 1886 to 1895), for example, 9.5 percent of the men attended college for at least one year whereas 8.9 percent of the women did. Attendance figures are only slightly higher for cohorts born around 1900 (1895 to 1900); see figure 2.1 and appendix table 2.1).[7] Graduation rates are somewhat further apart, when the definition of graduating college is attending for four years or more (see figure 2.2 and appendix table 2.1).[8] Of the cohort born around 1890, 5.0 percent of men graduated college whereas 3.4 percent of women did. Attendance rates were far higher for women relative to their graduation rates, but only in part because two-year colleges are included in the data.[9] Until recently far fewer women than men who attended college actually graduated. By the cohort born in 1905, even graduation rates had narrowed between the sexes; the ratio of graduating males to females was 1.24. The trend, however, was not to continue.

The two lines in figures 2.1 and 2.2 diverge with cohorts born around 1910, and they remain apart until the recent period. Some of the men in the cohorts born around 1920 delayed their college education during World War II; many others would not have received a college education were it not for the war. The GI Bill of Rights provided the first large dose

Figure 2.1   Percentage of White Males and Females Attending College,
              by Birth Cohort

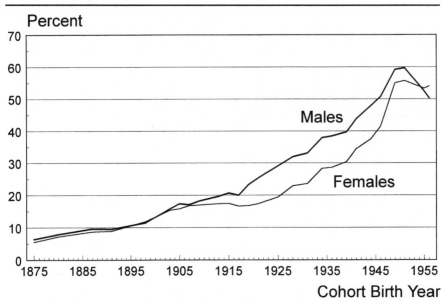

Sources: U.S. Bureau of the Census, series P-20, "Educational Attainment in the United States" (various years). See appendix table 2.1.
Notes: In virtually all cases only the responses of individuals aged 45–54 or 55–64 were used. For cohorts born since 1945 projections were made to 1995 or 1997 on the basis of changes for the preceding cohort that was aged 35–39 (30–34) in 1977 and 45–49 (40–44) in 1987.

of federal subsidization of college tuition and enticed a proportion of men in their 20s and early 30s to return to school.

Large differences between men and women in college graduation rates persisted until the cohorts born in the 1950s. The ratio of male to female graduates increased to 1.79 for the cohort born around 1930. It declined to 1.62 in the next ten years, but was still far higher than it had been earlier in the century. Attendance rates differed less than graduation rates, in part because men, whose tuition was subsidized after World War II, completed college at higher rates than women. Also, women attended two-year schools in somewhat greater numbers. The gap in both graduation and attendance eventually disappears. In 1980 more women than men were receiving B.A.s.

To summarize, cohort I attended college when few men and women went to college but when they attended in roughly similar shares to their populations. Cohort III attended college when the ratio of males to females in attendance was greater than at any time in the past hundred years. Finally, cohort V is attending college in an era of the greatest gender equality in both attendance and graduation rates.

FRAMEWORK FOR UNDERSTANDING CHANGE IN FAMILY AND CAREER DECISIONS

I have constructed a simple framework to demonstrate how the constraints facing college women changed across the past century. Changing constraints, more so than changing tastes, I believe, served to alter the decisions of college women with regard to family and career.

The framework contains three periods, each of which should be thought of as seven to ten years in length. All periods occur after a woman achieves her highest grade or degree (a B.A., or higher degree, in the case of college women). In each period a woman's time endowment (T) can be spent employed full time (e), with family full time (f), or involved in some combination of the two, each part time.[10] Utility is a function of T^f, time spent with family, and income, Y:

$$U = U(T^f, Y).$$

For college women, each period at full-time work can be used to earn at least

$$Y_i^e = w_i^e T.$$

If a college woman works *full time for two consecutive periods* she obtains a return to job experience (r), and she obtains an additional return (r) if she works full time for three periods. Lifetime earnings (in the case of no discounting) are simply

$$Y^e \leq w^e \times T + w^e \times T(1+r) + w^e \times T(1+r)^2.$$

A "career" is defined as working full time for at least two consecutive periods, thus accruing returns to job experience.[11] Women who do not graduate from college earn, at most, each period

$$Y_i^n = w_i^n T, \quad \text{where } w^e > w^n.$$

No return to job experience accrues to non–college-graduate women, and therefore a woman who does not graduate from college cannot have a "career." "Family" is defined as having at least one child. Each child requires a minimum fraction (k) of a time period that must be spent with family. Women cannot engage in "family time" unless they have children.

Figure 2.2   Percentage of White Males and Females Graduating from College, by Birth Cohort

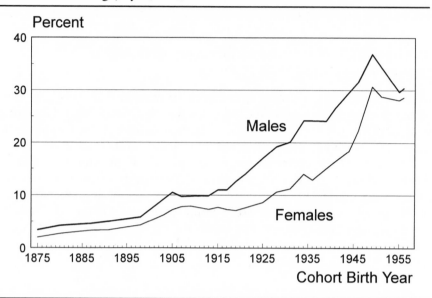

Sources: U.S. Bureau of the Census, series P-20, "Educational Attainment in the United States" (various years). See appendix table 2.1.

Notes: In virtually all cases only the responses of individuals aged 45–54 to 55–64 were used. For cohorts born since 1945 projections were made to 1995 or 1997 on the basis of changes for the preceding cohort that was aged 35–39 (30–34) in 1977 and 45–49 (40–44) in 1987.

I consider a woman's lifetime budget constraint (without possible husband's income).[12] Figure 2.3, panel A, depicts this constraint under the simple assumptions just made. The horizontal axis is time, of which there are three periods, of length T, which can be spent with family or in the labor force. Family time increases when moving from left to right; labor time increases in the opposite direction. Labor time earns at a wage, which depends on education and labor market experience, and the vertical axis shows income earned.

The points on and within the budget constraint contain every possible value of the lifetime allocation of a college woman's time. Beginning with the right-most point, (f, f, f) represents spending all periods full time with family and earning no income. Moving to the left, a woman can trade off any portion of this time to work in the market at wage rate w^c. The point (f, f, e) gives $w^c \times T$ income and $2T$ in family time. Moving farther to the left shows that when a woman works for two consecutive periods she

Figure 2.3   A Framework for Understanding Family and Career Choice

Panel A: Three-Period Budget Constraint

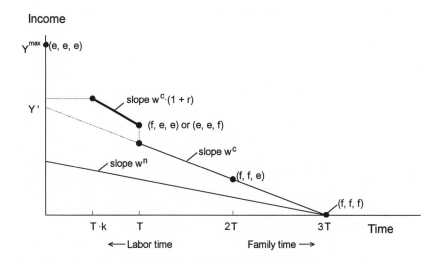

Panel B: Career and Family Choice

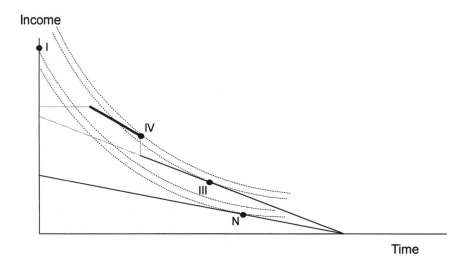

reaps a return of $r \times w^c \times T$ and the budget constraint has a break. This point can represent either (e, e, f) or (f, e, e). Note that all points between (f, f, f) and the break can be achieved by trading time with the market. Because children require only $T \times k$, all the points to the break are consistent with family and "job," although not necessarily with "family and career."

If a woman spends each of the three periods full time at one of the two activities (paid employment or family) there are eight combinations that are deemed rational. The ninth combination produces an interior point: (e, f, e), meaning two employment spells interrupted by family. It is dominated by either (f, e, e) or (e, e, f) because of the returns to continuous employment.[13] The budget constraint is invariant to the timing of the decisions, under the assumptions given.[14]

Allocations between $T \times k$ and T are of interest because it is the only range of "family and career." After a woman is in the labor force for two consecutive periods, she earns at the rate $w^c(1 + r)$. A woman who remains in the labor force for the entire three periods earns the maximum income (Y^{max}) at point (e, e, e). Given the assumptions of the framework, it would not be rational to spend a positive amount of time on family that was less than $T \times k$ and thus the budget constraint jumps to (e, e, e).[15]

The budget constraint in figure 2.3, panel A, has been drawn under the assumptions that $T = 7$ years, $k = 0.5$, and $r = 0.5$, a reasonable value if the return to experience is about 6 percent per year.[16] The darkened portion of the budget constraint and point (e, e, e) represent all possible time allocations that achieve a career. The (e, e, e) point is "career only," whereas the segment between $T \times k$ and T (which is also (f, e, e) or (e, e, f)) allows for "family and career."

The budget constraint gives the complete set of choices, possibly those facing college women today. But it does not represent those available to college women of past generations, for whom many segments of the budget constraint were off-limits. The women in cohort I were faced with a stark choice between two extreme points, (f, f, f), that is, $3T$, and (e, e, e) because married women generally did not work for pay.[17] The budget constraint takes shape with cohorts II and III when married women began to work for pay after their children were grown. But it would exclude the "family and career" portions. With cohort IV the "family and career" portion gets added. All of the changes in the budget constraint were due to the greater acceptance of married women, in general, in the labor force, not just college women.

How did college change the lives of these women? Without college, the budget constraint is the line with slope w^n in figure 2.3, panel A. With college, the budget constraint is first just the two extreme points, (f, f, f) and (e, e, e), then the line with slope w^c, and finally the broken line containing the "family and career" points.

Figure 2.3, panel B, shows that a set of homothetic indifference curves can generate equilibrium combinations chosen by many of the college graduate women in cohorts I, III, and IV. Changes in the constraints facing college graduate women, in the absence of changing tastes or self-selection, can generate changes across the past hundred years regarding work, career, and family. It should be clear why so many women in the first cohort opted for point (e, e, e) even if they had the same preferences as the non–college-graduate group who chose point N. It should also be transparent why, as more options became available, many shifted to a combination of "family and job" given by point III, and why, when the budget constraint includes the "family and career" segment, many desire to shift to point IV. It is not clear from this analysis, however, why so many women in cohort IV have not been successful in getting to point IV.[18]

COHORT I: FAMILY OR CAREER

The women of cohort I completed their B.A. degrees between 1900 and 1920. Although prior cohorts of female college graduates can be studied, the women of cohort I are the earliest for which data on education, occupation, fertility, marriage age, and husband's income can be found in the 1940 Public Use Microdata Sample (PUMS) of the federal population census.

The first college to open its doors to women was Oberlin in 1837, but it was not until the 1850s that opportunities for women in higher education expanded, particularly with the establishment of women's colleges. At that time, however, many of the institutions of higher learning open to women were not true colleges but were seminaries, often no more intellectually demanding than high schools and without rigorous entrance requirements. Only in the 1870s and 1880s with the establishment of such women's colleges as Vassar and Smith, and with the opening of various state universities to women, did the era of women's higher education truly begin. By 1910, 73 percent of all colleges were open to women, almost 80 percent of which were coeducational institutions (Newcomer 1959, 37). Most of the women's colleges that had the minimum age requirement of 16 were upstanding institutions that endeavored to provide to women what other colleges were giving to men: They strove for equality of curriculum (Woody 1929). Most colleges and universities taught a liberal arts curriculum in which there were basically two courses of study: classical and scientific. Thus, women and men took similar classes, even when they were not at the same institution.

Women's higher education had what Thomas Woody, the noted historian of education, viewed as an unanticipated consequence. By the 1890s it was clear that college women were marrying at decidedly lower rates than were those who did not attend college, and that, even if they married, they were having considerably fewer children than their less educated counterparts. The finding spawned an extensive literature, for it was alarming to many in an era of growing nativism.[19]

They, and current researchers, have faced the same problem in trying to ascertain how much of the difference in demographic experiences was due to sample selection and how much was due to the treatment effect of college. Although definitive evidence on the subject has not yet been unearthed, two independent findings, discussed below, are consistent with the notion that demographic differences were more a function of what college did for women than which women went to college. One is that the marriage rate of college women rose before there was a great expansion of college graduation rates for women. Another is that surveys of Radcliffe alumnae reveal their nuptiality and fertility trends to be similar to those of all college women despite the fact that Radcliffe women were drawn from a rather elite group. In fact, the proportion of Radcliffe undergraduates who came from private schools increased between cohorts I and III.

That said, it should be noted that many of the previous studies of the nuptiality rates of college women were not based on nationwide samples, but rather on alumnae surveys. Most, but not all, were surveys of women in the elite colleges of the Northeast, often women's colleges like Smith, Vassar, Radcliffe, Wellesley, and Bryn Mawr (see, for example, Van Kleeck 1918). Not only were the studies biased in their selection of schools, often known for their low marriage rates, but marriage rates for relatively recent graduates were given with no adjustment for time since graduation. Estimates in the previous studies were biased both by virtue of composition and in terms of incompleteness of spell.

The 1940 PUMS affords a more universal view of the nuptiality of college women, although the bias here is probably in the opposite direction. By accepting the recollections of older women and using the percentage who listed themselves as "never married," it is likely that the proportion who claimed to have ever married is overstated. Among those born around 1890, more than 30 percent never married by age 45.[20] For those born around 1900, about 25 percent never married by age 45 (see table 2.2).

A woman who attended but did not graduate from college (or who graduated from a two-year college) stood a somewhat higher probability of marrying by age 45. But the percentage who never married for either college group was considerably greater than for women who never attended college (see table 2.2). Female college graduates born around 1890 were 4 times more likely to remain single than their noncollege counterparts (31.1 percent against 7.8 percent). Those who were born around 1880 were 3.7 times more likely to remain single than their noncollege counterparts (computed for women aged 55–64). College graduate women in the years from about 1900 to 1927 had lifetime marriage probabilities that were fully 20 percentage points lower than those of their noncollege counterparts.

Table 2.2   Percentage Never Married for (White) Women with Four Years or More of College and No College, 1880–1960 Birth Cohorts

Approximate Year of Birth	Ages 25–34	Ages 35–44	Ages 45–54	Ages 55–64
≥ Four Years of College				
1880				30.3
1890			31.1	28.5
1900		28.7	24.7	26.7
1910	38.7	21.2	19.1	16.9
1920	26.5	14.3	12.2	10.6
1930	17.4	11.3	9.1	8.2
1940	18.4	10.4	7.3	
1950	25.6	12.2		
1960	31.5			
No College				
1880				8.10
1890			7.80	6.11
1900		8.80	5.90	6.85
1910	16.90	6.23	6.06	5.88
1920	9.84	5.26	4.80	4.14
1930	6.80	4.60	3.55	3.11
1940	7.01	3.95	3.77	
1950	9.51	5.80		
1960	16.00			

Sources: 1940 PUMS, 1/100; U.S., Bureau of the Census (1953, 1966, 1972, 1985); 1990 Current Population Survey, Outgoing Rotation Group, NBER-CPS extracts.

The general conclusion of the turn-of-the-century studies on nuptiality and college was that the college experience both caused and enabled women to have a lower marriage rate. College permitted women to be more discerning in their choice of lifestyle and husband. Further, the typical occupation for college graduate women, particularly in the East, was as a teacher in a private girls' school, and "there is no station in life (save that of a nun) so inimical to marriage as that of resident teacher in a girls' school" (Shinn 1895, 948). Finally, men, it was said, often disliked intellectual women. The possibility of sample selection was raised, and some noted that women who considered going to college formed a biased sample because they had not married young (Newcomer 1959, 212–213). But the notion that the college woman would not have married anyhow was generally, though not entirely, dismissed.

Not only did the college woman of the early twentieth century have a lower probability of marrying, she also stood a much higher probability of not having children even if she married. Just under 30 percent of female college graduates who were between ages 35 and 44 in 1940 (and were ever married) recorded no lifetime births. The percentage was 1.72 times that of women with no college education and was 11.7 percentage points higher (see table 2.3). Figure 2.4 graphs the percentage of ever-married (white) women having no births by ages 35–44 for college graduates, those with no college, and high school–only graduates.[21] Together with the data on marriage, those on children show that 50 percent of all female college graduates born between 1886 and 1895 either never married or had no children by the time they reached age 45 (see figure 2.5).

Female college graduates around the turn of the century made a distinct choice *between* family and career. About 50 percent did not opt for husband and children, whereas only 22 percent of those who did not attend college took that route.[22] College women of that era were twice as likely as women who did not attend college to take this atypical route in life. One is therefore led to ask what took the place of family.

Of those college graduate women who were between ages 45 and 54 in 1940 and who had never married, 88.4 percent were in the labor force in 1940, and the vast majority were teachers (60 percent in elementary and secondary schools and 4 percent in colleges). Even to contemporary commentators, their choice of occupation was viewed as peculiar: "If it be asked why college women marry less than others, it may very safely be answered . . . that it is *not* because they crave a more exciting and public life; for the majority of them are school-teachers (Shinn 1895, 947; emphasis in original). Of those aged 45–54 who had never had a birth but were in the ever-married group, 34.1 percent were in the labor force; of those who were currently married, 28.4 percent were in the labor force. Even for the college graduate woman with no children, marriage was a decisive factor in her employment.

College men were likely to have been drawn from the same families as the college women in cohort I, but their demographic fates were unaltered by their college experiences. In 1940, 10.2 percent of all college graduate white men aged 45–54 were never married, which is one third the rate for women. Of men in this age group with no college, 11.4 percent were never married, slightly higher than the rate for college graduates. In 1950 just under 7 percent of all college graduate men aged 45–54 had never married, or one quarter the rate for women. In 1960 the proportion for men was also 7 percent, or one third that for women, and in 1970 it was about 6 percent, or one half that for women.[23] The percentage of college graduate men who married by the time they reached age 45 was virtually identical to, indeed somewhat higher than, that of men with no college. Thus, the marriage rate of men was virtually unaffected by college, whereas that for women was reduced, at times substantially.

What accounts for the fact that 50 percent of female college graduates in cohort I either did not marry or did not have children by ages 45–54

Table 2.3   Percentage of (White) Ever-Married Women with No Births by Ages 35–44, for Various Educational Groups

Approximate Year of Birth	≥ Four Years of College	No College, High School Graduate	No College	> Four Years of College
1900	27.9	21.6	16.2	n.a.
1910	23.8	21.0	17.3	n.a.
1920	14.1	11.8	11.3	19.4
1930	10.1	7.5	7.2	14.0
1935	8.6	5.3	5.3	n.a.
1936	10.9	6.0	6.0	n.a.
1937	11.8	6.5	6.0	n.a.
1938	9.7	6.1	5.6	n.a.
1939	11.8	5.8	5.7	16.0
1940	14.1	6.2	5.9	20.6
1941	14.2	5.3	5.1	17.9
1942	15.7	7.0	6.8	20.8
1943	15.8	6.7	6.2	16.5
1944	16.1	7.9	7.2	18.3
1945	18.2	8.1	7.7	22.8
1946	18.1	8.5	7.9	20.4
1947	19.3	8.7	7.9	24.0
1948	18.9	8.6	8.2	23.8
1950	19.1	9.6	8.5	23.9
1952[a]	17.3	9.9	8.9	n.a.

Sources: U.S. Bureau of the Census (1955, 1964, 1973), series P-20, "Fertility of American Women" (various years, ending with no. 470, June 1992).

Notes: All data are for white women only. The educational categories change with P-20 no. 470 (June 1992). That may account for the decline in no births to women with ≥ 4 years of college when the other categories increase.

[a]A change in educational categories accompanied series P-20, no. 470 (June 1992). There is no longer a category of > four years of college and that for ≥ four years of college has been replaced by B.A. degree or higher. It is unclear whether the change in definition has caused the change in percentage childless or whether there has been an increase in births.

when the figure was 22 percent for women without college? Particularly since the percentage graduating from college was very low at the time, one cannot rule out the possibility that college women were a self-selected group who would have had the same demographic fate had they not attended college. Colleges like Bryn Mawr were known to have attracted young women who had no intention of marrying and to have provided them with a "higher calling." But the percentage from the land-grant institutions who did not marry was also high. Thus, the differences do not rest entirely on the type of college or the social backgrounds of the women.

The best evidence in support of the notion that college actually provided a "treatment effect" is that the percentage of female college gradu-

Figure 2.4   Percentages of Ever-Married White Women with No Births by Ages 35–44

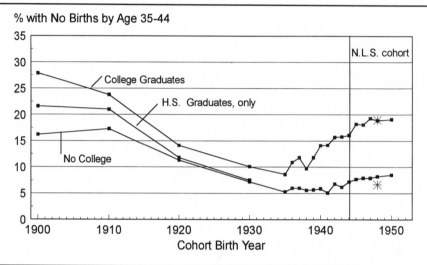

% with No Births by Age 35-44

Sources: 1940 PUMS 1/100 sample-line; U.S. Bureau of the Census (1955, 1964, 1973); post-1970: series P-20, "Fertility of American Women" (various years).

Notes: The stars are for the NLS cohort members for whom a measure of sample participation was nonmissing in 1988. College graduates have completed ≥ sixteen years of school.

ates who never married (at each age) decreased substantially even when there was no increase in the percentage of women who were college graduates. The percentage of women who attended or graduated from college, as can be seen in figures 2.1 and 2.2, remained fairly constant for the cohorts born between 1905 and 1920.[24] But the percentage who never married, as can be seen in figure 2.6, began to fall sometime after the cohort born in 1890. Despite the stability in the percentage graduating from college, the percentage never marrying plummeted from around 25 to 10 percent for cohorts born between 1905 and 1920. If attending college involved self-selection, the underlying process would have had to change drastically to produce this result. Thus, there is prima facie evidence that there was little or no self-selection because the demographic experiences of female college graduates changed by birth cohort before the increase in attendance and graduation rates.

Another way of establishing that self-selection cannot account for the high levels of nonmarriage among cohort I–women is to observe what happened in subsequent generations. Between cohort I and cohort III the percentage of the relevant female population who attended college for four years doubled; it increased from 7 to 14 percent (see appendix table 2.1) and the proportion among them who never married plummeted from

Figure 2.5   Percentages of White Women (All Marital Statuses) with No Births by Ages 35–44

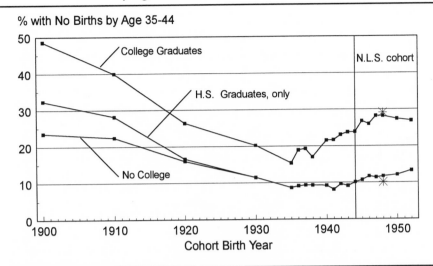

Sources: 1940 PUMS 1/100 sample-line; U.S. Bureau of the Census (1955, 1964, 1973), post-1970: series P-20, "Fertility of American Women" (various years); 1979 has been omitted because the columns in series P-20, giving the proportion ever married, do not sum properly.

Notes: For birth cohorts prior to 1941 the percentage with no births is given by: [(percent with no births among the ever married) × (percent ever married)] + (percent never married) because birth information was asked only of those who were ever married.

30 to 8 percent (at ages 55–64). I will construct a hypothetical case in which all never-married college graduate women in cohort I are self-selected and show that the change over time rejects the hypothesis.

Consider cohort I to consist of 100 women of whom 30 had self-selected to go to college *because* they did not want to marry. That is, college in this hypothetical case provides no "treatment effect" regarding marriage. If we double the number of college graduate women to 200 we are duplicating what happened in the move from cohort I to cohort III. The 30 single women for whom college provided no "treatment" will remain in the group. As an extreme case, assume that of the additional 100 there is no woman who will eventually remain unmarried; that is, the process that generates nonmarriage is not random. The percentage of women in cohort III who remain single should fall from 30 to 15 percent. But it fell to 8 percent—half the amount. The 30 women in cohort I could not have been self-selected from a population in which the desire to remain single remained constant. There must have been another set of factors accounting for the change in the proportion of college women who ever married.

Figure 2.6   Percentage Never Married, White College Graduate Women

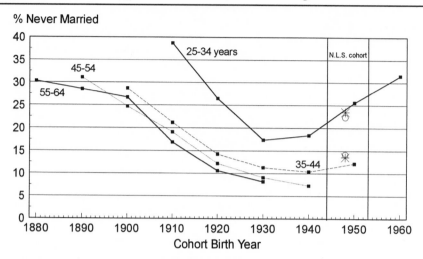

% Never Married

Sources: See table 2.2

Notes: It is not clear why the figure for those aged 55–64 (for the cohort born in 1900) is greater than that for those aged 45–54. The same reversal appears in the data for those having no college. The stars are for the NLS women with ≥ sixteen years of school completed; the circles are for those with a B.A. degree. The census data refer to years of school completed.

Other evidence in support of the claim that self-selection was not the primary factor in the low marriage rate among cohort I can be found in alumnae records. An extensive set of alumnae surveys from Radcliffe College reveals that the percentage never marrying among Radcliffe graduates tracks the national average very closely between 1890 and the 1970s. But the economic and social backgrounds of the Radcliffe graduates remained fairly constant. If anything, because there was an increase in the proportion of Radcliffe students drawn from private, as opposed to public, secondary schools between 1910 and 1960, they may have come from more, rather than less, elite families. Yet their marriage rates increased.[25]

Why, then, did the first cohort of college women marry at low rates and why did the rates begin to increase with subsequent cohorts? An important clue is found in what educated women, in particular educated married women, were allowed to do at the time. Educated women were, by and large, teachers, and, beginning around the end of the nineteenth century, school districts adopted policies restricting the hiring of married women and firing single women who married in service. These "marriage bars" increased slowly to the 1920s and then, with the necessity to ration jobs during the Great Depression, they escalated in the 1930s in teaching, office work, government jobs, and various other positions (Goldin 1990, 1991). Many of the college women who taught when married were employed by private schools or found public school positions in some of the nation's large cities that had reversed their marriage bars earlier in the century or never had such policies. There was also considerable social opprobrium regarding the employment of married women, even those in white collar jobs before the 1940s.

For many of the college-educated women of cohort I, their era left them little choice. They could marry *or* they could have a career in teaching, but they could not easily do both. Marriage bars in teaching were largely removed after 1941 when both the exigencies of the war and the, possibly related, spate of state supreme court rulings declared marriage bars to be "capricious and unjust" (see Goldin 1990, 170).

Even though the percentage of college women who never married by ages 45–54 decreased to 19.1 percent by the cohort born around 1910, it was 6.1 percent for those who were not college-educated. Although it plummeted to 7.3 percent by the cohort born around 1940, it decreased to just 3.8 percent for those with no college education. College women were following a trend in nuptiality that was sweeping the nation, a trend apparent in figure 2.7 for noncollege women. The second factor, then, to have increased the marriage rates of college women was the general increase in marriage and family after the Great Depression. College women were enabled to have both family and job and were enticed to do so by a new norm that had, for a time, universal appeal.

COHORT III: FAMILY THEN JOB

By cohort III, college women had joined a bandwagon. All Americans, independent of educational attainment, were marrying at their highest rates in the twentieth century (see figure 2.7). And college women were not only increasing their marriage rates, but they were also increasing their numbers in proportion to the female population. During the twenty-year expanse of this cohort, graduation and attendance rates doubled (see appendix table 2.1). Women followed the lead of men into college, but the increase of men was so rapid that by the end of the 1940s men substantially outnumbered women.[26] In 1925 there were as many female undergraduates as male undergraduates, and for the ten years preceding there had been more women than men undergraduates (see figure 2.8).[27] But by 1950 there were two men for every woman in college. Even after the peak in postwar enrollments, say in 1960, male undergraduates outnumbered female undergraduates by 1.5 to 1. Because the statistics in figure 2.8 are from contemporaneous data, whereas those in figures 2.1 and 2.2 are for birth cohorts, they more accurately reflect the proportions of males and females in college during a particular year.

Figure 2.7   Percentage Never Married, White Women with No College

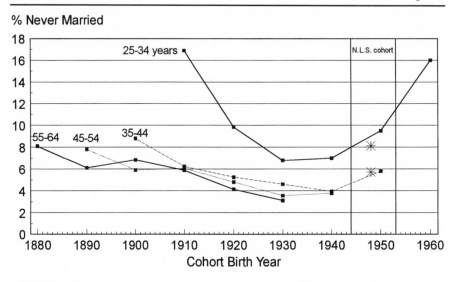

Sources: See table 2.2.

Notes: It is not clear why the figure for those aged 55–64 (for the cohort born in 1900) is greater than that for those aged 45–54. The same reversal appears in the data for those attending college.

Family, not just marriage, took the country by storm in the post–World War II era, and college women were not left out of this trend either. Among the college women who did marry, a far smaller proportion were not having children. About 10 percent, or a third the level for the first cohort, did not have a baby by ages 35–44 in the cohort born between 1926 and 1935. Thus, for the second cohort, 17.5 percent were either not marrying, not having children, or both, compared with 50 percent for the previous cohort.[28] College women had become part of the American mainstream in various ways. College was considerably more open to the masses, college women were marrying at a greater rate, and they were bearing far more children when married. But I emphasize that the timing of these changes is important to the argument and that the change in marriage and fertility rates preceded the increase in college attendance and graduation rates. Further, as noted above, the marriage and fertility increases were quantitatively larger than the increase in the proportion of women who graduated from college. Self-selection, with increasing enrollments, could not be the sole driving force in the changing demography of college women.

After World War II college became more accessible to and desired by Americans from most walks of life. The college enrollment of men soared

Figure 2.8   Ratio of Male to Female Undergraduates

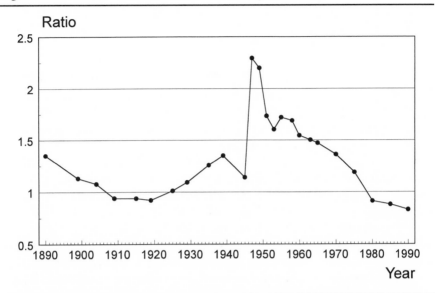

Sources: 1889 to 1953: U.S. Bureau of Education or Office of Education or U.S. Department of Health, Education, and Welfare, *Biennial Survey of Education* (various years); 1960 to 1965: U.S. Department of Health, Education, and Welfare, OFE (various years); 1970 to 1988: U.S. Department of Education and U.S. Department of Health, Education, and Welfare, *Digest of Education Statistics* (various years).

Notes: Undergraduate enrollments include colleges, universities, junior colleges or two-year colleges, normal schools, and teachers colleges. They do not include summer sessions. Part-time and full-time students are treated equally, and some of the rise of female attendance in the most recent period is due to the large enrollment of women who attend college on a part-time basis. Enrollment in graduate school and for professional degrees has been subtracted. Various assumptions have been employed and interpolations used in several years. All underlying data are available upon request from the author.

in the 1950s when they outnumbered women about 2 to 1, as can be seen in figure 2.8. With the decline in the marriage age for all Americans, college became, de facto, an active marriage market in which the supply of husbands greatly outstripped the demand. In general, as the age at first marriage declines and that at leaving school increases, the probability of meeting one's spouse in school increases. Among the college graduates in cohort III who eventually married, 57.2 percent did so before or within a year of college graduation.[29] Marrying a college man—and there was a large financial gain from doing so—was made far more likely through the route of college attendance.

Whether the direct pecuniary return to college was greater than some appropriate alternative rate is relevant for all cohorts. Various factors make the question of particular importance for cohort III. When elites dominated college classes, the "country club" provided the preferred marriage market. But when "ordinary Joe" went to college, the only place for "ordinary Jane" to meet him was at college, and the campus took the place of the country club.

The direct pecuniary returns for the median female graduate probably fell short of the alternative rate of return. But the indirect pecuniary returns through the marriage market could have more than made up for the shortfall and may have been the initial impetus for the subsequent increase in the college attendance of women.

One can easily compute the rate of return to a woman's college education under a number of reasonable assumptions. The median female college graduate in the mid 1950s married in her year of graduation and, if she married, she worked for four years and then exited the labor force for about eight years.[30] She reentered the labor force, therefore, at about age 35. A high school graduate, it will be assumed, also exited from the labor force after four years but remained out for ten years or two years more than the college graduate. The ratio of a college graduate woman's earnings to a high school graduate's was about 1.3 when the college woman entered the labor market and increased to about 1.4 by midlife for both of them.[31] In nominal amounts the college woman, at the moment of her graduation in 1960, earned about $4,000 whereas the high school graduate of 1956 earned about $3,000. The direct expense for each of the four years of college was $837 for public universities and $1,552 for private universities.[32] Both the high school and college graduate women are assumed to work continuously after they reenter the work force until age 60, and their reentry earnings are taken to be those at the time of exit. Under these assumptions, the internal rate of return to the four years of college investment was between 4 and 6 percent.[33] The internal rate of return to college for men at that time exceeded 10 percent, or about double that for women (Freeman 1977). Even though the return to college for men and women—given by the ratio of wages earned by a college graduate to those of a high school graduate—was comparable, the internal rate of return for women was half that for men because of their briefer employment.

But the simple calculation does not consider that college affected a woman's future resources through the man she married, what I will term the "indirect" return to college. In 1960 the probability that a woman aged 30–39 married a college graduate was vastly increased by her having graduated from college. Almost two thirds of all college graduate women (aged 30–39 and married), and more than one third of those who attended college but did not graduate from a four-year school, were married to a college graduate. Only 10 percent of the high school graduate women were married to a college graduate (see Goldin 1992, table 3).

Not only did college-educated women face a much higher probability of marrying a college man, but they also married men with higher incomes within each educational level. Further, among the women who attended college and married college men, those who married during college or immediately following graduation had husbands whose later earnings exceeded those of women who married college men later. The early birds got the bigger worms. On the negative side, however, college women still had a somewhat lower probability of ever getting married, although it was considerably higher than it had been for the previous cohorts.[34]

The indirect computation is quite simple and uses the 1960 PUMS. A standard log earnings equation is estimated for the husbands, to which are added variables concerning wife's education and the timing of their marriage in relation to her education (see Goldin 1992, table 4). The thought experiment involves taking a high school graduate woman in the 1950s, giving her four years of college, and then observing her husband's income in 1960 when she was between ages 30 and 39. The total impact is to increase her husband's income by almost 40 percent.[35] The largest component (66.5 percent of the 40 percent increase) comes from altering the probability that she will marry a more educated man. The likelihood that she will marry a man who attended or graduated from college increases, whereas the likelihood that she will marry at all other levels decreases. This change, then, increases husband's income by 27 percent.

But increasing her education results in another effect. The college graduate woman married the higher-income-earning man at all levels of his education. This factor accounts for 22.5 percent of the total 40 percent, or a 9 percent gain in husband's income for the college graduate woman over that of the high school graduate. Because almost 80 percent of all college graduate women married a man who attended some college, the effect can be thought of as part of the gains from the college marriage market. Another possible interpretation is that women with more education were better able to assist their husbands and thereby directly enhanced their income.[36] Finally, a third effect involves the fact that marrying early, either in college or upon graduation, also increases one's earnings. The "early bird" effect adds the remaining 11 percent of the total 40 percent, or about a 4 percent gain in income for the college graduate woman. Overall, therefore, the thought experiment of giving a high school graduate woman a college education in the 1950s increased her income through the marriage market by 40 percent.[37]

Following the logic of treating the indirect gain as one does the direct gains from education and assuming that a woman marries and does not divorce, the total returns to her education are now greatly augmented and, under reasonable assumptions, double. The total return to college for the second cohort, rather than being in the range of 4 to 6 percent, is now closer to 10 or 11 percent. Thus, the full return to women's college education in the 1950s is increased from a value that is somewhat less than the real return to assets to one that is more in line with the returns to college education for men. Families, therefore, should have been willing to send a daughter to college if they viewed her marriage prospects as being enhanced by the experience. Thus, it would not be surprising if many families refused to pay for their daughter's education if they thought she would simply marry the "boy next door."

The majority of women in cohort III, like most in cohort I, prepared to be teachers. The percentage who were teachers in 1960 decreased slightly from that of the previous group, but was still between 50 and 60 percent. And the proportion who taught at some time in their lives must have been considerably greater. The employment rates of married women in cohort III were not much higher than those of the women in the previous cohort when they were young (29.6 percent versus 25.3 percent) and did not greatly exceed those of women who did not attend college (29.6 percent versus 26.7 percent).[38] But their employment rates greatly exceeded those of women who did not attend college when both groups were older. That is, college women who married and had children were now having family and employment *serially—first* family and *then*, when their children were teenagers, employment.

To recap, cohort III women had substantially higher marriage and fertility rates than cohort I women, were in the labor force considerably more when older but not much more when younger, and were teachers to almost the same degree. The women of cohort III benefited by the substantial decrease in barriers to their employment. Before the 1940s the vast majority of school districts and many employers of office workers had "marriage bars"—stated policies that married women would not be hired and that single women would be fired upon marriage (see Goldin 1990, 1991). Added to the marriage bars were reinforcing and pervasive norms restricting the ability of married women to work for pay. Of additional importance is that the number of men entering college increased substantially in the 1940s and 1950s. Finally, all Americans were marrying earlier and having more children, and these changes affected the college-educated as well. The three changes were reinforcing. College women no longer had to treat marriage and employment as alternatives in life, and college was no longer just a place to learn for it was, de facto, transformed into a place to meet one's spouse.

But as this cohort aged it became less content with its small victories, and successive generations of college women launched a campaign for more equality and finally for real equality. Cohort III included the women who were awakened and provoked by *The Feminine Mystique* (1963), Betty Friedan's description of the experiences of her own generation who graduated from college in the 1940s. Feminism sprang from this group who knew they were as able as their male friends in college but who encountered a world outside college that was not ready for them.

COHORT IV: CAREER THEN FAMILY

Cohort IV—graduating between 1966 and 1979 and born between 1944 and 1957—was the first to enter the labor force in the era of modern feminism. I characterize it as having desired "career then family" because it has delayed marriage and children while it has pursued career. But in consequence, it has experienced a high rate of childlessness. I will also show that its success rate in the employment arena has not been stellar. In the popular press it is often portrayed as trying to combine career with family, juggling both with little spousal help at home.

The *Current Population Reports*, series P-20, reveals that among those with four years or more of college, 27.4 percent of this cohort have not yet had a first birth by 1990.[39] And among those with more than four years of college, 33.3 percent have not. Although not as extreme as those for cohort I, these figures are higher than are those for any cohort since then, and the proportion of women graduating from college is almost ten times what it was in 1910. The statistics do not look good for the "family and career" route, if family is defined as having had at least one birth.[40] But in comparison with previous cohorts, a far higher proportion of cohort IV has been employed since college graduation. Even though many of them have not yet had a first birth, a substantial proportion could be "having it all."[41]

Longitudinal data are needed to gauge the success of the group at attaining career goals. The National Longitudinal Survey for Young Women (NLS-YW) is precisely the cohort of interest and at last interview, in 1991, it was between ages 37 and 47. The survey began in 1968 with about 5,000 participants, but through attrition has been whittled down to about 2,400 in 1988 when the group was between ages 34 and 44. The sample in 1988 of white women who earned a B.A. degree was 600 and 646 for those with four years or more of college. Yet, amazingly enough giving the small sample and its possible attrition bias, its demographic features are very similar to those in the relevant Current Population Survey (CPS) group.

Figures 2.4 and 2.5, giving the proportion of college women having no births by ages 35–44, contain a demarcated area for the NLS cohort and data points for the NLS cohort in 1988. Among white, NLS ever-married women with four years or more of college and aged 35–44 in 1988, 19 percent had not yet had a first birth (figure 2.4); the figure in the relevant CPS is 18.9 percent. For all marital groups the NLS figure is 29.1 percent (figure 2.5), whereas that in the CPS is 28.2 percent. Similarly, for the data on proportion never married by ages 25–34 and 35–44, figure 2.6 shows the close agreement between the NLS data and that in the 1980 census.[42]

Gauging whether a woman has achieved a "career" is considerably less objective than determining whether she had a first birth. Any measure will be arbitrary. Because careers are generally assessed against a male standard,

I begin by defining a "career" as attaining an earnings path that some group of men has achieved. I use the earnings of women in their late 30s and early 40s, when both family and schooling investments were generally complete. The standard will be the man at the 25th percentile in the male distribution. For women to achieve a "career" will not even require that they reach the median of male hourly earnings in any one year. It should be noted at the outset that the wage standard chosen is virtually identical to one that uses, instead, the median wage of the women themselves. Therefore, the standard could be equally expressed in terms of a female, not a male, norm.

I first define a "career" for the NLS women with four years or more of college to be an earnings path for a series of years (say 1987 and 1988) during which their hourly earnings exceed that of the 25th percentile male (in the relevant CPS) also with four years or more of college. I restrict the NLS sample to women who are represented for all the years under consideration (see also notes to tables 2.4 and 2.5 for other exclusions).

Mean and median hourly earnings for women with four years or more of college are fairly similar in the CPS and NLS for the 1980–1988 period, even though neither sample has been weighted in any comparable manner (see table 2.4).[43] Further, it is interesting to note that the medians for women are in the range of the 25th percentile in the male distribution.

The results on "career" are presented in table 2.5 in two ways: Part A includes only women with positive hourly earnings in each of the years considered, that is, only those in the labor force and not self-employed; part B accounts for women who were not in the labor force in any one or all of the years. Thus, if one wants the percentage of all college graduate women who attained "career," the numbers in part B should be used; if one wants the same for women who were in the labor force, part A should be used. Given the definition of a "career," 43 percent of all (white) women with four years or more of college *employed in both 1987 and 1988* are above the mark. Self-employed women are excluded from both the numerator and denominator but are included below in another measure of "career."[44] The comparable figure is 35 percent for women who had at least one child and 56 percent for those who did not. Restricting the definition to attaining the same cutoff for 1985, 1987, and 1988 gives 30 percent for women with children and 47 percent for those without. Note that the percentages just given are for women who were employed in each of the years considered.

But some of the women in this cohort were not in the labor force in one or all of the years considered. Part B of table 2.5 adjusts for the labor force participation rate (for those not self-employed). Using the two-year definition gives 24 percent for women with children and 54 percent for those without. Employing the three-year definition gives 18 percent for women with children and 45 percent for those without.[45] Similar estimates are obtained by using income, rather than hourly earnings, and the income measure enables the inclusion of the self-employed as well as others whose hourly earnings are omitted.

Table 2.4   Hourly Earnings in the Current Population Survey and the National Longitudinal Survey of Young Women

	Males in CPS			Females in CPS			Females in NLS		
Year	Median	25th	N	Median	Mean	N	Median	Mean	N
1980	8.750	6.500	8,977	6.528	7.245	5,793	6.440	6.763	355
1982	10.83	7.778	7,887	8.108	8.896	5,179	7.690	8.443	342
1983	11.43	8.262	7,753	8.750	9.562	5,170	8.560	9.185	345
1985	13.25	10.00	7,781	10.00	10.98	5,360	9.665	10.36	350
1987	15.00	10.91	7,577	11.00	12.10	5,501	11.06	11.99	345
1988	15.63	11.25	7,175	11.25	12.68	5,212	12.16	12.73	340
1991	18.25	13.20	7,155	13.50	14.82	5,717	15.38	15.90	349

Sources: Current Population Survey, Outgoing Rotation Group, NBER-CPS extracts; NLS-YW.

Notes: For CPS: Ages 14–24 in 1968; college graduate = sixteen years attended and completed last year; top-coded values are assigned $1.4 \times$ top amount; hourly earnings is (weekly earnings)/(usual hours worked per week); observation is excluded if hourly earnings < one half relevant minimum wage; race = white. No top code issues are addressed for 1991.

For NLS: Same restrictions on education, race, age, use of one half minimum wage on an hourly basis for exclusion. Data are given for observations containing a nonmissing value for (computed) job experience in 1985. Hourly earnings in NLS is hourly rate of pay in current or last job derived by the NLS from "rate of pay" and "time unit rate of pay" variables. Various extreme outliers are coded as missing values (but are recorded as their actual values in the computation of the career variables in table 2.5). The NLS changed its procedure in 1991, which increased the "rate of pay" by factoring in separate time period information collected from teachers. In both the CPS and NLS earnings from self-employment are excluded.

The percentage of these women who attained family *and* career can be seen in table 2.6 for four definitions of career: the two-year and three-year measures for both the hourly wage and annual income data.[46] The conclusions are not substantially affected by the choice of earnings variable and I will make reference only to the hourly earnings results. Using the three-year definition, only 13 percent of the group attained both "family and career." Another 13 percent had career but no family, and 74 percent did not attain career of whom 78 percent had family. Using the two-year definition, 17 percent attained both "family and career," and another 16 percent had career but no family. For every woman who attained family and career there was another woman who attained career but had no family, using any of the definitions.[47]

The definitions of career just employed may be subject to the criticism that they adopt a male income standard. But, as I noted before, the results are identical if I chose, instead, the standard of the median wage or earnings of all college graduate women in the cohort. If career is meant to proxy success as judged by the individual, a personal standard would be

Table 2.5   Career Attainment Among College Graduate Women: National Longitudinal Survey of Young Women

	Total	Women With Children	Women Without Children
A: Percentage attaining career for white women with ≥ sixteen years school, only for those in labor force 1985, 1987, 1988			
Career: 1987, 1988	43	35	56
Career: 1985, 1987, 1988	37	30	47
B: Percentage attaining career for white women with ≥ sixteen years school, for those in *and* out of labor force			
Career: 1987, 1988	33	24	54
Career: 1985, 1987, 1988	26	18	45

Source: NLS-YW.

Notes: Career is defined as having hourly earnings exceeding that of the 25th percentile male (white, ≥ sixteen years schooling) in the CPS of the relevant year (see table 2.4). NLS women are included if they are in the sample for all of the years considered (for example, 1987 and 1988) and have earnings data that are not missing. The self-employed are excluded from both numerator and denominator, as are those who refused to answer questions on their earnings. Children born to women until the end of the survey (1991, although there are only seventeen first births after 1985) are included. The figures that are unconditional on labor force participation give a zero value to career for women who are out of the labor force in any of the years considered. Women whose hourly earnings are below one half the minimum wage are considered to be out of the labor force. Had they been included in the labor force, the career percentages conditional on labor force participation would be somewhat lower and closer to those unconditional on labor force participation.

more appropriate. But the intent is not to discern whether women found contentment in their paid work. Rather, it is to assess whether those observing them judge that they attained careers. Another potential criticism is that life continues after age 40 and careers for many begin in midlife. Once again, the issue here is whether cohort IV has achieved "family and career" by midlife, an oft-stated goal of many in cohorts IV and V.

Other definitions can be devised that do not use an income standard. Consider, for example, a definition of career based on employment and full-time commitment, with no income or hourly wage cutoff. More concretely, consider a woman to have a career if she is in the labor force for each of three years (1985, 1987, and 1988) during which time she is generally a full-time worker (as an employee or self-employed).[48] Among those in the sample who had at least one child, 31 percent had careers using this definition, and among those who did not have a child 67 percent had careers. But only 22 percent of the total group had "family and

Table 2.6   Family and Career for Cohort IV: Four Definitions of Career

Career	Family	
	Children	No Children
Using hourly wage measure: 1985, 1987, 1988 ($N = 482$)		
No	57.7%	16.2%
Yes	13.1	13.1
Using hourly wage measure: 1987, 1988 ($N = 511$)		
No	53.6%	13.5%
Yes	17.0	15.9
Using income measure: 1985, 1987, 1988 ($N = 585$)		
No	60.7%	15.6%
Yes	12.1	11.6
Using income measure: 1987, 1988 ($N = 611$)		
No	54.7%	12.3%
Yes	17.3	15.7

Source: NLS-YW.

Notes: See tables 2.4 and 2.5. The definition of career using income is similar to that using the hourly wage. The cutoff point uses the data for men in table 2.4 multiplied by 2,000 hours. Women in the NLS who were self-employed and others with missing hours information are included in the earnings data. Earnings is the aggregate of wage and salary, and business, professional, and farm income.

career" using this definition. The percentage is higher than that obtained using the income or hourly wage cutoff, but it still implies that one college graduate woman in 4.5 attained "family and career" by age 40.

Defining career as (usually) full-time, although not necessarily year-round, employment during each of three years, is not what is generally meant by career. More than 40 percent of the women deemed to have a career using this definition did not, in 1985, attain the income level of a college graduate man at the 25th percentile of the male distribution; just 53 percent of these "career" women attained the income level of the college graduate man at the 25th percentile of the male distribution in both 1985 and 1987.[49] Why the figure for "family and career" is low even when lenient criteria are used can be understood by a decomposition. First is the fact that 28 percent of the women in the group did not have children, implying that the percentage with "family and career" cannot exceed 72 percent using any standard for career. Further, among those who had children, 46 percent were in the labor force for all three years (1985, 1987, and 1988). The full-time commitment criterion brings the final figure down to 22 percent.

One may wonder what percentage of men would pass the "career" standard imposed here. The NLS for Young Men was terminated in 1983 owing to attrition but a substitute can be found in the Panel Study of Income Dynamics (see Moffitt and Gottschalk 1993).[50] The probability that a man above the 20th percentile remained in that position for another year was 92 percent, the probability that he would stay for two years was 85 percent, and for four years was 78 percent. If the same probabilities held for the man above the 25th percentile (and held for college men to the same degree as for all men), 64 percent of men would have been above the mark using the two-year definition, whereas 43 percent of all college women were in the NLS.

The most generous interpretation of the data is that between one fifth and one quarter of all college graduate women with children attained career as they neared midlife. And about one half of the women without children have achieved career. But because almost 30 percent of the cohort has not yet had its first birth, between 17 percent (0.712×24 percent) and 13 percent (0.712×18 percent) of the cohort have realized the goal of "family and career."

It is difficult to say what factors encouraged and enabled the women in this cohort to attain "family and career." Slightly more of the career women than the noncareer women expressed a desire when they were 15 to 25 years old for paid employment when 35 years old (60.3 percent versus 56.7 percent in 1969). But most of the difference comes from the group who never had children among those attaining career (63.5 percent versus 57.1 percent).[51] That is, those eventually attaining career and no family were more apt to have expressed an early desire for paid employment.

Divorce was considerably more common among the ever-married women who attained career than among those who did not (37.5 percent versus 23.0 percent using hourly earnings; 43.9 percent versus 22.5 percent using income). And conditioning on having children does not change the difference much (33.3 percent versus 16.9 percent using hourly earnings; 37.1 percent versus 18.1 percent using income). It was career, not children, that somehow affected divorce, or vice versa. College graduate women with both family and career had a divorce rate 20 to 30 percent higher than average for the entire group of college women.[52] Not only was divorce more common, but marriage was less frequent among college women who would eventually attain career. Among those who achieved career, 76 percent married by 1988, whereas among those who did not attain career 87 percent married.[53] Thus, in 1985 only 53 percent of the career group was currently married, whereas 79 percent of the noncareer group was. I would like to emphasize, however, that the determination of "family and career" does not require that the college woman was currently married nor that she ever married.

Women with careers, not surprisingly, had more years of education than average college women (64 percent of those with careers had more than sixteen years versus 39 percent of those without careers). But there is no clear separation between those who attained their career with children and without (59 percent of those with children had more than sixteen years of schooling whereas 68 percent of those without children did). The NLS, despite its richness, does not hold the answer to the question in the minds of many college women today: What is the key to "family and career"? There are no obvious early differences and those that develop later in life, for example, with regard to the timing of marriage and children, may be correlated with unobservable differences across individuals.

When today's young college women observe the experiences of cohort IV, it is clear why they express considerable frustration. Only 17 percent of the college graduate women in that cohort have achieved *both* "family and career" using the two-year definition and just 13 percent have using the three-year definition.[54] Looking on the bright side, however, one might consider these numbers to be nontrivial proportions of the cohort. And not only are they nontrivial, but they are probably much higher than achieved by cohort III. That is, cohort IV is probably the first in U.S. history to contain even a small group who managed to reach midlife with both family and career. But the proportion is sufficiently small that young women today have judged cohort IV to have failed at "having it all."

But are college women today judging the success or failure of cohort IV by their own standards, not those of cohort IV? The NLS surveyed its participants concerning the desire for future births. Beginning in 1978 the question was asked of all women, rather than just those who were ever married. Among those who remained in the sample to 1991 and who did not have a first birth by 1991, 48.4 percent had desired one in 1978. For those in the group who were aged 24–29 in 1978, 62.9 percent did. If the older group had been similarly inclined when they were aged 24–29, a considerable proportion (19 percent = 63 percent × 30 percent, where 30 percent = percentage with no births by 1991) of the entire cohort was disappointed with the "family" outcome. That is, a greater percentage of the group (19 percent) was disappointed with not having children than eventually achieved the "family and career" outcome (between 13 and 17 percent).

SUMMARY AND CONCLUSIONS

The demographic and labor force experiences of college women changed considerably across the past century. In the first cohort of college women studied (graduating c. 1910), 50 percent either never married or never had a first birth. But by the third cohort (graduating c. 1955), college graduate women were marrying and having children at rates that were high both by absolute standards and relative to other women their age. Cohort IV (graduating c. 1972) is the most recent to have nearly completed its fertility history and rates of childlessness appear to have climbed once again, although they are far lower than for cohort I. Yet among women in this cohort who attained "career" status, using my definitions, nearly 50 percent were childless by ages 37–47. "Career" still entails large costs.

I have emphasized altered social constraints surrounding women's paid employment as generating many of the changes across the cohorts. There is at least one important complication. College women themselves fought for many of these changes. Around the turn of the century a small proportion of men and women attended and graduated from college. Attendance for men climbed considerably just after World War II when college men outnumbered women by about 2 to 1. Some time during the 1940s women realized that they could have family and job—albeit serially timed—and that college could enable and enhance both. Although the direct returns to college for women probably did not justify their increased enrollments, the heightened indirect returns through the marriage market did. Thus, some portion of the increase in college attendance and graduation rates of the women in cohort III was due to the simple fact that they followed men into college. By today's standards, that is not a kind characterization. But, paradoxically, profound social change was set in motion by cohort III, women who probably entered college with the least motivation for academically serious studies and whose "Mrs." degrees were worth nearly half of the total returns from their B.A.s.[55]

Cohort IV was the recipient of cohort III's legacy: considerably loosened constraints in educational and labor market choices. But, as these women reach midlife perhaps one sixth have thus far achieved "family and career." Is it no wonder that the women of cohort V are nervous about reaching that elusive goal?

ACKNOWLEDGMENTS

This paper derives from "The Meaning of College in the Lives of American Women: The Past Hundred Years," National Bureau of Economic Research Working Paper No. 4099. I repeat the acknowledgments made in that paper by thanking the students of Economics 1356 (Spring 1991) for furnishing the stimulus for this study, and the participants of public lectures at numerous colleges and universities, among them Wellesley College, Bates College, Simmons College, Bard College, Tufts University, the University of Pittsburgh, the University of Iowa, and Queen's University, Ontario, for their comments. The earlier paper was presented at the Conference on Women's Human Capital and Development, May 18–22, 1992, Bellagio, Italy, and I acknowledge the helpful comments of the discussants, John Strauss and Barbara Torrey, as well as those of the other participants. I thank Boris Simkovich for his research assistance on the earlier version and Rohini Somanathan and Linda Tuch for their research assistance on this version. Larry Katz commented on both drafts. I was prompted to write this paper by Fran Blau's comments on the previous version: "I would love to see you do a similar type of analysis for "the intermediate cohort" [cohort IV]—That is, our cohort!"

APPENDIX

Appendix Table 2.1   College Attendance and Graduation Rates by Sex, for Cohorts Born 1875–1955

Birth Year	White Males		White Females				
	Attended College (1)	Graduated from College (2)	Attended College (3)	Graduated from College (4)	(3)/(1)	(4)/(2)	(2)/(1)− (4)/(3)
1875	6.4%	3.4%	5.5%	2.0%	.86	.59	16.8
1880.5	7.9	4.2	7.2	2.7	.91	.64	15.7
1887.5	9.6	4.6	8.7	3.3	.91	.72	10.0
1890.5	9.5	5.0	8.9	3.4	.94	.68	14.4
1897.5	11.4	5.8	11.8	4.3	.97	.74	14.4
1902.5	15.8	9.2	15.4	6.2	.97	.67	18.0
1904.5	17.4	10.5	15.8	7.2	.91	.69	14.8
1906.5	17.1	9.7	16.8	7.8	.98	.80	10.3
1908.5	18.2	9.8	17.0	7.9	.93	.78	7.4
1912.5	19.7	9.9	17.4	7.3	.88	.74	8.3
1914.5	20.7	11.0	17.5	7.7	.85	.70	9.1
1916.5	20.0	11.0	16.6	7.3	.83	.66	11.0
1918.5	23.3	12.6	16.8	7.1	.72	.56	11.8
1920.5	25.4	13.9	17.4	7.6	.69	.55	11.0
1924.5	29.1	17.0	19.4	8.6	.67	.51	14.1
1927	31.9	19.2	22.9	10.6	.72	.55	13.9
1930	33.1	20.1	23.6	11.2	.71	.56	13.3
1933	37.9	24.2	28.3	14.0	.75	.58	14.4
1935	38.4	24.2	28.6	12.9	.74	.53	17.9
1938	39.7	24.1	30.3	15.0	.76	.62	11.2
1940	43.8	26.6	34.4	16.4	.79	.62	13.0
1943	47.9	29.6	37.5	18.4	.78	.62	12.7
1945	50.7	31.6	41.4	22.3	.82	.71	8.5
1948[a]	59.2	36.9	55.0	30.7	.93	.83	6.5
1950[a]	59.7	34.4	55.7	28.8	.93	.84	5.9
1954[a]	52.5	29.7	53.3	28.1	1.02	.95	3.9
1955[a]	50.3	30.4	54.0	28.6	1.07	.94	7.5

Sources: U.S. Bureau of the Census, series P-20, "Educational Attainment in the United States" (various years).

Notes: In virtually all cases only the responses of individuals aged 45–54 or 55–64 were used. For cohorts born since 1945 projections were made to 1995 or 1997 on the basis of changes for the preceding cohort that was aged 35–39 (30–34) in 1977 and 45–49 (40–44) in 1987.

[a]Projections to 1995 or 1997 based on the experiences of the previous cohorts.

NOTES

1. The ratio of men to women in professional schools was 23.4 in 1960 but 1.66 in 1988. The ratio in graduate schools was 2.48 in 1960 but 0.90 in 1988 (U.S. Department of Education, Digest 1988; U.S. Department of H.E.W., O.F.E. 1960).

2. The 50 percent figure is for the cohort born c. 1890: 31.1 percent (= percent never married) + [27.6 percent (= percent having no children by ages 35–44) × 68.9 percent (= percent ever married)].

3. When I refer to selection bias I mean that regarding marriage and family only. The issue is whether the college women in cohort I married and had children at lower rates because they were initially a self-selected group. Under that assumption, college enabled them to fulfill their desires. Alternatively, college could have had a true treatment effect. In this case, if a random group of bright women were allowed to go to college, they would alter their marriage and family goals because they would be given a chance to have a career, under the constraints of the day that family and career were incompatible.

4. The figure is 28.8 percent for no first births by 1991 for white women with ≥ sixteen years of education (28.6 percent for white women with B.A. degrees) conditional on being in the sample in 1991.

5. This conclusion is based, admittedly, on a small sample—those in my Economics 1356 class, other undergraduates with whom I have spoken, and the impressions of friends who teach generation X.

6. It should be noted at the outset that in all of the empirical work that follows only white men and women are considered because of the considerably smaller number of nonwhites who attended college in the past. A similar study of African American college women could be done using alumnae records of all-black universities and colleges, but I have not yet done it.

7. The percentage attending college may be exaggerated for the older cohorts, although differences by sex could be accurate. I suspect the figures are exaggerated because the data for high school graduates are overstated in the 1940 census (see Goldin 1994).

8. Both the graduation rates and the attendance rates are as of ages 45–54 or 55–64. See figures 2.1 and 2.2 for sources and notes.

9. In 1962, for example, two-year colleges accounted for 14 percent of all college enrollees for both males and females. Yet the ratio of graduation rates to attendance rates was 61 percent for males but 48 percent for females in the birth cohort of 1940 (see appendix table 2.1). Thus, the differences in graduation rates between males and females must be accounted for by differential graduation from four-year colleges. The same is probably not the case for earlier cohorts. Graduation rates were much lower for women in the cohorts born before 1905, thus graduating before about 1927. A large proportion of the women in these cohorts who attended college were in teachers colleges and normal

schools, but it is difficult to separate data for the two-year normal schools from those for the four-year teachers colleges in those years. Normal schools are of little importance after the 1940s.

10. "Full time" here, means without interruption (nonintermittently) and full time, in the usual manner (meaning at least 35 to 40 hours a week).

11. Career earnings are akin to a large bonus at the end of the second and, possibly, third years.

12. The model can be expanded to account for why the women in cohort III went to college even when the increase in their earnings did not result in a sufficiently high rate of return. If college gained them entry to a lucrative "marriage market," as I claim below, their budget constraint will be shifted upwards.

13. By (e, f, e) is meant that the first period is spent in the labor force full time, the second at home with family full time, and the third and final period in the labor force full time. The allocation produces an interior point because the gains from job experience accrue only when experience is continuous.

14. The budget constraint may not be invariant when, as in this framework, there is a return to experience for a portion of the last period or a portion of the first. The invariant portion will involve a "timing error," similar to the excluded combination (e, f, e). That is, a woman can work two consecutive periods and have a child in either the first or the last period. The minimum time required for a child is $T \times k$, leaving $T \times (1 - k)$ for paid employment. If the $T \times (1 - k)$ portion is taken at the start of the first period, it earns at only w^e, and the budget constraint will not include the portion with slope $w^e(1 + r)$.

15. The reason is simply an assumption of the framework that a child requires $k \times T$ time and that anything less will not produce a family.

16. This is because $(1.06)^7 = 0.50$.

17. The maximum income for this cohort might be thought of as Y', which is full-time work for three periods but no career.

18. The problem might be that if point IV is attempted through the (e, e, f) route, marriage and children are put off too long, and biological clocks determine outcomes. One would have to add stochastic terms into a more elaborate model. Alternatively, when point IV is attempted through the (f, e, e) route, children often consume the time demands of career.

19. See Cookingham (1984) for references.

20. I focus on college graduates to get around the problem that college attendance includes those at two-year colleges and normal schools. I have assumed that women graduated from college at age 22, but that is generally a minimum, and the age for the earlier cohorts was probably much higher.

21. The age group is determined by the demands of the most recent data.

22. These figures are for women aged 45–54. It should be emphasized that even women in this cohort who did not attend college also had a rather low rate of ever marrying.

  I use the language of choice (for example, opt) even though I contend that many cohorts of college women were extremely constrained in their choice set. Many faced a stark choice of having family *or* having a career. The language of choice may be imperfect for all women. The reader should take the use of words, such as choice and opt, as a shorthand to mean that choices are subject to various constraints. In addition, it is always the case that some women, college and noncollege, may not have made intentional and volitional choices.

23. U.S. Bureau of the Census (1953, 1966, 1972) and the 1940 PUMS.

24. I do not yet know what accounts for the sharp increase in college graduation rates, and to a lesser extent college attendance rates, with cohorts born around 1897. It is possible that the World War I military draft accounts for the rise.

25. These findings come from a project using two extraordinary surveys of Radcliffe graduates: the Centennial Survey (covering graduating cohorts from 1910 to 1975) and that taken during the semicentennial in 1928 (covering graduating cohorts from around 1890). I will be using these surveys in future research on college women. The percentage graduating from public secondary schools was 67 percent for the 1910–1919 graduating cohort but 49.4 percent for the 1950–1959 graduating cohort. See Solomon (1985) for a discussion of the semicentennial survey; the data are held by the Henry Murray Research Center of Radcliffe College.

26. It should be noted that World War II also affected women's presence in the academy because they were allowed to enroll in far greater numbers during the shortage of male students. Many universities, such as Harvard, changed their rules during World War II, allowing women to take classes previously reserved for men only.

27. Attendance at both junior colleges and normal schools could inflate the statistics for women more than for men. Both were intended for less than a four-year period. As a percentage of total undergraduate enrollment by sex, junior (or two-year) colleges have been attended by men to the same degree as women. That was not the case for normal schools, a teacher-training program that did not culminate in a degree. Women, to a far greater extent than men, attended normal schools and state teachers colleges, although the latter were four-year institutions. The education statistics for the pre-1940s, however, do not conveniently separate individuals who attended normal schools from those who attended state teachers colleges. Data for 1929 to 1930 indicate that among all female undergraduates in state teachers colleges and normal schools only 20 percent were in normal schools. The same data also indicate that about 30 percent of all female undergraduates who began in teachers colleges finished the four-year program and graduated (U.S. Bureau of Education Biennial Survey 1928–1930).

28. Only 8.2 percent of the cohort born between 1926 and 1935 never married by ages 55–64. The 17.5 percent figure is: 8.2 percent (= percent

never married) + [91.8 percent × 10.1 percent (= percent with no children among those ever married, by ages 35–44)].

29. See Goldin (1992), table 2. The figure is computed from the 1960 PUMS by defining "marriage before or in year of school completion" as: (years of school attended + 6) ≥ age at first marriage.

30. In a sample of about 700 female graduates of the class of 1957, 42 percent married before or within eight months of graduation (see Goldin 1992). Of those who were married by 1964, or seven years after graduation, the median woman worked until 1961, or for four years after graduation. In 1964 the median graduate had one 3-year-old and an infant (or was probably expecting one). Among those without children, more than 80 percent were in the labor force. The addition of a child under age 3 reduced participation to 26 percent and a 3-to-5-year-old reduced it to 35 percent. There were too few women with children ages 6 and over to observe when women, in this sample, began to reenter the labor market. I assume here that most reentered when their children began first grade. Thus, they exited after four years and remained out for eight years, or long enough for the younger of the two to be 5 or 6 years old. My sense is that, for various reasons, this is an underestimate of the median time spent out and will, therefore, result in an overstatement of the rate of return.

31. The annual starting income for college graduates in the class of 1957 was about $3,800 (1957 dollar), close to the figure from the 1960 PUMS for college graduate women, assuming an annual increase, in nominal terms, of about 2.5 percent. The ratio of a college graduate's annual income to a high school graduate's was 1.3, in the 1960 PUMS, for those aged 25–29, but 1.4 for those aged 44–49.

32. Figures are for tuition, room, and (seven-day) board (U.S. Department of Health, Education, and Welfare 1960).

33. The calculation solves for r in the standard equation:

$$\Sigma C_t / (1+r)^t + \Sigma \Upsilon_t^c (1+r)^t = \Sigma \Upsilon_t^{hs} / (1+r)^t,$$

where C = direct costs of college, Υ^c = income of a college-educated woman, Υ^{hs} = income of a high school–educated woman. A woman is assumed to graduate from high school at age 18, work until she exits from the labor force at age 22 (presumably to raise a family), reenter the labor force at age 32, and retire at age 60. If she, instead, graduates from college, she works from 22 to 26, exits at 26, reenters at 34, and retires at 60. Wages for both high school and college graduate women rise with job experience so that the ratio begins at 1.3 but rises to 1.4 by midlife.

34. For women aged 30–39 in 1960, 6 percent of those who graduated from high school but did not attend college had never married. Of those who attended college, but did not complete four years, 7.1 percent had not married. Of those who graduated from college, 15.1 percent were still in the never-married group in 1960, although by the 1980s only 8 percent of this group had never married.

35. The total change in (the log of) income from is 0.334 and exp(0.334) = 1.3965, or about 40 percent. The 0.334 figure is almost identical to the difference in the coefficients on wife's education (college minus high school graduate = 0.324) in a regression on her husband's income, not including any other covariates.

36. Because the factor "married in college" is not of importance for the group aged 50–59 (see Goldin 1992), the marriage market hypothesis seems more compelling.

    Benham (1974) estimates a similar equation, using the 1960 PUMS, but with a different purpose. He interprets the positive coefficient on women's education in the male earnings equation as indicating the greater productivity of more educated women in the home and their impact on their husband's earnings. To distinguish between the marriage market and productivity hypotheses, Benham includes the wife's age at marriage in the husband's earnings equation, together with their respective levels of education. Women who marry later given their level of education have a higher probability of having finished their education after marriage. Under the selectivity hypothesis husband's earnings should be unaffected by postmarriage education, whereas it might be affected under the productivity hypothesis. Benham finds a negative coefficient on the age at marriage and interprets it as not supporting the selectivity hypothesis. But women who marry later, given their level of education, were less likely to have taken advantage of the marriage market in college or high school. That is, Benham's variable is picking up part of the "early bird" effect.

    More important, my way of separating the productivity hypothesis from that concerning the marriage market is to note that the productivity hypothesis can take effect only within educational groups. The largest single effect on a woman's income from going to college was from marrying a college-educated man. That effect cannot be due to her enhancing his productivity but must, instead, be sought in a marriage market model.

37. How one treats this income depends on various assumptions concerning whether husbands and wives share all income equally, how long a woman remains married, and whether, should she divorce, she receives alimony in proportion to her husband's income.

38. The 25.3 percent figure is for those graduating around 1928 to 1937, whereas the 29.6 percent figure is for those graduating around 1948 to 1957.

39. The figure for those with a B.A. degree is 26.9 percent in 1992, although the educational categories change from 1990 to 1992. There is a decrease in those without a first birth moving from the measure $\geq$ four years of college to having a B.A. degree that can be duplicated, to some extent, in the NLS data.

40. I also include, below, adopted children and stepchildren (see endnote 47).

41. I am adopting the language of the women in cohort IV and the popular press in defining "having it all" as children and career. Many women find happiness without children and some, with children, would also

want to include having a loving husband. I am not denying the diversity of opinion on what constitutes personal happiness. I am, however, using the most common and least restrictive definition of family by those in cohort IV and others who describe its aspirations.

42. I use ≥ sixteen years of schooling, as the definition of college graduate, when making comparisons with the CPS but a B.A. degree when not. When the *Current Population Reports* series P-20 refers to 35-to-44-year-olds, I drop the youngest age in the NLS for comparison. Consistency is attempted with any data set in making comparisons with the NLS.

43. The NLS calculated hourly earnings differently in 1991 than before (see table 2.4). For that reason, I do not use 1991 in the calculation of "career."

44. The self-employed are also excluded from the hourly earnings figures in the CPS.

45. Note that the three-year definition really spans four years because of the absence of data for 1986.

46. The income measure is almost exactly the same as the hourly wage measure. It uses the hourly wage of the male at the 25th percentile multiplied by 2,000 hours. The group of women included expands, in part, because it includes the self-employed.

47. In the definition of family, only "own" births have been included. Including adopted children increases the "family and career" group minimally to between 13.3 and 17.4 percent of the total (using the hourly earnings measure); adding stepchildren plus adopted children increases the group to between 14.7 and 19.6 percent.

48. The criteria are applied to white women, with highest grade completed equal to sixteen years or more. The women must have been in the labor force in 1985, 1987, and 1988 (using the CPS definition of labor force participation), and their usual hours worked weekly in the preceding year must have exceeded 39. Because hours and labor force participation apply to different years, there are some cases of missing values for usual hours worked for women considered in the labor force. These cases have been coded as "career" as long as usual hours in other years exceeds 39 a week or is missing. This decision rule results in an upper bound estimate of the percentage with "career."

49. See the note to table 2.6 for the procedure used to obtain the income at the 25th percentile of the male distribution.

50. The Moffitt and Gottschalk (1993) data are not given by educational group. I am using the transition matrix for the entire sample. In addition, they give quintiles not quartiles.

51. These data use the three-year, hourly-earnings definition of career. See table 2.5.

52. I have conditioned the entire group on remaining in the sample in 1987. A range is given for the hourly and annual income measures using the three-year definition.

53. The data throughout this section use the three-year hourly wage measure of career described above and given in tables 2.5 and 2.6.

54. The 13 and 17 percent figures are derived from the underlying data, but could also be obtained by multiplying the percentage of women attaining careers who had a first birth by the percentage having a first birth.

55. By academically serious studies I am relying on the distribution of college majors and the fact that cohort III included the greatest percentage of education majors of any of the cohorts. One could, of course, make similar claims about the recent generation of college men and women who are majoring in business and commerce. I am also basing the statement on the comments on contemporary college guidance counselors who noted the problems of keeping young women in college when the pull of marriage and family was so strong.

Commentary on Chapter 2

Ileen A. DeVault

In "Career and Family," as she has done many times before, Claudia Goldin provides us with firm economic evidence that allows us to expand on arguments that social historians have made. Historians of women's education have long suspected and discussed the patterns pointed out here by Goldin. In particular, I thought of Margaret Rossiter's work (1982) on the history of women scientists since the late nineteenth century. Rossiter found that the never-married women of Goldin's cohort I created careers for themselves despite institutional hostility, while the married women scientists of the mid-twentieth century (especially Goldin's cohort III) failed to gain full careers or to be taken seriously.

Goldin makes a convincing and interesting argument about the "treatment effect" of college education for women. She also weaves the historiography of women's education very effectively into her discussion of women's changing life plans. On the other hand, it seems to me that we have to talk not only about changes in women's life plans and goals, but also about changes (or lack of changes!) in men—and men's life plans. This might help explain the unusually high divorce rate Goldin finds for her cohort IV: In Goldin's analysis, "family" is represented by children, but the high divorce rate reminds us that "family"—and family-related tasks—includes husbands as well. Historians, sociologists, and economists have found, for example, that there has been much less change over the past twenty to thirty years in men's participation in housework than in women's. Historians and sociologists have also argued in recent years that the very definition of "family" has changed over time. To give just one example relevant to Goldin's argument, recent research suggests that cohort I women such as the founder of Cornell's School of Home Economics, Martha Van Rensselaer, and her life partner, Flora Rose, may have formed a type of alternative family. Certainly their relationship helped to sustain their long and productive careers (see Babbitt 1995). It is hard to know how to analyze these shifting forms and definitions of alternative "families"—especially in economics. After all, standard data sources such as the U.S. Census do not acknowledge such alternatives. But perhaps cohort V needs to know that "family" can be whoever you love; happiness does not have to equal a husband and 2.6 (or 1.8) children.

One of the intriguing lessons brought home to me by Goldin's discussion of these five different cohorts of college women was the reminder that not only does each cohort serve as a role model for the following cohort, but each cohort is also, either literally or figuratively, made up of daughters of the previous cohort. In other words, each cohort passes on—directly or indirectly—their expectations and experiences to the next generation.

This is, in fact, the problematic situation that led Goldin to develop this paper in the first place: the frustration expressed by today's college women when they look toward those of us in cohort IV for role models. Today's college women are *not* planning on a career that will give them an income equivalent to that of the 25th percentile of men (or on a median salary substantially *below* that of men). Cohort V women have much grander plans for themselves. I think of the Cornell senior who, a few years ago, informed me that her career goal was to become "the CEO of a major corporation, such as General Motors." What is the advice or lesson that we in cohort IV can give to the young women we teach and mentor? Yes, we can urge them to attempt to achieve their ideal of career and family—but they will need to remember as they make that attempt what *we* have all learned about functioning in male-dominated hierarchies (whether they be corporate or academic!): that it is virtually never as simple and straightforward as we would have liked. And slamming into the glass ceiling can be quite painful.

Commentary on Chapter 2

Myra H. Strober

"Career and Family" is a rich paper with much to be learned from a careful reading of its tables, figures, and text. Of major interest are the historical data on women's college attendance and graduation and on marriage and birth rates for women with various levels of educational attainment.

Data on birth rates that put current-day laments about women's low rates of fertility into historical perspective are particularly valuable. The paper also develops a useful indifference curve—budget constraint model of college women graduates' work and family choices. In her empirical work, Goldin presents the very interesting finding that only about half of the economic return to college for women in cohort III (those born between approximately 1924 and 1943 and graduating from college between 1946 and 1965) resulted from an increase in their own earnings. The other half resulted from the increased probability of marrying a high-earning husband who was a college graduate.

Goldin motivates her study of earlier cohorts by discussing the frustration in combining work and family experienced by the current cohort of college women in cohort V (born between 1958 and 1973 and graduating from college between 1980 and 1995). She finds that very few women even in the directly preceding generation, cohort IV (born between 1944 and 1957 and graduating from college between 1966 and 1979), were able to attain the kind of life she believes women in cohort V hope to lead. In the first place, Goldin argues, women in cohort IV sought to attain career first and then have a family, whereas women in cohort V want to do the two simultaneously. In the second place, according to Goldin's definitions, very few in cohort IV (between one fifth and one quarter, "using the most generous interpretation of the data") had attained both family and career by the time they had reached age 40. Goldin concludes that the lack of success of women in previous cohorts in achieving family and career may make women in cohort V nervous about reaching that elusive goal themselves.

My discussion of Goldin's paper focuses primarily on the experience of women in cohort V and has three parts. First, I argue that cohort V women might deem more cohort IV women as having careers than Goldin does.

Second, I question whether cohort V and cohort IV differ with respect to the timing of career and family in the way that Goldin suggests. Finally, I examine the various causes of cohort V's dissatisfactions.

WHO HAS A CAREER AND WHO DOESN'T?

The definitions of career and family are important to understanding Goldin's argument. The paper provides several definitions of having achieved "career," but all of them require having several years (two or three) of continuous labor force participation. They also require either having earnings that exceed that of the 25th percentile for male college graduates or having worked full time (at least 40 hours a week) for three years. The definition of having achieved "family" is having at least one birth.

Career is a slippery concept to operationalize, particularly without data on occupation and work history. The dictionary defines a career as "a chosen pursuit; life work" (*American Heritage Dictionary*) or "a course of professional life or employment, which affords opportunity for progress or advancement in the world" (*Oxford English Dictionary*). Careers are generally distinguished from jobs in terms of both worker commitment and opportunity for advancement.

Who decides whether someone is in a career or not is a key question. Clearly, with respect to Goldin's argument, it must be women in cohort V that decide. In making such a determination about a particular older woman, a young woman would have more information than Goldin has, especially information about occupation, work history, and the woman's degree of commitment to a profession or organization. Collectively, using their own criteria, young women might well have a more inclusive definition of career than Goldin does.

For example, young women might well deem someone as having a career even if she did not earn above the 25th percentile of the wage distribution for male college graduates (which, in dollar terms, is equivalent to being above the median for women college graduates). A woman with a commitment to a low-paying, predominantly female profession (nursery school teaching, child care work, social work, as examples) or one of the arts (photographer, actress, writer), might well earn below the median for college women, particularly if she worked part time. Can a woman be considered to have attained a career if she works part time in a low-paid occupation?

It is likely that a young woman's answer to that question would depend upon what she wants for her own future. If she is seeking a full-time, "high-powered" career with high income in a formerly all-male occupation, then she would probably categorize women with part-time careers in traditionally female occupations as "not having a career." It may be that the young women at high-prestige institutions, the ones that Goldin talks to at Harvard or the ones I talk to at Stanford, are seeking nontraditional careers.[1] But the fact is that large numbers of college women are continuing to enter traditionally female careers in fields that do not pay high salaries and permit part-time or part-year work. My guess is that if we asked a random sample of young women in cohort V whether they knew women who had careers of the kind they were seeking and also had children, the percentage would be greater than that suggested by Goldin's definitions.

TIMING OF CAREER AND FAMILY

What about the contention that cohort IV members sought to have work and family serially while cohort V members want them simultaneously? It is not at all clear to me that the goals of cohort V with respect to the timing of work and family are in fact different from those of cohort IV.

In my study of the Stanford graduates of the class of 1981 (members of cohort V), I find that nine years after graduation, at about age 31, although two thirds of the women in the sample are married, only one third have children. In other words, at least 40 percent of the married women are postponing having children (some, of course, may be "postponing" it permanently) in order to concentrate first on career (see Strober and Chan 1996).

COHORT V'S FRUSTRATIONS

If cohort V women are frustrated, their uneasiness may have as much to do with their own experiences as with what they have observed about cohort IV. In my consulting in corporations with women in management, young women tell me that certainly a part of their distress stems from the absence of women in high-level management positions, that there seems to be a "glass ceiling" through which almost no women have yet passed. But there seem to be three aspects of their lives that are at least as important to them as the absence of women in high-level positions.

The first concerns the home front. Although Goldin defines "family" as having children, many of the women I talk to do not simply want career and family. They want a family life that includes a "happy" and egalitarian marriage and parenting. They are not interested in being a part of a dual career couple where the wife has sole responsibility for housework and childrearing. Nor are they interested in having children and career if the combination means they wind up with a divorce and single-parenthood. What is distressing to them is that they have difficulty getting their own partners to be egalitarian with respect to child care or that they see so few egalitarian parenting relationships in their *own* cohort, never mind some preceding cohort.[2]

Second, young women managers are distressed by the inequalities of pay between women and men in their workplaces. Beyond wanting a career in a traditionally male field, they want a career in which they are paid the same as their male colleagues. Although there has been much celebration of the decline in the female-male earnings differential, the fact is that young women and men in the professions and management still face gender pay inequity. Just one example: At a high-tech Fortune 500 company at which I consulted recently, young women scientists and engineers received an average increase of 11 to 14 percent after the women insisted that management do a study of pay equity.

Finally, young women managers report that almost nobody in a corporate setting sits down and talks with them about their likely career path. In my experience very few young managers, male or female, get formal mentoring in companies. But men often get informal advice; young women rarely do. Thus, in the absence of a senior manager who wants to help them succeed at dealing with sexism or combining work and family, young women become frustrated with the corporate sector or the large law firm and exit in substantial numbers.

Goldin's results imply that women in cohort V have few role models, but it is not necessary to have role models to succeed (although it certainly makes it easier). Women pioneers, no matter what their cohort, who have combined raising a family with medicine, law, business, academia, or science had no role models to lead the way. Somebody always has to be first. What I think feels so difficult for women in cohort V is not so much the absence of substantial numbers of role models who have combined career and children, but the fact that it is proving so difficult for their own generation to have equity in the workplace combined with a sustained egalitarian relationship that includes egalitarian parenting. Combining career and family among women college graduates is still a tough assignment, in part because cohort V has raised the ante for success.

NOTES

1. Of the women from Stanford's class of 1981 who responded to my 1990 survey, the majority, 57 percent, were in formerly all-male occupations, such as physician, lawyer, professor, engineer/scientist, or manager. See Strober and Chan (1996). Anne Machung (1989) found in her 1985 survey of senior women at U.C. Berkeley that 90 percent were planning to earn graduate degrees in law, medicine, science, or business.

2. The Stanford sample I referred to earlier indicates that at least some members of cohort V who have children and work full time are having some success in getting their spouses to share household tasks. Among the married women with children who worked full time, 61.0 percent reported that they shared household tasks equally with their husbands. Among married women with children who did not work full time, only 21.6 percent reported that their husbands shared equally in household tasks.

Chapter 3

Labor Supply Effects of State Maternity Leave Legislation

Jacob Alex Klerman and Arleen Leibowitz

This paper develops a theory of the labor supply effects of maternity leave statutes. The theory predicts that both employment and leave will increase with the passage of maternity leave legislation, but the direction of the legislation's effect on work is ambiguous. We test these hypotheses using data from the 1980 and 1990 censuses. The results are sensitive to the controls for state and year effects and to the controls for the characteristics of sampled women. The estimates provide some evidence that maternity leave statutes increased leave, but had insignificant positive effects on employment and work.

The employment of new mothers rose dramatically over the 1980s. Currently, about 45 percent of mothers of 1-month-olds are in the labor force (Klerman and Leibowitz 1994). While *employment* of mothers of newborns is high, actual levels of *work* are much lower. The difference between employment and work is accounted for by women who are on paid and unpaid leave. Among employed mothers with a 1-month-old child, only about one third are actually at work; fully one quarter of all mothers of newborns are on paid or unpaid leave. This "employed, but not at work" group shrinks quickly as the child grows older, so that leave is essentially at the level for mothers of toddlers by the time the child is 4 months old (Klerman and Leibowitz 1994).

Beginning in 1987, a number of states responded to these changed labor supply patterns by passing a maternity leave statute (hereafter MLS).[1] This movement culminated in January 1993 when, as one of his first official acts, President Clinton signed into law the federal Family and Medical Leave Act (hereafter FMLA). Such MLSs guarantee to qualifying recent mothers a right to return to the job held in pregnancy after an unpaid leave. Table 3.1 tabulates the terms of the state and federal statutes.

The state laws provide only for unpaid leave, as does the FMLA. The various statutes apply only to firms with a minimum of between 10 and 250 employees (50 in the FMLA), and require that firms allow leaves of

Table 3.1   Maternity Leave Statutes

	First Implemented	Weeks Guaranteed[a]	Firm Size[b]	Births (1,000s)
Minnesota	7/87	6	21	68
Rhode Island	7/87	13	50	15
Oregon	1/88	12	25	41
Wisconsin	4/88	6	50	72
Maine	4/88	8	25	17
Washington	9/89	12	100	73
New Jersey	4/90	12	100	122
Connecticut	7/90	12	250	49
District of Columbia	4/91	16	50	22
California	1/92	17	50	557
Vermont	7/92	12	10	8
Hawaii	1/94	4	100	19
Federal	7/93	12	50	4,041

Sources: Abstracted from Helitzer (1990), Women's Legal Defense Fund (1992), and Strumberg, Steinschneider, and Elser (n.d).

Note: Weeks and firm size are for the law as initially implemented.

[a]Maximum length of protected leave in weeks.

[b]Smallest firm to which law applied.

between four and seventeen weeks (twelve in the FMLA). In comparison to maternity leaves of up to twelve months in western Europe, these guaranteed leaves are quite short.

Nonetheless, the state laws often guarantee the right to a leave considerably longer than new American mothers typically take. In the absence of legislation, leaves tend to be quite short. Klerman (1993) estimates that about one third of all new mothers take maternity leave. Among these women, only one quarter have leaves longer than eight weeks. Thus, it is plausible that state legislation could increase the length of maternity leave. Since the legislated maternity leave is unpaid, it is unclear whether women can "afford" to take advantage of these statutory guarantees and for how long.

Advocates for children supported federal maternity leave legislation, arguing that a period of guaranteed maternity leave would allow mothers the time to develop healthy, secure relationships with their infants in the months immediately following childbirth without forcing the mothers to quit their jobs. (Brazelton 1986; Zigler, Frank, and Emmel 1988). For the most part, they did not question that guaranteed maternity leave would increase the amount of time that mothers remained at home with their newborns.

In this paper we develop an economic model that shows that maternity leave legislation may result in either increases or decreases in the amount of time mothers spend at home with their newborns. We show that MLSs increase both leave and employment among new mothers. However, the increase in employment occurs because some women who would have quit their jobs instead remain employed and return to work earlier than they otherwise would have. Thus, maternity leave legislation could result in mothers spending less time at home with their infants.

The implementation of MLSs in several states in the late 1980s provides an opportunity to estimate the effect of these laws on employment, leave, and work. This paper explores theoretically and empirically the labor supply effects of such state MLSs. The next section develops a model of the effects of an MLS on several dimensions of labor supply. The third and fourth sections describe our methods and present the results of our empirical examination. The paper concludes with a summary and discussion of directions for future research.

THEORY

Much of the labor supply literature treats a woman's decision about whether or not to work as a choice made in a spot market; in that is, a woman would make her daily labor supply decision by comparing her value of leisure today with the offered wage. However, the right to return to the preleave job guaranteed by maternity leave legislation is only meaningful in a labor market with enduring employment relations, in which the decision to stay away from work longer than her employer's leave policy allows requires her to quit the current job and forfeit her accumulated firm-specific human capital. In that case, when she returns to work after a longer hiatus, she will bear the costs of searching for a new job that will probably pay less.

From the firm's perspective, the optimal leave policy balances several considerations. On the one side, having a worker on leave disrupts the normal production process, imposing additional costs. Such disruption may be more severe for maternity leave than for vacations because the leave is often longer and its timing is not under the control of the firm. On the other side, maternity leaves have two advantages for employers. First, because employers also make investments in workers, leaves that maintain the employment relation keep the firm from forfeiting its investment in the worker and bearing search costs for a new employee. Second, the physical rigors of childbirth and the demands of a very young infant are likely to reduce the productivity of a woman in the weeks following childbirth. By offering unpaid leave (or allowing the use of accumulated vacation time or sick leave), employers can avoid paying full wages during this period of reduced productivity. This consideration alone is likely to make offering some leave optimal for most employers.

Nevertheless, the employer is likely to offer only a short leave. Thus, a new mother must choose between returning to her previous employer at the current wage after a relatively short leave or quitting her job and spending more time not working; but when she returns to work, she is likely to earn a lower wage. An MLS changes the new mother's choice set and, for some women, the labor supply decision. In this section, we set out a simple theory of the choices that a woman faces given long-lasting employment relations, and how those choices are affected by the implementation of an MLS.

We consider the choice that mothers make about when to return to work following childbirth. Some women will choose to return to work after an interval of a few weeks; others may not work for years after childbirth. In this section we characterize how that choice depends on the wage available to the woman at the job held before the birth (w_o), on the wage at an alternative job (w_a), and on employer provisions for maternity leave and state maternity leave laws.

We conceptualize the labor supply choice as binary: New mothers either work full time or not at all (there is no hours choice). Women have exactly one child, whose birth date is exogenous. We assume that the marginal utility of leisure is strictly decreasing (that is, the value of leisure—nonwork—falls) with the child's age and that the woman's wage offer is constant, independent of the age of the child. In that case, the maternal labor supply decision can be fully characterized by the date on which the woman returns to work. She does not work until that date; she works continuously after that date.[2]

Figure 3.1 depicts the basic spot market problem given these assumptions. The vertical axis measures the market and reservation wages in dollars (per hour). The horizontal axis measures weeks since childbirth. We assume for convenience of graphical exposition that leave begins with delivery.

It is useful to think of the heavy diagonal line as the woman's reservation wage.[3] Presumably leisure is more valuable when children are younger, so the reservation wage declines as the child grows older. Then, in a spot market world, each morning the woman gets up, compares her reservation wage with the offered market wage, and decides whether or not to go to work. Figure 3.1 draws a constant market wage of w_o with a corresponding return to work date of sixteen weeks. Since the reservation wage is monotonically declining and the wage offer is constant, she will not work at all until her child is sixteen weeks old, and will work continuously thereafter.

We can also draw iso-utility curves that represent the utility the woman gets from remaining away from work for x weeks, during which she receives no wage, and earning a wage of w for the remainder of her working life. Note that higher wage rates correspond to greater utility, but the change in utility with length of leave is not monotonic. As drawn, the util-

Figure 3.1   Women's Return to Work in a Spot Market

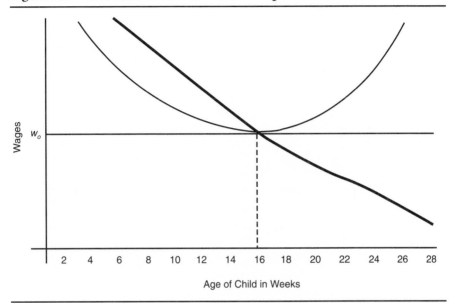

ity curve implies that at w_o, both leaves shorter than sixteen weeks and leaves longer than sixteen weeks are strictly worse than a leave of exactly sixteen weeks.

The reservation wage line passes through the minimum of the drawn iso-utility curve. It traces out all such minima (for a given woman, for varying levels of utility). It gives the woman's optimal leave length in a spot market, conditional on market wages.

If the employer offers a maternity leave of at least sixteen weeks, the woman will return to work after a leave that corresponds to the crossing of w_o and the reservation wage curve (that is, sixteen weeks). However, even though the woman may prefer a sixteen-week leave from the job she held in pregnancy (at wage w_o), her employer may limit leave to less than sixteen weeks. In that case, the choice (w_o, 16) is not feasible. This situation is graphed in figure 3.2. The woman will necessarily be at a lower utility level than her preferred position on the higher utility curve. She can choose to return to her old employer or she can quit and take a new job when she is ready to return to work. However, on the new job she would earn the lower alternative wage, w_a. By revealed preference, we know that $w_a \leq w_o$. Since skills are acquired through firm-specific training, w_a is likely to be considerably lower than w_o, which incorporates the return to training. Similarly, the relevant w_a is net of the search cost required to find the new job.

Figure 3.2 captures the essence of the constrained all-or-nothing choice facing the new mother. To the spot market plot, it adds a horizontal line

Figure 3.2   Women's Decision to Quit or Take Maternity Leave

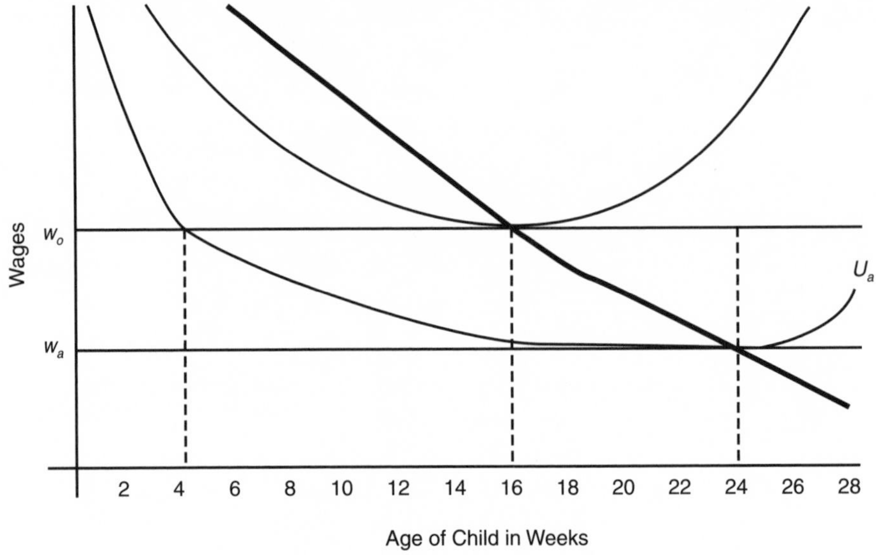

at the alternative wage w_a, and the utility curve corresponding to w_a. That lower utility curve, U_a, has a minimum at twenty-four weeks. By construction, the reservation wage curve also passes through this minimum.

This lower utility curve also intersects the w_o line. As drawn, that intersection occurs at four weeks. Thus, the new mother is indifferent between a leave of four weeks followed by return to her old job and quitting her job followed by return to work at a new job, at the lower wage w_a, but with an unconstrained leave length (as drawn, she will take twenty-four weeks). Thus, if her prebirth employer offers a leave of four weeks or less, the new mother will quit her job. If the firm offers a leave of four to sixteen weeks, the new mother will take as much leave as the firm offers. If the firm offers more than sixteen weeks, the woman will still take only sixteen weeks. Thus, under certain conditions women will return to their old job after a maternity leave that is shorter than they would have preferred had they not been constrained by the limit set by their employer.

An MLS guaranteeing a leave longer than the firm's allowed leave will change the new mother's choice set. Figure 3.3 illustrates how an MLS guaranteeing twelve weeks of leave affects the choices of a woman whose employer previously offered only four weeks of leave. This figure adds a new iso-utility curve passing through w_o at twelve weeks. As drawn, this point is preferable both to quitting and to taking the employer's offer of four weeks, though it is still inferior to what the woman would have chosen if she were

**Figure 3.3   Women's Maternity Leave Decision with a Maternity
Leave Statute**

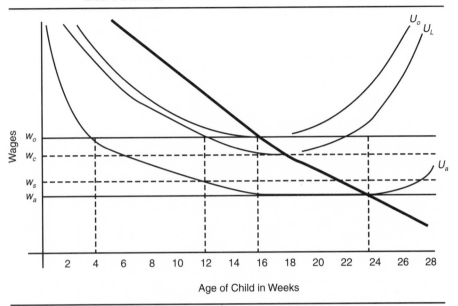

unconstrained (namely, sixteen weeks). Thus, firms that previously offered leaves of less than four weeks and saw their workers quit will now see some of those workers taking the statutory leave of twelve weeks and then returning to their preleave job. Similarly, firms that offered four to twelve weeks of leave will now see employees taking the full statutory guaranteed leave. Firms that offered leaves longer than the statutory leave will be unaffected.

Figure 3.4 illustrates how women with varying initial wage offers respond to the statutory leave, holding preferences, the firm's leave, the statutory leave, and the alternate wage fixed. We plot several wages; w_b is the market wage at which the woman would have chosen four weeks of leave; w_c is the "critical" wage such that the woman is indifferent to the choice between taking a firm's offer of four weeks leave and quitting and coming back at twenty-four weeks at wage w_a. In the absence of a statute, women with wages between w_b and w_c take the longest allowed leave of four weeks. Women with initial wage offers between w_c and w_a quit and return at twenty-four weeks. We add the critical wage under the statutory leave (w_s), which is the wage at which the new mother is indifferent between the leave guaranteed by statute and quitting her job. There are four regions to consider. For wages above w_b, the leave taken is always the unconstrained leave choice (which is less than the firm's offered leave). Women with wages between w_b and w_c would have chosen the firm's offered leave before the law, but lengthen their leave to the statutory

Figure 3.4　Leave with a Maternity Leave Statute, as a Function of the Current Wage

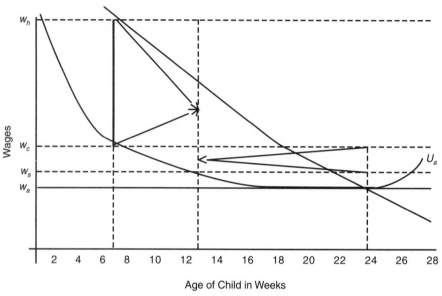

amount after the law is implemented. In the absence of the statute, women with wage offers between w_c and w_a would have quit their job to take longer leaves and wages of w_a. With a statutory guarantee of twelve weeks, women with wage offers between w_c and w_s return to work at twelve weeks, which is earlier than they would have in the absence of the law. Finally, women with wages between w_s and w_a quit their job both before and after the statute's implementation.

This graphical development implies that the number of women quitting a job to spend more time at home falls. Thus, an MLS will unambiguously increase employment. The number of women on leave—that is, employed but not at work—also clearly rises. However, the total effect on time at home with the child is ambiguous. Some women (with wages between w_h and w_c) return to work later than they would have without the law, while others (with wages between w_c and w_s) return earlier.[4]

Thinking of the model's two wages as the discounted lifetime earnings if the woman quits or takes leave, we could develop a *ceteris paribus* theory of who takes maternity leave. Women with more firm-specific training would face a larger cut in pay if they left their job, and, therefore, should be more likely to take whatever leave is offered rather than quit. A similar argument applies to women with "rarer" jobs, so that their cost of searching for a new job would be higher. Finally, women who expect to stay in a given job longer after the birth of their child should be less likely to quit. They will collect higher wages on the prepregnancy job over a longer period. Any direct test of such a theory of which new mothers take maternity leave would be open to objections concerning the endogeneity of the characteristics used to proxy for specific training, rare jobs, expected job durations, and so on. Instruments for these regressors are not readily apparent.

This is a partial equilibrium analysis. It does not allow for changes in the current or alternative wage with the implementation of an MLS. If women take the leave and it is expensive for firms, the costs may be shifted to women workers, whose wages may fall (Gruber and Krueger 1990; Gruber 1994). Similarly, women's choice of job, or even career/occupation, might be affected by the protection of an MLS. Such changes are unlikely to occur unless the state maternity laws stimulate labor supply changes for new mothers. Here, we test for a direct response to MLSs. Under the null hypothesis of no effects on labor supply there will be no changes in wages or job choice. If there are large labor supply effects, then examining equilibrium adjustments and second-order effects would be an attractive direction for future research.

The theory developed here has clear sign predictions for many of the outcomes of interest. In the next section we test how employment, work, and leave from work changed as a result of the implementation of the state MLSs.

DATA AND METHODS

This section describes the data and statistical techniques that will be used in the empirical work.

PUMS DATA

The data for our analysis come from the census Public Use Microdata Sample (PUMS) files. They provide a 5 percent sample of U.S. households for 1980 and 1990. Since all of the state MLSs were implemented after 1980, these two census years give us "before" and "after" data. A more direct test would examine the year before and year after implementation. However, because the states that passed maternity leave legislation before 1990 were relatively small with correspondingly few births (see table 3.1), only the 5 percent sample of the census provides sufficient sample size. The longer interval also allows time for adjustments to the law to occur. The census data have another advantage over most other data sets. They clearly distinguish between women who are at work in the census week and those who are employed but not at work, that is, those who are on leave (see Klerman and Leibowitz 1994).[5]

Although work status of the mother is precisely measured in the PUMS data, the age of her child is not. The 1980 PUMS data include calendar quarter of birth. The 1990 PUMS do not. However, in 1990, children under age 1 are clearly coded. Even for data aggregated over an interval including both time during and after the maternity leave guarantee period, our theory has unambiguous predictions about employment and leave. Thus, we consider the effect of MLSs on the woman's labor market status in the child's entire first year of life. Although the maternity leave effect may be diluted, the very large sample of new mothers makes the PUMS a preferable data set for testing the effects of maternity leave.

The PUMS is hierarchically arranged, with families and households clearly identified. This structure allows us to link all resident children to their mothers. We can thus code women by the age of their youngest child in the household. Similarly, we can identify mothers of older children as a control group (we use 2- and 3-year-olds). Appendix tables 3.1 and 3.2 give the sample means.

STATISTICAL METHODS

The PUMS data allow three types of contrasts that shed light on the effects of MLS. First, in 1990 we can compare labor supply of new mothers in MLS states with labor supply of new mothers in non-MLS states. Second, for states with an MLS in 1990, we can compare pre-MLS labor supply patterns in 1980 with labor supply patterns in 1990. Third, we can compare mothers of infants (under age 1) with mothers of older children who should not be affected by the short amount of leave guaranteed by an MLS.

Recent empirical work in policy analysis has emphasized the potential endogeneity of government policies (Gruber and Krueger 1990; Card 1992; Gruber 1994; Moffitt 1990). There are several reasons that cross-sectional comparisons of work patterns in states with an MLS and those without an MLS might be problematic. States that passed an MLS may have different patterns of female labor force participation (even in the absence of an MLS) than those that did not. States with higher levels of female employment may have a bigger political constituency for passing an MLS. Perhaps states with more progressive beliefs are both more likely to pass maternity leave legislation and also have more positive attitudes toward maternal work. For these reasons, it is important to control for pre-existing differences among states and not to rely on only the simple cross-sectional difference in 1990.

Comparisons of labor supply in MLS states before and after the passage of the legislation also do not provide a strong test of the effect of an MLS. Historically, MLSs were implemented in the latter half of the 1980s. Yet, the 1980s was a decade of major increases in female employment, especially for mothers of young children. Some of the increase in women's employment may have been due to the MLSs, but much of it was due to other forces. Thus, the pure increase in employment over time in states that implemented an MLS would overstate the effect of the legislation.

Finally, it is not sufficient to compare labor supply of mothers of younger children, who would be protected by an MLS, with that of mothers of older children alone. It continues to be true that employment rises with the age of the youngest child. Thus, simple comparisons of mothers of older and younger children will spuriously imply that an MLS lowers employment.

Rather than using any of these three simple differences, we account for differences across state and year as well as the passage of an MLS using a difference-of-differences (DoD) approach (Card 1992; Gruber 1994). We compare the proportion of women in each labor force status (employed, at work, or on leave), in states that have implemented an MLS, using data from before the MLS and after. We compare the change in employment in these MLS states with the change in employment among women living in states that did not pass an MLS. The change over time in a state controls for persistent differences across states. The comparisons of growth over time in MLS and non-MLS states control for nationwide secular trends in labor force behaviors. If MLSs have increased employment, we expect greater growth in employment over time in MLS states than in non-MLS states.

This DoD estimator controls for persistent differences across states and for nationwide secular changes in women's labor supply. It does not, however, control for variation within a state across years (not correlated with the national secular trends). The most obvious source of such variation is local labor market conditions. Perhaps states with expanding economies were more likely to pass MLSs. We control for this variation by using the labor supply of mothers of older children to control for state-year specific shifts in local labor markets. This yields a difference-of-difference-of-differences (DoDoD) estimator (Gruber 1994).

The identification conditions for this DoDoD approach are quite weak (Gruber 1994). The comparison with mothers of toddlers is with similar women in the same state and year. Since the mothers of infants and mothers of toddlers share the same cultural and political climate and local labor market conditions, this DoDoD approach should control for state conditions that might simultaneously result in the passage of an MLS and changes in labor market patterns.

RESULTS

SIMPLE DIFFERENCE ESTIMATORS

We report tables with weighted cell means for each of three labor supply measures—employment, leave, and work, for 1980 and 1990—in states that passed an MLS between 1980 and 1990 and in control states, which did not. The upper panel in tables 3.2–3.4 presents labor supply results for mothers of children under age one for 1980, the same for 1990, the difference between 1990 and 1980, and the t-statistic for the difference. The middle panel contains the same information for mothers of two- and three-year olds (pooled). The lower panel shows the differences across women with younger versus older children and presents the *t*-statistic for this difference. Each panel is divided into three sets of columns, showing data for states with an MLS (experimental states), states without an MLS (control states), and the differences in average labor force status between experimental and control states.

Looking first at the results for 1990, we find that, consistent with the theory, both employment and leave are significantly higher among mothers of infants in states that had passed an MLS before 1990 than in states that had not. The percentage of women working in these states is also higher. However, looking at labor supply in 1980, we find that employment and work were higher in MLS states even before they passed MLS legislation. To control for these underlying differences across the states, we next compare the *changes* between 1980 and 1990 in employment, leave, and work in MLS and non-MLS states.

We begin with the results for employment. Our theory predicts that employment will increase with an MLS, because women who otherwise would have quit instead take leave. The time they would have been away from work accounts for a net increase in employment. Consistent with the large secular increases in female labor force participation, employment increased substantially in both the experimental and control states over the decade from 1980 to 1990. Table 3.2 shows a growth of 16.3 percentage points in MLS states and 13.8 percentage points in control states. Consistent with the theory, the increase was larger in the experimental states, resulting in a DoD estimate of 2.6 percentage points, which is strongly significant.

Table 3.3 presents the results for leave from work, defined as "with a job, but not at work." Women who quit their job are not classified as "on leave." Our theory predicts that leave will increase with an MLS because some women who would have quit take short leaves if an MLS is present. In addition, some women who would not have quit (either before or after the law) now take longer leaves.

Leave among mothers of infants increased significantly between 1980 and 1990—by 1.5 percentage points in the experimental states and 1.2 percentage points in the control states. As predicted by the theory, the increase was larger in the experimental states than in the control states. Although the MLS states had significantly greater proportions of women on leave in 1990 than the control states, the difference in the growth in leave over time between experimental and control states was only 0.3 percentage points, which is positive, but not statistically significant.

Table 3.4 presents the equivalent analysis for work. The theory suggests that for women who would have quit, but now take leave, the net effect is to increase work, but for others the net effect is to decrease work. For women who would not quit whether or not there were an MLS, the net effect is to decrease work. Assuming, as did the proponents of the FMLA

Table 3.2 Percentage of Mothers Employed, by Age of Youngest Child, Maternity Leave Statute, and Year

	States With MLS			States Without MLS			With-Without (Difference-of-Differences)		
	%	s.d.	N	%	s.d.	N	%	s.d.	t
Age: <1 year									
1980	0.3333	0.0041	13,327	0.3179	0.0012	150,320	0.0156	0.0043	3.7
1990	0.4969	0.0047	11,444	0.4555	0.0014	134,925	0.0414	0.0049	8.5
Difference 1990–1980	0.1634	0.0062		0.1376	0.0018		0.0258	0.0065	4.0
t (1990–1980)		26.3			76.0			4.0	
Age: 2 and 3 years									
1980	0.4495	0.0039	16,624	0.4394	0.0011	196,518	0.0101	0.0040	2.5
1990	0.6151	0.0035	19,294	0.5621	0.0010	229,799	0.0530	0.0037	14.5
Difference 1990–1980	0.1656	0.0052		0.1227	0.0015		0.0429	0.0054	7.9
t		31.8			80.5			7.9	
Difference-of-Difference-of-Differences									
0-(2 and 3)	-0.0022	0.0081		0.0149	0.0024		-0.0171	0.0084	-2.0
t		-0.3			6.3			-2.0	

Table 3.3 Percentage of Mothers on Leave, by Age of Youngest Child, Maternity Leave Statute, and Year

	States With MLS			States Without MLS			With-Without (Difference-of-Differences)		
	%	s.d.	N	%	s.d.	N	%	s.d.	t
Age: <1 year									
1980	0.0454	0.0018	13,327	0.0442	0.0005	150,320	0.0012	0.0019	0.6
1990	0.0606	0.0022	11,444	0.0560	0.0006	134,925	0.0046	0.0023	2.0
Difference 1990–1980	0.0152	0.0029		0.0118	0.0008		0.0034	0.0030	1.1
t (1990–1980)	5.3			14.4			1.1		
Age: 2 and 3 years									
1980	0.0109	0.0008	16,624	0.0126	0.0003	196,518	-0.0017	0.0008	-2.0
1990	0.0108	0.0007	19,294	0.0114	0.0002	229,799	-0.0006	0.0008	-0.8
Difference 1990–1980	-0.0001	0.0011		-0.0012	0.0003		0.0011	0.0011	1.0
t (1990–1980)	-0.1			-3.6			1.0		
Difference-of-Difference-of-Differences									
0-(2 and 3)	0.0153	0.0031		0.0130	0.0009		0.0023	0.0032	0.7
t	5.0			14.7			0.7		

(Brazelton 1986; Zigler, Frank, and Emmel 1988), that maternal care is important in the first few months of life, work would have to decrease for an MLS to have a direct, positive effect on child development.[6]

Table 3.4 documents large increases in work for mothers of children of all ages in both experimental and control states between 1980 and 1990. The increase is larger in the experimental states than in the control states by 2.24 percentage points, and this difference is significant (t = 3.5). Since both employment and work grew more in MLS states, it is possible that labor markets were stronger in these states than in non-MLS states. To control for within-state demands we turn to the DoDoD analysis.

The DoDoD analysis of employment suggests that the large increase in employment among mothers of infants may not be due to the MLS. Employment among mothers of two- and three-year-olds in the MLS states also increased considerably over the decade, rising by 16.6 percentage points. This increase was 4.3 percentage points larger than in the control states, where employment grew by only 12.3 percentage points. This differential growth rate between experimental and control states is larger for mothers of 2- and 3-year-olds than for mothers of infants (4.3 versus 2.6). Thus, against the predictions of our theory, the DoDoD estimate implies that the MLS decreased employment by 1.7 percentage points, which is statistically significant.

One interpretation of the reversal in sign is that perhaps states with booming economies passed an MLS and that those with weaker economies did not. Strong demand for labor in the states that passed an MLS would have caused employment to rise for mothers of both infants and toddlers. If this interpretation is correct, then the DoD estimator spuriously attributes the increased employment to an MLS, when in fact the causation runs from the strong economy to both the passage of an MLS and increased employment.

The DoDoD results on leave (Table 3.3) also show positive but insignificant effects. The theory suggests that an MLS should have essentially no effect on labor supply decisions of mothers of two- and three-year-olds. Leave among mothers of older children actually declined slightly between 1980 and 1990 by 0.01 percentage points in the experimental states (not significant) and by 0.12 percentage points in the control states (significant, t = 3.6). However, the difference between MLS and control states is not significantly different from zero. Differencing again, the DoDoD estimate of the effect of an MLS on leave provides a test of whether leave grew faster in MLS states than in control states for mothers of infants compared with mothers of toddlers. The difference of 0.2 percentage points is not significantly different from zero.

REGRESSION ESTIMATORS

Table 3.5 presents linear probability model estimates of the effect of an MLS on employment, leave, and work.[7] Three different model specifications are presented for each outcome. The DoD model in column 1 com-

Table 3.4 Percentage of Mothers at Work, by Age of Youngest Child, Maternity Leave Statute, and Year

	States With MLS			States Without MLS			With-Without (Difference-of-Differences)		
	%	s.d.	N	%	s.d.	N	%	s.d.	t
Age: <1 year									
1980	0.2881	0.0039	13,327	0.2737	0.0011	150,320	0.0144	0.0041	3.5
1990	0.4363	0.0046	11,444	0.3995	0.0013	134,925	0.0368	0.0048	7.6
Difference 1990–1980	0.1482	0.0061		0.1258	0.0018		0.0224	0.0063	3.5
t (1990–1980)	24.4			71.4			3.5		
Age: 2 and 3 years									
1980	0.4386	0.0038	16,624	0.4268	0.0011	196,518	0.0118	0.0040	2.9
1990	0.6042	0.0035	19,294	0.5507	0.0010	229,799	0.0535	0.0037	14.6
Difference 1990–1980	0.1656	0.0052		0.1239	0.0015		0.0417	0.0054	7.7
t (1990–1980)	31.7			81.3			7.7		
Difference-of-Difference-of-Differences									
0–(2 and 3)	−0.0174	0.0080		0.0019	0.0023		−0.0193	0.0083	−2.3
t	−2.2			0.8			−2.3		0.0

pares employment, leave, and work for mothers of infants in 1980 and 1990 in states that did and did not pass on MLS.

The regressions in the first column include variables that control for heterogeneity of the sampled women. The regressions include measures of a woman's race, age, education, parity, and marital status as well as interactions of these variables with state and year indicators. (Means of the variables are in appendix tables 3.1 and 3.2.) The regressions in column 2 add the state unemployment rate in the corresponding census years to the list of explanatory variables. Column 3 corresponds to the DoDoD estimates. These models are estimated on a sample of mothers of infants and mothers of two- and three-year-olds. These models contain the demographic controls listed above, but do not include state unemployment rates. Rather, the labor supply of mothers of toddlers implicitly controls for the demand for labor.

We find a significant, positive effect of MLSs on employment, even after controlling for demographic factors (Table 3.5, row 1, column 1). To test the hypothesis that this effect is spurious because an MLS was more likely to be passed in states with booming economies, the results in column 2 include the state unemployment rate. Consistent with our expectation, controlling in this way for the demand for labor lowers the estimated effect of an MLS on employment. Controlling for labor demand by including mothers of two- and three-year-olds in the sample (column 3) also results in a positive estimate that is not significantly different from zero.

The theory predicts that an MLS should increase leave. The results in column 1 show a statistically significant positive effect of MLS on leave, even after controlling for women's characteristics. The significant positive effect of MLS on leave remains even after controlling for the unemployment rate. However, with the alternate control obtained by examining the contrast between mothers of younger and older children (the DoDoD results reported in column 3), an MLS does not appear to increase leave-taking significantly.

The bottom row of table 3.5 reports the regression estimates for work. The theoretical effect of an MLS on work is ambiguous. Note, however, that work is arguably the crucial outcome. Our definition of work implies that time not spent working is time at home with the new baby (whether on leave or because the woman is not employed). The results are similar to those for employment. The DoD point estimate is positive and significant. Inclusion of the unemployment rate cuts the point estimate by one third, and the effect is no longer statistically significant. The DoDoD specification in column 3 also shows a positive effect that is not significantly different from zero. Since well over 90 percent of employment is work, this similarity between the results for employment and work is not surprising.

Table 3.5   Effect of State Maternity Leave Statutes on Employment, Leave, and Work (Regression Coefficients and Standard Errors)

	Demographic Controls (DoD)	Demographic Controls Plus Unemployment Rate (DoD)	Demographic Controls Plus State Labor Market (DoDoD)
Employment	0.01422**	0.00508	0.00802
	(0.00629)	(0.00640)	(0.00836)
Leave	0.00800***	0.00776***	0.00371
	(0.00258)	(0.00265)	(0.00390)
Work	0.01523**	0.00964	0.00678
	(0.00631)	(0.00647)	(0.00850)

Note: * –p < 0.10; ** –p < 0.05, *** p < 0.01.

CONCLUSION

This paper has presented a theory of the labor market effects of maternity leave statutes and tested the predictions of the theory using a generalized difference-of-difference-of-differences procedure. The theory predicts that both employment and leave will increase, but the direction of the effect on work is ambiguous. The presumption in the legislative debate appears to have been that the MLSs would cause work to decrease, and its complement, home time, to increase. Proponents of the state MLSs and the federal FMLA argued that this increase in home time would improve developmental outcomes for infants. The empirical results are very sensitive to the exact specification.

While some results are consistent with the theory, our preferred results (Difference-of-Difference-of-Differences with demographic controls) imply that the MLSs have no statistically significant effect on employment, leave, or work. Some of the sensitivity appears to be due to the fact that states with booming economies were more likely to pass MLSs. Thus, simple specifications are biased toward concluding that MLSs increased all three labor market outcomes, when improved economic conditions led to at least some of the increase. In addition, some of the sensitivity relates to the change in characteristics of mothers between the two census dates (Leibowitz and Klerman 1995).

ACKNOWLEDGMENTS

This research is funded by the National Institute for Child Health and Human Development, Center for Population Research Grant 2-P-50-HD-12639. The views expressed here do not necessarily represent the position of NICHD.

Earlier versions of this paper were presented at RAND, the annual meetings of the Population Association of America, and the ILR-Cornell Institute for Labor Market Policies Conference "Gender and Family Issues in the Workplace."

Jerene Kelly, Natasha Kostan, and Edie Nichols did an excellent job of preparing the document. Kim McGuigan, Patricia St. Clair, and Bob Young provided programming support. Robert Bell provided a crucial statistical insight. Jonathan Gruber provided some of the information about maternity leave legislation. The responsibility for all remaining errors remains, of course, with the authors.

APPENDIX

Appendix Table 3.1   Sample Means: 1980 and 1990

Mother's Characteristics	All States: 1980–1990 Age = 0, 2, 3	Control States: 1980 Age = 0	Control States: 1980 Age = 2, 3	MLS States: 1980 Age = 0	MLS States: 1980 Age = 2, 3
Race					
White (and other)	0.777	0.763	0.762	0.945	0.948
Black	0.121	0.135	0.140	0.028	0.028
Hispanic	0.102	0.102	0.048	0.024	0.024
Age					
15–19	0.044	0.090	0.021	0.070	0.012
20–24	0.211	0.316	0.209	0.317	0.188
25–29	0.323	0.335	0.342	0.366	0.360
30–34	0.301	0.203	0.313	0.205	0.337
35+	0.121	0.056	0.115	0.042	0.102
Education (years)					
<12	0.190	0.244	0.235	0.155	0.138
12	0.400	0.428	0.451	0.464	0.498
13–15	0.247	0.185	0.182	0.228	0.219
16+	0.163	0.142	0.131	0.153	0.144
Parity					
1	0.372	0.405	0.356	0.476	0.329
2	0.371	0.347	0.383	0.348	0.462
3	0.173	0.163	0.176	0.161	0.187
4+	0.083	0.088	0.085	0.075	0.082
Marital status					
Never married	0.085	0.072	0.059	0.000	0.037
Currently married	0.829	0.873	0.833	0.411	0.862
Once married	0.085	0.055	0.107	0.041	0.100
N	772,251	150,320	196,518	13,327	16,624

Appendix Table 3.2   Sample Means: 1990

	Control States: 1990		MLS States: 1990	
Mother's Characteristics	Age = 0	Age = 2, 3	Age = 0	Age = 2, 3
Race				
White (and other)	0.762	0.762	0.942	0.946
Black	0.120	0.123	0.022	0.024
Hispanic	0.118	0.115	0.035	0.030
Age				
15–19	0.072	0.019	0.052	0.012
20–24	0.221	0.141	0.222	0.118
25–29	0.322	0.295	0.350	0.301
30–34	0.285	0.360	0.283	0.390
35+	0.099	0.184	0.094	0.180
Education (years)				
<12	0.166	0.146	0.115	0.089
12	0.346	0.364	0.361	0.374
13–15	0.292	0.305	0.330	0.349
16+	0.196	0.184	0.193	0.189
Parity				
1	0.389	0.360	0.374	0.316
2	0.351	0.390	0.359	0.400
3	0.173	0.176	0.179	0.196
4+	0.047	0.074	0.089	0.088
Marital status				
Never married	0.127	0.099	0.094	0.069
Currently married	0.815	0.797	0.859	0.840
Once married	0.057	0.105	0.047	0.090
N	134,925	229,799	11,444	14,294

NOTES

1. Since the Pregnancy Discrimination Act of 1978, all firms that provide medical disability leaves must cover pregnancy like any other disability.

2. Formally, the graphical representation is consistent with a model in which households maximize lifetime utility over consumption and leisure; leisure is dichotomous (the mother either works or does not work), and the utility of leisure declines as the child ages. This choice structure can be derived from a standard intertemporally separable utility function (except that the utility of leisure varies with the age of the child) and perfect capital markets. We do not explore what more general technical assumptions about the primitive properties of the decision problem (that is, conditions on the budget set and preferences)

would be sufficient. The graphical and formal argument presented in the text is considerably more general than the standard neoclassical development (for example, it does not require constant wage opportunities or perfect capital markets).

3. In the presence of income effects, the reservation wage interpretation is not strictly correct. The reservation wage in one period will be a function of lifetime earnings, which will be a function of labor supply decisions in other periods. Therefore, in a multiperiod model, there is no single reservation wage curve. Even so, this line (which we will refer to as the reservation wage curve) is well defined and plays a central role in the theory below.

4. This point was noted by Gill (1991). He states that mandated unpaid, job-protected leave for employed parents of infants (under age 1) could lead to not more but less parental care for young children. Guaranteed leaves may tie the mother more closely to the employing firm and encourage her to return to work sooner, rather than quitting this job and taking a different job much later.

5. The Current Population Survey (CPS), used in Klerman and Leibowitz (1995a), also makes this distinction; most other standard surveys do not (for example, the National Longitudinal Survey, the Panel Study of Income Dynamics, and the Survey of Income and Program Participation).

6. This assumption is the subject of debate in the literature. The proponents' claim is consistent with Belsky (1988), but inconsistent with Clarke-Stewart (1991). More recent analyses also come to mixed conclusions (for example, Hill and O'Neill 1994; Caughy, DiPietro, and Strobino 1994).

7. The linear probability model is ordinary least squares regression applied to a binary dependent variable (for example, work yes/no). The resulting regressions are heteroscedastic. The results in the body of the paper are estimated using an appropriate GLS correction for this heteroscedasticity.

Commentary on Chapter 3

Lawrence F. Katz

Jacob Klerman and Arleen Leibowitz have produced an insightful and well-executed paper that theoretically and empirically examines the effects of maternity leave statutes on the labor supply of new mothers. The analysis is motivated by the recent passage and implementation in the United States of laws at both the state and federal level that provide a substantial proportion of employed women with the right to job-protected, unpaid maternity leaves of limited duration (up to twelve weeks under the federal Family and Medical Leave Act of 1993). These statutes attempt to address the rapid secular rise in the labor force attachment of mothers of young children and growing concerns about the ability of parents of young children to balance parenting and work responsibilities.

Klerman and Leibowitz make the important point that maternity leave statutes are relevant only in labor markets with enduring employment relationships (presumably arising from firm-specific human capital investments) such that total compensation is higher on a woman's preleave job than on the outside labor market. The authors develop a simple but illuminating theoretical model to examine the first-order effects of maternity leave legislation on the choices of previously employed new mothers with respect to working, staying on leave but retaining their preleave job, or quitting their previous job to take more time off from work than permitted by either their company's leave policy or the maternity leave statute. The model demonstrates that the first-order effect of a maternity leave statute is to increase the time spent on leave and reduce quit rates (thereby increasing the employment rates of mothers of newborns). The impact on work time is ambiguous since more women will get longer leaves and retain their preleave jobs (reducing work), but others who without a statute would have quit their jobs will take less time off to retain their previous employment relationship. The model ignores the general equilibrium effects of changes in labor supply behavior and employer costs on wages. It also does not examine changes in hours of work and the longer-term impacts of the statutes on women's occupational choices and labor supply when their children are older.

Klerman and Leibowitz use data from the 1980 and 1990 census Public Use Microdata Sample (PUMS) files to analyze the impact of the initial state maternity leave laws (six laws in relatively small states passed from 1987 to 1989) on the labor supply of mothers with children under age 1. The major advantage of the PUMS is that it is the only data set available with large enough sample sizes to be able to usefully examine differences in the labor supply behavior at the state level of mothers with very young children. The authors present both (1) difference-of-differences (DoD) estimates, in which changes in the labor supply of mothers of newborns from 1980 to 1990 are compared in experimental states (those that implemented maternity leave statutes) and nonexperimental states (those without such laws); and (2) difference-of-differences-of-differences (DoDoD) estimates, in which these cross-state differences are presented relative to control groups (mothers with 2- and 3-year-olds) in both the experimental and nonexperimental states. The DoD estimates provide modest support for their theoretical framework and suggest slight increases in employment (work plus leave) and leave rates for new mothers in states passing maternity leave laws and some evidence of an increase in work. But the results are not robust to the inclusion of controls for demographics and labor market conditions and often look quite different in the more methodologically convincing DoDoD estimates. The authors emphasize that most of their estimates imply some increased work (and thereby possibly reduced time with children) for mothers with newborns. In summary, the estimates are fairly ambiguous and suggest relatively small initial impacts of state maternity leave statutes on labor supply behavior.

I have several concerns with the authors' empirical approach. First, the PUMS data, by providing information only for 1980 and 1990, do not allow one to determine whether difference in changes in labor supply behavior across states over the 1980s occurred before or after the passage of the state maternity leave laws that are the focus of the authors' analysis. The estimates of increases in employment, leave, and work for new mothers attributed to the laws by the authors in their DoD analysis could merely be picking up pre-existing trends that were present before the passage of the laws. It is plausible that laws would pass first in more progressive states already experiencing increases in female labor supply. One could potentially supplement the authors' analysis with data from the annual Current Population Surveys to look at differences in changes in labor supply across states by mothers of young children in the first and second half of the 1980s (although small sample sizes would make it difficult to detect small changes in labor supply behavior). On the other hand, the authors could underestimate the impacts of law changes if the states passing maternity leave laws had weaker pre-existing trends and were motivated by their lack of progress in expanding leave opportunities for new mothers. It would be useful to at least see how the 1980 to 1990 results would be affected by controlling for earlier trends (possibly from 1970 to 1980 using PUMS data) in labor supply for treatment and control groups by state.

Second, the authors compare the six states that passed maternity leave laws in the 1980s with all other states. There are many other unmeasured differences in economic and social trends across states that could drive differences in labor supply trends for mothers of young children. It would be nice to see a comparison of the states that changed laws with a smaller set of more comparable nonexperimental states (perhaps those more like the law-changing states in terms of pre-existing trends in the labor supply of mothers of young children).

Third, the authors' DoD finding of increased changes in work probabilities for mothers of children under age 1 in states passing maternity leave laws does not necessarily mean that these mothers are spending increasingly less time with their children. A discrete variable for work does not tell one how many hours these women are spending at work. More light could be shed on this issue by examining usual weekly hours as well as the discrete labor force status indicator studied by the authors. Furthermore, maternity leave laws could increase leave-taking and time spent at home with newborns in the first several months after birth, but increase time at work after the child is 6 months old or so by allowing mothers to better maintain their previous jobs and career trajectories. The Klerman and Leibowitz results on work could be driven by composition effects of reduced work immediately after childbirth but increased employment opportunities after the legal leave-taking period is over.

Despite the ambiguity of their exploratory empirical results, Klerman and Leibowitz have developed a theoretical model and empirical framework that can usefully guide future work analyzing the labor supply impacts of changes in laws by larger states (such as California) and the federal government in the 1990s.

Commentary on Chapter 3

Marjorie Honig

Attempting to identify the effects of public policy is always a risky undertaking. Programs are usually not substantial enough to evoke a large response, and they are rarely adopted in settings that would qualify as natural experiments. The authors of this paper are to be congratulated for extracting as much as they have on the effect of state maternity leave statutes on the employment, leave-taking, and work of mothers with infants. In the end, however, a firm conclusion eludes them. Their results are weak and the data do not permit them to distinguish among a number of alternative explanations for their findings.

I will focus on employment effects, although my comments generalize to leaves and work as well. The theoretical expectation is that the employment of mothers with infants should have increased more between 1980 and 1990 in states with maternity leave statutes (MLSs) than in non-MLS states and that the employment of mothers with toddlers, included to control for state-specific changes in labor market conditions over the period, should have been unaffected by these statutes. Findings on raw cell means indicate, however, that the employment of the control group not only increased more in MLS states than in non-MLS states, but by more than that of mothers with infants.

The authors suggest that this unexpected result may be explained by a greater increase in the demand for labor in MLS states during the period under study. In regression analyses that account for changes in the characteristics of women with infants over time and for differences between 1980 and 1990 due to sampling variability, the authors use two alternative measures of shifts in labor demand across states: changes in the statewide unemployment rate and in the employment of mothers with toddlers. Both measures produce the same result: When the full set of covariates and interactions are included, the coefficient of the dummy variable for the presence of maternity leave statutes has the correct positive sign, but is small and its t-value is somewhat less than one.

Neither of the authors' controls for changes in labor demand is ideal, of course, and stronger effects of the statutes may be obtained with a better measure of the local labor market conditions facing mothers with infants. Information in the PUMS on detailed geographic areas within states could be used to develop person-specific estimates of local demand conditions.

Indications from the results on cell means, however, are not promising. In the absence of any reason why favorable market conditions in MLS states should have increased the employment of mothers with toddlers more than that of mothers with infants, the effect of the statutes still should have been a larger relative increase in the employment of the latter group. Changes in labor demand, in other words, do not appear to be the whole story.

Even assuming that the controls for shifts in labor demand are adequate, at least two explanations are consistent with these weak measured effects of maternity statutes. One explanation suggests that the maternity leave statues examined in this paper were unlikely to have had significant effects on the employment of mothers with infants; the other suggests that maternity leave statutes may have had employment effects but broader than those proposed by the authors. The first explanation suggests that MLS states differ from non-MLS states in more than labor demand. Only six states enacted MLSs in the late 1980s, and four of them—Minnesota, Wisconsin, Oregon, and Washington—are progressive (Maine and Rhode Island may belong in this category as well). Thus, MLSs in these states may be endogenous, the result of favorable attitudes toward the employment of mothers with young children and, very possibly, widespread private-sector provisions of maternity leave as early as 1980. If public mandates for maternity leave were modeled after private-sector provisions (normally two or three months), they would not add to the choices available to women who wanted short leaves and would not tip the balance for women who wanted leaves of longer duration. Thus, there would have been few new incentives provided by the statutes in these states.

The second explanation allows for the possibility that maternity leave statutes may be effective, but carries the implication that mothers of toddlers may not be an appropriate group to control for labor demand changes. If MLSs affected the employment of mothers with toddlers as well, there may be little additional variation remaining once the employment of this group is controlled for. The passage of statutes in the late 1980s may have provided mothers who had previously left jobs at childbirth with an incentive to cut short their time out of the labor force while anticipating the birth of their next child. Women with 2- and 3-year-olds are likely to be anticipating additional births. Those with general human capital that does not depreciate with extended absences from the labor force may have preferred to remain out of the labor force from the birth of the first child until completion of childbearing, rather than incur search costs and suffer wage declines from the loss of their firm-specific capital. By 1990, maternity leave statutes had reduced the costs of subsequent births and thus may have encouraged mothers with "pre-MLS" toddlers to reenter the labor force.

Additional states have passed maternity leave statutes since 1990, which offers the possibility of an expanded sample. The endogeneity of the statutes is likely to remain a problem, however. At a minimum, a better measure of local labor demand would eliminate the need for a demographic control group whose behavioral response to maternity leave statutes is uncertain and would provide a better test of whether, once demand conditions are accounted for, there is an independent impact of publicly mandated maternity leaves.

Chapter 4

Working Mothers Then and Now: A Cross-Cohort Analysis of the Effects of Maternity Leave on Women's Pay

Jane Waldfogel

This paper uses two young cohorts from the National Longitudinal Surveys of Young Women and of Youth (NLS-YW and NLSY) to investigate the importance of family status as a component of the gender gap and the potential impact of job-protected maternity leave as a remedy for the pay penalties associated with motherhood. The results suggest that despite the narrowing of the gender gap over the 1980s, family status continues to be quite important in explaining the lower pay of working mothers. The results also suggest that maternity leave policies can have an important effect on women's pay. In both cohorts, employment continuity over the period of childbirth is associated with higher pay because women who maintain employment continuity over childbirth have higher wages to start and also because returning to the prior employer after childbirth leads to gains in work experience and job tenure. In the NLSY, women who were covered by a formal maternity leave policy and returned to their original employers after their most recent birth have higher current pay, all else equal, than other working mothers. Although the higher pay of these women is explained in part by higher prebirth wages, there are also positive returns to having maternity leave coverage and returning to a prebirth employer. Coverage, even if not used to maintain employment continuity, is associated with higher pay, perhaps reflecting covered women's superior position in the labor market relative to women without coverage.

American women have made progress in recent years in narrowing the gender gap in pay. Despite this progress, a substantial gap persists between the earnings of mothers and others. Using two cohorts from the National Longitudinal Surveys, this paper explores at two different points in time the importance of family status in explaining the gender gap among young adults and the extent to which maternity leave coverage and employment continuity over childbirth are effective remedies for the pay penalties associated with motherhood.

PREVIOUS RESEARCH AND THE MOTIVATION
FOR THIS RESEARCH

One of the most remarkable features of the U.S. labor market in recent years has been the narrowing of the gender gap in pay. Throughout the 1960s and 1970s women's earnings, on average, were 59 percent of men's earnings, but since 1979 this ratio has changed considerably, and women's earnings are now over 70 percent of men's earnings (Blau and Ferber 1992).

The closing of the gender gap in the 1980s and the reasons for it have been well documented (Goldin 1990; O'Neill and Polachek 1993; Blau and Kahn 1994). Less well documented, however, is the importance of family status (defined here as marital status and parental status) as a contributing factor to the gender gap.[1] It is well known that married men receive higher pay, all else equal (Korenman and Neumark 1991), and that women with children receive lower pay, all else equal (Korenman and Neumark 1992; Neumark and Korenman 1994; Waldfogel 1994a, 1997). How much of the gender gap in pay is due to the differential returns that men and women receive for marital status and parental status? Wood, Corcoran, and Courant (1993), in their study of young lawyers, concluded that family responsibilities account for 40 percent of the gender gap in pay. Waldfogel (1994b) concluded that family status accounts for over 50 percent of the gender gap for American young women and a similar proportion of the gender gap for British young women.

This study uses two young cohorts, observed in 1980 and 1991, to ask the following question: As the gender gap in pay was falling over the 1980s, how did the percentage of the gap accounted for by family status change? If the progress in narrowing the gender gap was equally shared among women without regard to family status, then the proportion of the gap accounted for by family status should have held relatively constant over the 1980s. If, on the other hand, it was women without family responsibilities who chiefly gained relative to men, then the portion of the gender gap due to family status should have grown over the decade.

If there are negative effects of children on women's pay, and if such effects persist in 1991, then it is extremely important to consider policies that might mitigate these effects. This paper considers one such policy: job-protected maternity leave. There is evidence that work interruptions at childbirth have lasting negative effects on women's pay (see, for example, Jacobsen and Levin 1995), but there has been little research on the potential positive wage effects of having maternity leave coverage and maintaining employment continuity over childbirth.

Two recent studies have investigated the wage effects of labor force participation postbirth and employment continuity over childbirth among

American women. Shapiro and Mott (1994), using a sample of women aged 33–43 from the National Longitudinal Survey of Young Women, found that women who worked (with either the same employer or a different one) within six months following their first birth had higher wages in 1987, primarily owing to higher levels of lifetime work experience. Waldfogel (1994a), using a sample of women aged 27–34 from the National Longitudinal Survey of Youth, found that women who returned to work for the same employer within twelve months following their most recent birth had higher wages in 1991. These higher wages were not entirely explained by work experience; rather, there was a positive return to maintaining employment continuity over childbirth above and beyond its effect on experience.[2]

There has also been one recent study of the wage effects of maternity leave coverage. Waldfogel (1994b) found that women who had maternity leave coverage at their most recent birth had higher wages in 1991, with the largest wage boost for those who had been covered and who returned to work for the prebirth employer, even after controlling for current employer characteristics (such as employer size and union status) that are associated with maternity leave coverage.

Comparing the effects of maternity leave at two points in time is important, because maternity leave coverage and usage have changed and are continuing to change in the United States. In contrast to the majority of industrialized countries (see, for example, Kamerman and Kahn 1995, 1991; Ruhm and Teague in this volume), the United States had no national maternity leave policy until 1993. The only federal legislation related to childbirth prior to that date was the Pregnancy Discrimination Act (PDA) of 1978, which prohibited discrimination on the basis of pregnancy and also required employers who had short-term paid disability leave plans to cover pregnancy and childbirth on the same terms as other types of disability. This law was particularly important for women working in medium-sized and large firms since they usually had such plans; in 1988, for example, 89 percent of full-time employees in firms with one hundred employees or more were covered by disability plans (Blau and Ferber 1992). The PDA was also important in the five states with state-run temporary disability insurance plans as they, too, were now required to cover pregnancy and childbirth as they did other disabilities (Kamerman, Kahn, and Kingston 1995).

In the absence of national maternity leave legislation prior to 1993, a number of states passed their own laws (Klerman and Leibowitz in this volume). As a result of the state laws, as well as union contracts and voluntary employer policies, maternity leave coverage has become more common, with an estimated 40 to 60 percent of women covered by a formal maternity leave policy by 1991 (Waldfogel 1994b) compared with 40 percent or less in the 1970s and early 1980s (Kamerman, Kahn, and Kingston 1983). According to one study (U.S. Department of Labor 1993), maternity leave coverage for young women aged 26–34 increased even more sharply, from 28 to 45 percent (depending on educational qualifications) in 1978 to 56 to 82 percent (again depending on qualifications) in 1991. Over the same period, the percentage of full-time working women using some form of maternity leave (whether formal or informal) and returning to work for their previous employer rose from 38 percent in 1975 to 51 percent in 1980 and 68 percent in 1984 (O'Connell 1990). By the late 1980s nearly 75 percent of young women working full time were returning to work after childbirth (Garrett, Lubeck, and Wenk 1987), and by the early 1990s this figure exceeded 75 percent (Klerman and Leibowitz 1994).

Maternity leave is now undergoing further change as a consequence of the passage of the Family and Medical Leave Act (FMLA) in 1993. This legislation guarantees a job-protected, unpaid maternity leave of twelve weeks to women working for firms with fifty employees or more; it also provides for continued health insurance coverage during the leave for those whose employers offer such coverage. To the extent that this law extends the right to a job-protected maternity leave to previously uncovered women and to the extent that these newly covered women choose to utilize it, we should see a further expansion of both coverage and usage post-FMLA. This provides an important motivation for attempting to better understand the effects of maternity leave coverage and employment continuity over childbirth on women's pay.

DATA

This study uses two young female cohorts (with mean age 30), from the National Longitudinal Survey of Young Women (NLS-YW) and the National Longitudinal Survey of Youth (NLSY). The NLS-YW sample contains 2,934 women who are observed working in 1980 (or if not working in 1980, then in 1978, 1977, or 1975). The NLSY sample consists of 4,334 women who are observed working in 1991 (or if not working in 1991, then in 1990, 1989, 1988, or 1987). Two young male cohorts (also mean age 30) are used for comparison purposes: a sample of 2,374 men from the National Longitudinal Survey of Young Men (NLS-YM), with wage observations from 1980 (or 1978, 1976, or 1975), and a sample of 4,771 men from the NLSY, with wage observations from 1991 (or 1990, 1989, 1988, or 1987). Means for all four samples are shown in appendix table 4.1.

The empirical strategy is to use the NLS-YW/YM and NLSY cohorts to compare the situation of young women and men at two points in time: 1980 and 1991. The advantage of using these two NLS cohorts is that the information collected is similar across the two surveys. Thus, these NLS data sets offer comparable samples of young women and men at two points in time.

IMPORTANCE OF FAMILY STATUS IN ACCOUNTING FOR THE GENDER GAP

In both cohorts, the wages of mothers are markedly lower than the wages of nonmothers and men, as can be seen in figure 4.1 and table 4.1. While the overall female-male pay ratio rose a full 20 percentage points from 64 to 84 percent over the period for these young cohorts, mothers' wages rose less sharply (from 60 percent of men's pay to 75 percent) than non-mothers' wages (from 72 percent of men's pay to 95 percent) and thus continued to lag much further behind.[3]

Human capital differences are likely to be important in accounting for at least some of these wage differences between mothers and others. Therefore, to estimate the effects of family status on men's and women's wages and the role that family status plays in explaining wage differences between mothers and nonmothers and men, this study uses a human capital earnings function, in which all the coefficients are allowed to vary by gender:

$$
\begin{aligned}
lw_i = {} & \beta_0 + \beta_1 age_i + \beta_2 age_i * wom + \beta_3 exp_i + \beta_4 exp_i * wom \\
& + \beta_5 ed1_i + \beta_6 ed1_i * wom + \beta_7 ed2_i + \beta_8 ed2_i * wom \\
& + \beta_9 ed3_i + \beta_{10} ed3_i * wom + \beta_{11} mar_i + \beta_{12} mar_i * wom \\
& + \beta_{13} prev_i + \beta_{14} prev_i * wom + \beta_{15} kid_i + \beta_{16} kid_i * wom \\
& + \beta_{17} twokids_i + \beta_{18} twokids_i * wom + \beta_{19} black_i \\
& + \beta_{20} black_i * wom + \beta_{21} hisp_i + \beta_{22} hisp_i * wom + \mu_i \qquad (1)
\end{aligned}
$$

where

lw = the log of hourly wage, in 1991 dollars,
age = age in years,
wom = dummy variable (0,1) for women,
exp = actual work experience in years,
$ed1$ = dummy variable (0,1) for college education or higher,
$ed2$ = dummy variable (0,1) for some college,
$ed3$ = dummy variable (0,1) for high school only,
mar = dummy variable (0,1) for currently married,
$prev$ = dummy variable (0,1) for previously married,
kid = dummy variable (0,1) for parent of only one child,
$twokids$ = dummy variable (0,1) for parent of two children or more,
$black$ = dummy variable (0,1) for African American,
$hisp$ = dummy variable (0,1) for Hispanic, and
μ = disturbance term, with mean 0 and variance σ^2.

Figure 4.1   Female-Male Wage Ratios at Age 30

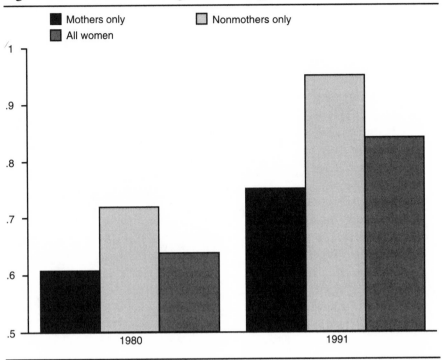

Table 4.1   Wages for Young Women and Men at Age 30: 1980 and 1991

	Men	Women	Nonmothers	Mothers
NLS-YW/YM: 1980	(N = 2,374)	(N = 2,934)	(N = 992)	(N = 1,942)
Wage at age 30	13.74	8.83	9.93	8.27
Female-male wage ratio	(na)	64%	72%	60%
NLSY: 1991	(N = 4,771)	(N = 4,334)	(N = 1,573)	(N = 2,761)
Wage at age 30	11.24	9.40	10.71	8.65
Female-male wage ratio	(na)	84%	95%	75%

Notes: In the NLS-YW and NLS-YM sample, wages are from 1980 for those working in 1980; for those not working in 1980, the wage is from the most recent survey year not earlier than 1975 in which the individual was working.

In the NLSY sample, wages are from 1991 for those working in 1991; for those not working in 1991, the wage is from the most recent survey year not earlier than 1987 in which the individual was working. All wages are in 1991 dollars.

Na = not applicable.

Because some of the wage observations are from years prior to the refer-ence year (1980 in the NLS-YW/YM and 1991 in the NLSY), the model includes controls for year. The model also includes a constant term, but not a separate one for women, because a separate constant term for women was not significantly different from zero. This suggests that all of the gender effects are being picked up by the "interaction" terms (that is, the different coefficients for women). Quadratic terms in age and experi-ence were also not significant for these young cohorts.

This model was estimated using ordinary least squares (OLS) for both the NLS-YW/YM and NLSY cohorts, and the results of the estimation are shown in table 4.2. It is apparent that women and men do receive differ-ent returns to some characteristics and that these gender differences changed over the 1980s. A look at the family status coefficients shows that men in both years received a positive return for being married and, in 1980 only, men also received a positive return for having previously been mar-ried and for currently having children. Women, in contrast, received a markedly smaller return to being married as well as significant negative returns to being parents in both years, even after controlling for human capital characteristics such as age, experience, and education.

How much did these differential returns to family status contribute to the gender gap? I use the regression results from table 4.2 to decompose the gender gap for the cohorts in 1980 and 1991 into four components (family status, age and experience, education, and race and ethnicity), not-ing in table 4.3 that portion due to differences in characteristics, differen-tial returns, and the combined effect of characteristics and returns for each component; the combined effects by component are shown in figure 4.2. This decomposition reveals that family status accounted for a large part of the gender gap in 1980 and an even larger part in 1991 (although, of course, the overall gap to be explained was much smaller in 1991). In 1980, 36 percent of the gender gap was accounted for by family status (almost entirely due to the differential returns to family status characteris-tics for women and men); in 1991, the proportion due to family status (again, due to differences in returns) had risen to 53 percent. Gender dif-ferences in age and levels of work experience and in returns to age and experience, while still extremely important, accounted for slightly less of the gender gap in 1991 than they had in 1980: 56 percent versus 62 per-cent. Together, the direct (family status) and indirect (age and experience) effects of marriage and childbearing explain nearly all of the gender gap in both of these cohorts.

The other two components of the gap are education and race and eth-nicity. Education (both differences in the level of qualifications and differ-ential returns to those qualifications) became less important in accounting for the gender gap, falling from 11 percent of the gap in 1980 to only

Table 4.2   Ordinary Least Squares Wage Equations for Young Women and Men in 1980 and 1991

	NLS-YW/YM 1980	NLSY 1991
Age	0.0055	−0.0085*
	(0.0029)	(0.0027)
Age*woman	−0.0105*	−0.0084*
	(0.0020)	(0.0015)
Actual work experience	0.0202*	0.0390*
	(0.0032)	(0.0030)
Experience*woman	0.0074	0.0083*
	(0.0039)	(0.0040)
College degree	0.4283*	0.5832*
	(0.0287)	(0.0220)
College*woman	0.0421	−0.0055
	(0.0390)	(0.0325)
Some college	0.3200*	0.2463*
	(0.0269)	(0.0191)
Some college*woman	−0.0471	−0.0053
	(0.0366)	(0.0292)
High school only	0.2129*	0.1271*
	(0.0252)	(0.0189)
High school only*woman	−0.0663*	−0.0738*
	(0.0328)	(0.0278)
Married	0.1078*	0.1154*
	(0.0279)	(0.0167)
Married*woman	−0.0798*	−0.0820*
	(0.0353)	(0.0250)
Previously married	0.1112*	0.0419
	(0.0294)	(0.0224)
Previously married*woman	−0.0415	−0.0183
	(0.0388)	(0.0321)
One child	0.0403	0.0095
	(0.0274)	(0.0195)
One child*woman	−0.0814*	−0.0939*
	(0.0349)	(0.0276)
Two children or more	0.0951*	0.0176
	(0.0249)	(0.0186)
Two children or more*woman	−0.1868*	−0.1088*
	(0.0326)	(0.0265)
African American	−0.1807*	−0.1287*
	(0.0196)	(0.0174)
African American*woman	0.1431*	0.0754*
	(0.0258)	(0.0254)

Table 4.2 *Continued*

	NLS-YW/YM 1980	NLSY 1991
Hispanic	−0.0370	−0.0145
	(0.0624)	(0.0191)
Hispanic*woman	0.0784	0.0595*
	(0.0795)	(0.0277)
Adj. R^2	.3479	.2692
Observations (N)	5,308	9,105

Notes: Model also includes an intercept and controls for year. Dependent variable is the log of hourly wage. In the NLS-YW and NLS-YM sample, wages are from 1980 for those working in 1980; for those not working in 1980, the wage is from the most recent survey year not earlier than 1975 in which the individual was working. In the NLSY sample, wages are from 1991 for those working in 1991; for those not working in 1991, the wage is from the most recent survey year not earlier than 1987 in which the individual was working. All wages are in 1991 dollars.

* = statistically significant (t-statistic > 1.96).

6 percent in 1991. In 1991, in fact, women had on average higher educational qualifications than men, but women still received slightly lower returns than men for their qualifications in the labor market. Race and ethnicity, on the other hand, became a more important positive feature for women relative to men: If women received the same negative returns to being African American or Hispanic as men, the gender gap would have been 9 percent larger in 1980 and 15 percent larger in 1991.

MATERNITY LEAVE COVERAGE AND EMPLOYMENT CONTINUITY OVER CHILDBIRTH

Since family responsibilities evidently continue to have quite important effects on women's pay, it is of interest to assess the impact of a policy intervention that might mitigate those effects. Maternity leave is particularly interesting as it could have an impact on both the indirect (experience) and direct (family status) effects noted above. This study looks at both maternity leave coverage and employment continuity over childbirth.

Maternity leave coverage refers to whether or not a woman's employer had a formal policy offering a job-protected maternity leave, whether paid or unpaid. In this study, coverage information is available for the NLSY cohort only.[4] The coverage variable is set to 1 if a woman reported being covered by a formal maternity leave policy at the job at which she was working six months prior to her most recent birth; it is set to 0 if she reported that her employer did not have a formal maternity leave policy.

Table 4.3   Accounting for the Gender Gap at Age 30

	NLS-YW/ YM 1980	NLSY 1991
Female wage	8.83	9.40
Male wage	13.74	11.24
Gender gap	36%	16%
Decomposition of gender gap		
Education		
Characteristics alone	6%	–6%
Characteristics and returns	11	6
Age and experience		
Characteristics alone	10	13
Characteristics and returns	62	56
Family status		
Characteristics alone	1	0
Characteristics and returns	36	53
Race and ethnicity		
Characteristics alone	0	–1
Characteristics and returns	–9	–15
Total		
Characteristics alone	17	6
Characteristics and returns	100	100

Note: Decompositions are based on regression results shown in table 4.2.

Maintaining employment continuity over childbirth refers to whether or not a woman returned to work for her previous employer postbirth, either as a result of using a formal maternity leave or as a result of making other arrangements (for example, using informal maternity leave, using other time off, taking no time off at all, leaving temporarily and then resuming work as a new hire). This variable is set to 1 if a woman was working six months prior to her most recent birth and was working for the same employer twelve months subsequent to the birth; it is set to 0 if she was not working for the same employer twelve months postbirth.[5] Employment six months prior to the birth is commonly used as an indication of a woman's labor force status prebirth (see, for example, Shapiro and Mott 1994). Although most women maintaining employment continuity return to work not later than four months after the birth (Klerman and Leibowitz 1994), this study looks at employment status twelve months after the birth so as not to miss the small group of women who take extended (six- or even twelve-month) maternity leaves and then return to their previous employer. Note, then, that the "returned to work" group includes women who have taken a leave (or other type of time off) of varying duration (from the one extreme of virtually no time off at all to the other extreme of a year-long leave), but that all have main-

Figure 4.2　Components of the Gender Gap at Age 30

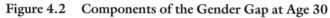

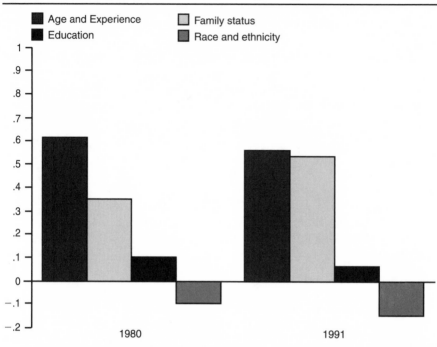

tained employment continuity with their prebirth employer, returning to work by no later than twelve months postbirth.

What are the likely wage effects of maternity leave coverage and usage?[6] As Blau and Kahn (1992) note, the answer is unclear *a priori*. In large part, this is because the answer depends on what the alternative to maternity leave would have been. If, in the absence of leave, women would have taken a very short break for childbirth and almost immediately returned to work, then the effects of leave could well be negative owing to the lost work experience associated with a twelve-week as opposed to, say, a two-week leave, although the size of such effects would likely be extremely small. (If the return to a year of experience is on the order of 2 to 4 percent, then the penalty to losing ten weeks of experience would be only about .5 percent). If, on the other hand, women without leave would have left their job, spent some time (perhaps more than twelve weeks) at home, and then at some point reentered the labor market as new employees, then the wage effects of leave should be positive, owing to experience and tenure effects. There might also be a job-matching effect; that is, maternity leave might allow workers to maintain good employment matches that might otherwise be disrupted by childbirth.[7] If this were the case, there might be a positive effect of coverage even if a woman did not take advantage of it to return to the employer, as presumably she would leave the firm only if a better option existed.[8]

It is important to note that while returning to work for the same employer postbirth is more common among covered women, it is not limited to them. Even women not covered by a formal maternity leave policy might in some instances return to their previous employer postbirth. For example, an employee who does not have access to a job-protected leave might negotiate a leave on an individual basis, or she might simply resume work with the former employer as a new applicant. These employees are, on average, unlikely to do as well as those who had maternity leave rights. As a result, we might expect to see a lower return to maintaining employment continuity among the non-covered than among the covered.[9]

In sum, if maternity leave allows women to maintain good job matches, then coverage together with returning to work should have positive effects on women's pay. Even coverage alone might have a positive effect if it gives women more and better choices in the labor market or if it reflects some other characteristic of the prebirth job, such as a commitment to promoting women, which is associated with more rapid wage growth for covered women in the future. Returning to work for those without coverage, on the other hand, might have less of a positive wage effect if such women are negotiating individual deals or are reentering as new applicants.

MATERNITY LEAVE COVERAGE AND EMPLOYMENT CONTINUITY IN THE TWO COHORTS

As can be seen in table 4.4, 58 percent of the young women in the NLS-YW cohort who have had children by age 30 were working when pregnant with their most recent child, and this proportion rose slightly to 63 percent in the NLSY cohort. More highly educated women were more likely to be working when pregnant, and this difference became more pronounced over the decade, as shown in figure 4.3. Only 46 percent of high school dropouts were working when pregnant in the NLS-YW cohort, and this proportion was virtually the same (47 percent) in the NLSY cohort. In contrast, 70 percent of college graduates were working when pregnant in the NLS-YW and this grew to 84 percent in the NLSY.

Coverage rates in the NLSY cohort also vary by educational level, as shown in table 4.4 and figure 4.4. Overall, 58 percent of those who were working when pregnant with their most recent child were covered by a formal maternity leave policy. More highly educated women were more likely to be covered: 68 percent of college graduates versus 57 percent of those with some college or only a high school diploma versus 50 percent of high

Figure 4.3   Mothers' Employment Prebirth and Postbirth

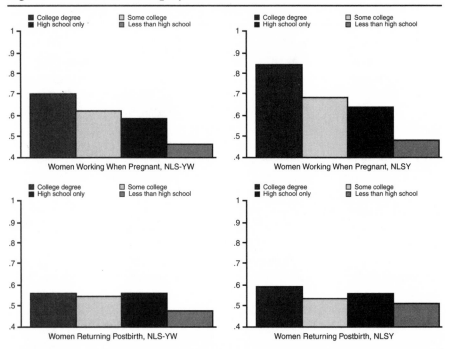

school dropouts. Comparable coverage data are not available for the NLS-YW cohort, but it is likely (given the aggregate statistics on coverage in the 1970s and 1980s cited earlier) that overall coverage rates were lower.

Table 4.4 (and figures 4.3 and 4.4) also show return to work rates for the two cohorts, and, perhaps surprisingly, the overall rate of maintaining employment continuity is fairly constant: 53 percent in the earlier cohort versus 54 percent in the later cohort. Again, education matters. Within each cohort, more-educated women are more likely to return to their employers after childbirth. In the NLS-YW, 55 percent of college graduates maintained their prebirth employment compared with only 47 percent of high school dropouts; in the NLSY, 58 percent of college graduates maintained their prebirth employment compared with 50 percent of dropouts.

Women in the NLSY who were covered were more likely to return to their original employer than those who were not covered. Among women who were covered by a formal policy, education had little effect on returning to work (for example, 61 percent of covered college graduates returned to their original employer as opposed to 59 percent of covered high school dropouts). Among those who lacked formal coverage, education mattered a great deal. College graduates who lacked formal coverage

Table 4.4 Mothers' Employment Prebirth and Postbirth

	All	College Degree	Some College	High School	Dropouts
NLS-YW mothers					
Working six months prior to most recent birth	(N = 1,803) 58% (8)	(N = 238) 70% (7)	(N = 359) 62% (7)	(N = 957) 58% (8)	(N = 388) 46% (11)
Returned within twelve months after birth, if worked when pregnant	53 (5)	55 (5)	54 (5)	55 (4)	47 (5)
NLSY mothers					
Working six months prior to most recent birth	(N = 2,648) 63%	(N = 341) 84%	(N = 647) 68%	(N = 1,020) 63%	(N = 640) 47%
Covered prebirth, if worked when pregnant	58 (15)	68 (8)	57 (15)	57 (16)	50 (21)
Returned postbirth, if worked when pregnant	54	58	52	55	50
Returned, if covered	60	61	58	63	59
Returned, if not covered	47	57	48	46	43

Notes: Figures in parentheses indicate the percentage of cases with missing data. Cases with missing data on work status when pregnant are excluded from the analysis; those with missing maternity leave data usage or coverage data are included and treated as a separate category. Return variable is set to 1 if a woman is working for her prior employer twelve months postbirth. Coverage variable is set to 1 if a woman reported that her employer six months prebirth had a formal maternity leave policy.

Figure 4.4   Maternity Leave Coverage and Employment Continuity, NLSY

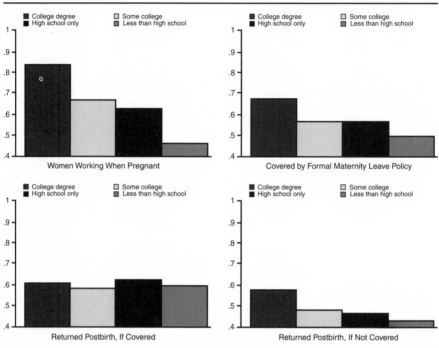

were nearly as likely to maintain employment over childbirth (57 percent) as those who had coverage (61 percent), in contrast to high school dropouts, who were much less likely to return to their prebirth employer if uncovered (43 percent) than if covered (59 percent). This differential might reflect a greater ability on the part of more-educated women to negotiate leave on an individual basis and/or a greater willingness on the part of their employer to agree to such arrangements.

Overall, the similarities across these two cohorts are more striking than the differences. Women in the NLS-YW and NLSY cohorts are about equally likely to have been working when pregnant, although the overall percentages mask the sharp rise in the percentage working when pregnant among more-educated women. Contingent on working when pregnant, women in the NLS-YW cohort were as likely to maintain employment continuity over childbirth as were women in the later cohort, but given the lower likely coverage rates, probably more of them were using informal as opposed to formal leave. In both cohorts, more highly educated women were much more likely to have been working when pregnant (and more likely to be covered in the NLSY); contingent on working when pregnant, more-educated women were somewhat more likely to return to their original employer postbirth than were less-educated women, with an especially pronounced difference among the women not covered by formal maternity leave policies.

EFFECTS OF MATERNITY LEAVE COVERAGE AND EMPLOYMENT CONTINUITY ON WOMEN'S PAY

This paper investigates two questions concerning the effects of maternity leave coverage and employment continuity on women's pay. First, for both cohorts, how does employment continuity over the period of childbirth affect women's wages and wage growth, all else equal? Second, for the NLSY cohort only, how do maternity leave coverage and employment continuity jointly affect women's wages and wage growth, all else equal?

For this analysis, I use a sample of "working mothers" only, that is, women who have had children by age 30 and were working when pregnant with their most recent child. It is important to restrict the sample to those working when pregnant because these are the women who might or might not have been covered by a formal policy, and who might or might not have returned to work for the prebirth employer. The sample is also restricted to those women who have wage observations prebirth and postbirth, so that a difference specification can be used to control for unobserved heterogeneity (as detailed below). To create a two-wage sample in the NLSY, a current wage is taken from 1991 (or the 1987–1990 period for those not working in 1991) and an early wage is taken from 1983 (or the 1979–1982 or 1984–1986 period for those not working in 1983). The NLSY women are on average 30 years old at the time of the current wage (with a maximum age of 34) and 22 at the time of the early wage (with a minimum age of 18). Similarly, in the NLS-YW, a current wage is taken from 1980 (or 1975–1978) and an early wage is taken from 1972 (or 1968–1971 or 1973–1975). The NLS-YW women are on average 30 years old at the time of the current wage (with a maximum age of 36) and 22 at the time of the early wage (with a minimum age of 18). Finally, the sample is limited to those who have no missing work experience or tenure data. These criteria yield a subsample of 634 "working mothers" from the NLS-YW and 1,453 "working mothers" from the NLSY, all of whom have two wage observations, have had at least one child between wage observations, and were working when pregnant with the most recent child. Means for the two "working mothers" samples are shown in appendix table 4.2.

COMPARING WOMEN WHO DID AND DID NOT
MAINTAIN EMPLOYMENT CONTINUITY

Figures 4.5–4.8 (and table 4.5) provide a first indication of how working mothers who returned to their original employers postbirth differ from working mothers who did not. In the NLS-YW, "returners" have somewhat higher wages than "nonreturners" at both age 22 (before their most recent birth) and age 30 (after the most recent birth), suggesting that preexisting differences in characteristics, including some (such as productivity or ability) that may be unobservable in the data sets, may be important. Not surprisingly, women who maintained employment continuity over childbirth have higher levels of work experience and much higher levels of job tenure at age 30 than do women who had children but did not return to their prebirth employers. Interestingly, only a small proportion of the experience and tenure differentials is due to differences at age 22, as can be seen in table 4.5. This suggests that current work experience and current job tenure are likely to be more important than prebirth differences in early work experience and early job tenure in explaining wage differences between returners and nonreturners in the NLS-YW.

The picture is slightly different for the working mothers in the NLSY. As shown in figures 4.7 and 4.8, women who maintained employment with the prebirth employer and those who did not both have about the same wages at age 22 (prior to their most recent birth), but the wages of women who maintained employment continuity over childbirth rise more rapidly to age 30 (after the most recent birth) than do the wages of women who did not. Thus, heterogeneity in unobserved characteristics such as productivity or ability is likely to be less important in explaining wage differences between returners and nonreturners in this cohort than in the NLS-YW cohort. As in the NLS-YW, those who maintained employment continuity over childbirth have higher levels of experience and tenure at age 30 (although they were only slightly higher at age 22, as shown in table 4.5), suggesting that current work experience and current job tenure will be important factors in explaining wage differences in this cohort as well.

Figure 4.9 and 4.10 provide a first look at the variation in wages, experience, and tenure associated with the joint effects of maternity leave coverage and employment continuity in the NLSY. The raw data indicate that among the women who stayed with the prebirth employer in the NLSY, those who were covered by a formal policy have the steepest wage growth from age 22 (prebirth) to age 30 (postbirth). These women also have the highest levels of work experience and job tenure at age 30 (although they had only slightly higher levels of experience and tenure at age 22, as shown in table 4.5). Women who were covered but did not return to their pre-

(Text continued on p. 111.)

Figure 4.5   Wage Growth from Age 22 to Age 30 in NLS-YW

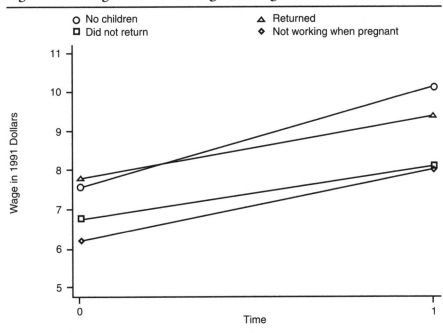

Figure 4.6   Experience and Tenure Levels at Age 30 in NLS-YW

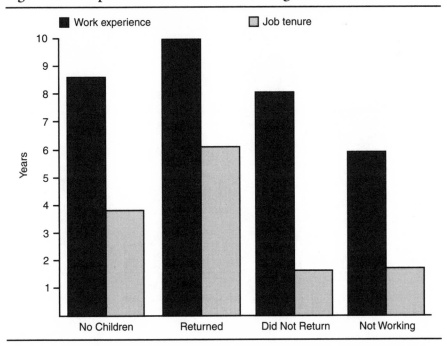

Figure 4.7   Wage Growth from Age 22 to Age 30 in NLSY

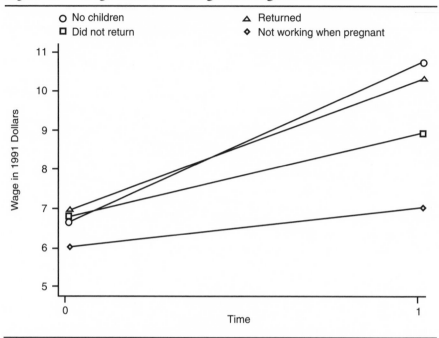

Figure 4.8   Experience and Tenure Levels at Age 30 in NLSY

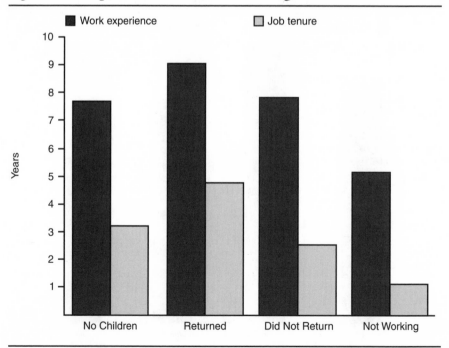

birth employer had fairly high starting wages at age 22 but less steep wage growth to age 30 compared with women who did maintain employment continuity without formal coverage, who had slightly lower starting wages but steeper wage growth. Maternity leave coverage, then, seems to be associated with higher starting wages, while maintaining employment continuity, particularly for those with formal maternity leave, seems to be associated with more rapid wage growth as well as higher subsequent levels of work experience and tenure.

ESTIMATING THE EFFECTS OF MATERNITY LEAVE COVERAGE AND EMPLOYMENT CONTINUITY ON WOMEN'S PAY

To estimate the effects of employment continuity controlling for other characteristics, I use a basic human capital wage equation, including a dummy variable for returning to work postbirth:

$$lw_i = \beta_0 + \beta_1 age_i + \beta_2 exp_i + \beta_3 ten_i + \beta_4 ed1_i + \beta_5 ed2_i + \beta_6 ed3_i + \beta_7 ch_i + \beta_8 ret_i + \beta_9 black + \beta_{10} hisp + \mu_i \qquad (2)$$

where

$\quad lw$ = the log of hourly wage, in 1991 dollars,
$\quad age$ = age in years,
$\quad exp$ = actual work experience in years,
$\quad ten$ = job tenure in years,
$\quad ed1$ = college education or higher,
$\quad ed2$ = some college,
$\quad ed3$ = high school only,
$\quad ch$ = number of children,
$\quad ret$ = working for the prebirth employer twelve months postbirth,
$\quad black$ = African American,
$\quad hisp$ = Hispanic, and
$\quad \mu$ = disturbance term.

The reference category in this model is a woman who was working when pregnant with her most recent child and did not return to her previous employer within twelve months after the child's birth. Because wage observations may be from different years, the model includes controls for year. The model also includes a control variable for those with missing data on whether or not they returned to work for the same employer (in the NLS-YW).[10]

To estimate the joint effects of maternity leave coverage and employment continuity in the NLSY controlling for other characteristics, I use a

(Text continued on p. 115.)

Table 4.5 Wages, Experience, and Tenure for Returners Versus Nonreturners

	Wage at Age 22	Wage at Age 30	Experience at Age 22	Experience at Age 30	Tenure at Age 22	Tenure at Age 30
NLS-YW women						
No children by age 30 (N = 889)	7.56	10.09	2.68	8.60	1.29	3.70
Returned to prebirth employer (N = 355)	7.78	9.39	2.98	9.95	1.59	5.70
Did not return (N = 237)	6.76	8.06	2.47	8.07	1.01	1.62
Did not work when pregnant (N = 165)	6.20	7.99	1.52	5.84	0.57	1.67
NLSY women						
No children by age 30 (N = 1573)	6.63	10.71	2.24	7.79	1.32	3.30
Returned to employer (N = 773)	6.92	10.29	2.85	9.15	1.69	4.84

Did not return (N = 771)	6.72	8.90	2.44	7.85	1.36	2.65
Did not work when pregnant (N = 737)	5.96	6.99	1.83	5.21	0.94	1.20
Covered and returned (N = 530)	7.02	10.76	2.96	9.48	1.80	5.57
Covered only (N = 429)	6.99	9.46	2.51	8.26	1.51	3.22
Returned only (N = 186)	6.86	9.83	2.69	8.65	1.49	3.74
Neither covered nor returned (N = 245)	6.33	7.89	2.40	7.35	1.18	1.94

Notes: Sample includes mothers who were working when pregnant with the most recent child, have wage observations prebirth and postbirth, and have no missing data. This table also includes some data on nonmothers (row 1) and mothers who did not work when pregnant (row 4).

Figure 4.9 Wage Growth from Age 22 to Age 30 in NLSY

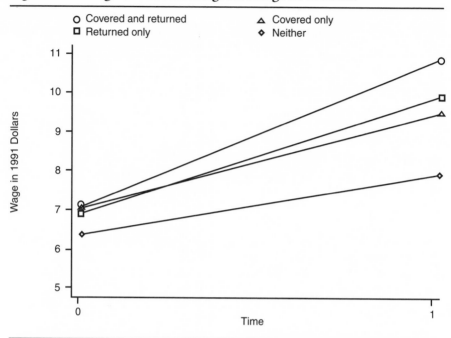

Figure 4.10 Experience and Tenure Levels at Age 30 in NLSY

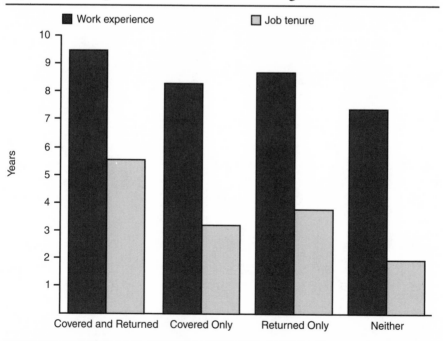

similar human capital wage equation, but with dummy variables for the joint effects of coverage and returning to work postbirth as follows:

$$lw_i = \beta_0 + \beta_1 age_i + \beta_2 exp_i + \beta_3 ten_i + \beta_4 ed1_i + \beta_5 ed2_i$$
$$+ \beta_6 ed3_i + \beta_7 ch_i + \beta_8 cov*ret_i + \beta_9 cov*noret_i$$
$$+ \beta_{10} nocov*ret_i + \beta_{11} black + \beta_{12} hisp + \mu_i \qquad (3)$$

where

cov*ret = covered by formal maternity leave policy and returned to prebirth employer within twelve months postbirth,

cov*noret = covered but did not return, and

nocov*ret = not covered but did return.

The omitted category in this model is a woman who was working when pregnant with her most recent child, was not covered by a formal maternity leave policy, and did not return to her previous employer within twelve months after childbirth. This model also includes controls for year as well as control variables for those with missing coverage data.

Results from these cross-sectional OLS models are shown in table 4.6. Column 1 (NLS-YW cohort) shows that, controlling only for age, education, number of children, race, ethnicity, and year, maintaining employment continuity by returning to the original employer postbirth is associated with about a 12.5 percent wage premium. It is clear that this premium reflects higher work experience and especially higher job tenure: After controlling for actual work experience (column 2), the returned to work premium falls to about 9 percent; and after controlling for tenure (column 3), the premium is no longer statistically different from zero. The premium to maintaining employment continuity in the NLSY is strikingly similar: Before controlling for experience and tenure, it is about 11 percent (column 4); and after controlling for experience and tenure (in models not shown here), it also falls to zero.[11]

The NLSY also permits us to look at the effects of usage and coverage together, and in these models (shown in columns 5–7), a consistent pattern emerges. By far the largest premium, at about 24.5 percent (column 5), is associated with employment continuity among those who had formal maternity leave coverage. About half this premium is due to experience and tenure, but a premium of about 12.5 percent remains even after controlling for experience and tenure (column 7). Coverage alone, when it is not used to maintain employment continuity with the prebirth employer, is also associated with moderately higher pay: 13 percent overall and 8 percent even after controlling for experience and tenure. Employment continuity alone, on the other hand, if no formal leave policy was available, has a positive but not significant effect on pay.

It is apparent from these results that there is a strong positive return to having formal maternity leave coverage and maintaining employment con-

(Text continued on p. 118.)

Table 4.6   Effects of Maternity Leave Coverage and Employment Continuity on Working Mothers' Wage Levels at Age 30

	NLS-YW (1)	NLS-YW (2)	NLS-YW (3)	NLSY (4)	NLSY (5)	NLSY (6)	NLSY (7)
Experience		0.0263* (0.0059)	0.0149* (0.0062)			0.0328* (0.0061)	0.0225* (0.0064)
Tenure			0.0280* (0.0052)				0.0235* (0.0043)
College degree	0.3668* (0.0616)	0.4349* (0.0626)	0.4085* (0.0614)	0.4955* (0.0441)	0.4757* (0.0438)	0.5122* (0.0439)	0.5000* (0.0436)
Some college	0.2457* (0.0569)	0.2646* (0.0563)	0.2415* (0.0553)	0.2456* (0.0399)	0.2388* (0.0396)	0.2210* (0.0393)	0.2189* (0.0389)
High school only	0.1345* (0.0496)	0.1534* (0.0491)	0.1220* (0.0484)	0.1157* (0.0373)	0.1069* (0.0369)	0.0782* (0.0369)	0.0723* (0.0366)
Number of children	-0.0283 (0.0157)	-0.0191 (0.0156)	-0.0173 (0.0152)	-0.0662* (0.0155)	-0.0592* (0.0154)	-0.0416* (0.0156)	-0.0441* (0.0154)
Returned postbirth	0.1256* (0.0317)	0.0919* (0.0322)	-0.0024 (0.0359)	0.1094* (0.0260)			
Covered and returned					0.2449* (0.0384)	0.1909* (0.0393)	0.1246* (0.0408)

Not covered but did return				0.0801 (0.0470)	0.0521 (0.0468)	0.0202 (0.0467)
Covered but did not return				0.1313* (0.0399)	0.0995* (0.0400)	0.0814* (0.0397)
Adj. R^2	.1606	.1848	.2205	.1796	.1995	.2145	.2301
Observations (N)	634	634	634	1,453	1,453	1,453	1,453

Notes: The dependent variable in all models is the log of hourly wage. All models include an intercept as well as variables for age, African American, Hispanic, and year. The working mothers sample includes all women who have had children, were working when pregnant with the most recent child, have wage observations prebirth and postbirth, and have no missing data. Means for working mothers are shown in appendix table 4.2.

* = statistically significant (t-statistic > 1.96).

tinuity when these occur together. There is also a moderately large positive return to coverage even when not used to maintain employment continuity. What explains these results? One possibility is that maternity leave coverage may raise women's pay. This could happen in two ways: first, by raising levels of work experience and job tenure for women who use the leave to return to work with their original employer postbirth; and, second, by improving the terms upon which women return to the labor market after childbirth, whether or not they return to their original employer.

Another possibility is that the higher wages of women who are covered by a maternity leave policy and maintain their prebirth employment reflect, at least in part, unobserved heterogeneity. That is, these women may have higher wages not as a result of maternity leave, but because they are more productive and able workers, who had higher wages to start.[12] For this reason, it is important to estimate the effects of coverage and employment continuity controlling for prebirth wages and other pre-existing characteristics. I do this by estimating two first-difference models, as follows:

$$\Delta lw_i = \beta_0 + \beta_1 \Delta age_i + \beta_2 \Delta \exp_i + \beta_3 \Delta ten_i + \beta_4 \Delta ed1_i$$
$$+ \beta_5 \Delta ed2_i + \beta_6 \Delta ed3_i + \beta_7 \Delta ch_i + \beta_8 ret_i + \Delta \alpha_i + \Delta \mu_i \quad (4)$$

and

$$\Delta lw_i = \beta_0 + \beta_1 \Delta age_i + \beta_2 \Delta \exp_i + \beta_3 \Delta ten_i + \beta_4 \Delta ed1_i +$$
$$+ \beta_5 \Delta ed2_i + \beta_6 \Delta ed3_i + \beta_7 \Delta ch_i + \beta_8 cov * ret_i$$
$$+ \beta_9 cov * noret_i + \beta_{10} nocov * ret_i + \Delta \alpha_i + \Delta \mu_i \quad (5)$$

where $\Delta lw_i = (lw_{i1} - lw_{i0})$, $\Delta age = age_{i1} - age_{i0})$, and so on, and where time is denoted by 0 or 1. As noted earlier, time 0 (when the women are on average age 22) is always prior to the birth of the most recent child, and time 1 (when the women are on average age 30) is always at least twelve months after the birth. In the NLS-YW, time 0 is from 1968 to 1978, and time 1 is from 1975 to 1980; in the NLSY, time 0 is from 1979 to 1986, and time 1 is from 1987 to 1991. The mean time elapsed between time 0 and time 1 is eight years, allowing the model to pick up long-term (rather than transitory or adjustment) effects. In this specification, all the independent variables are entered as differences, with the exception of the coverage and return terms, which apply only to the most recent birth. Note that the individual fixed effect α_i, which might be a characteristic like productivity or ability that is potentially correlated with the maternity leave coverage or usage variables, is assumed to be time-invariant, so differencing effectively removes it. Again, both models include controls for year (as well as for missing return to work or coverage data where applicable).

The first difference results are shown in table 4.7 (with alternative specifications shown in table 4.8). The results for employment continuity show that the overall premium is lower than that estimated in the levels equations (in fact, the NLS-YW premium is no longer significantly different from zero), and, as in the levels equations, experience and tenure fully account for the premium.

In the NLSY models that control for coverage as well as employment continuity (columns 5–7), the returns to maternity leave are also smaller, but the return to coverage among those who returned to work is still substantial. Before controlling for changes in experience and tenure but after controlling for changes in other characteristics (for example, age, education, number of children), the return to having formal maternity leave and returning to work for the prebirth employer is about 13 percent (column 5). This is twice as large as the approximately 6 percent penalty to having an additional child, suggesting that, all else equal, a woman having two children but having access to formal maternity leave and maintaining employment continuity with the most recent child would have wage growth no different from a woman who had no children over the period. As can be seen in columns 6 and 7, experience and particularly job tenure account for much of the returns to having and using formal maternity leave coverage, and, after controlling for experience and tenure, the effects of having coverage and maintaining employment continuity are positive but no longer significant.[13]

Taken together, these results suggest that there are probably (at least) three reasons why women who had access to formal maternity leave policies have higher pay at age 30: (1) These women were likely to have had higher wages to start; (2) if they returned to work for the prebirth employer, they subsequently have higher levels of work experience and job tenure; (3) whether or not they returned to the prebirth employer, having the right to a job-protected leave may have improved the terms upon which they reentered the labor market after childbirth.

CONCLUSION

This study used two young cohorts, observed in 1980 and 1991, to ask two sets of questions, the first concerning the role of family status as a component of the gender gap in pay and the second concerning the importance of maternity leave policy in mitigating the negative effects of parenthood on the pay of working mothers. Investigating these questions at these two points in time is important, because the gender gap narrowed a great deal between 1980 and 1991. Maternity leave coverage and employment postbirth also changed over the period, although less dramatically.

The results reported here suggest that family status is still an important component of the gender gap among young women and men. The differential returns that men and women receive in the labor market for being married, previously married, and parents account for a large part of the gender gap at age 30. The family status penalty for women did not diminish over the 1980s; in fact, it was larger as a component of the gender gap in 1991 (53 percent) than it was in 1980 (36 percent). Women's shortfall in work experience and lower returns to experience, also related to family

Table 4.7 Effects of Maternity Leave Coverage and Employment Continuity on Working Mothers' Wage Growth from Age 22 to Age 30: First-Difference Results

	NLS-YW (1)	NLS-YW (2)	NLS-YW (3)	NLSY (4)	NLSY (5)	NLSY (6)	NLSY (7)
ΔExperience		0.0104 (0.0080)	0.0011 (0.0082)			0.0171* (0.0093)	0.0072 (0.0095)
ΔTenure			0.0264* (0.0061)				0.0216* (0.0047)
ΔCollege degree	0.3107* (0.0731)	0.3178* (0.0734)	0.3177* (0.0724)	0.3447* (0.0496)	0.3307* (0.0496)	0.3487* (0.0505)	0.3464* (0.0502)
ΔSome college	0.1905* (0.0590)	0.1901* (0.0595)	0.1968* (0.0587)	0.0671 (0.0507)	0.0706 (0.0505)	0.0787 (0.0507)	0.0867 (0.0504)
ΔHigh school only	0.1212* (0.0631)	0.1210 (0.0631)	0.1247* (0.0622)	0.0520 (0.0687)	0.0590 (0.0686)	0.0731 (0.0689)	0.0693 (0.0685)
ΔNumber of children	-0.0624* (0.0276)	-0.0558* (0.0282)	-0.0532 (0.0278)	-0.0583* (0.0208)	-0.0622* (0.0209)	-0.0590* (0.0210)	-0.0590* (0.0208)
Returned postbirth	0.0408 (0.0368)	0.0269 (0.0382)	-0.0537 (0.0420)	0.0641* (0.0281)			

Covered and returned					0.1290* (0.0419)	0.1093* (0.0432)	0.0577 (0.0444)
Not covered but did return					0.0452 (0.0515)	0.0320 (0.0520)	0.0068 (0.0519)
Covered but did not return					0.0600 (0.0437)	0.0482 (0.0442)	0.0382 (0.0439)
Adj. R^2	.0458	.0463	.0729	.0673	.0736	.0751	.0876
Observations (N)	634	634	634	1,453	1,453	1,453	1,453

Notes: The dependent variable in all models is the difference in log hourly wage. In the NLS-YW, wage 1 is from 1975 to 1980 and wage 0 is from 1968 to 1978; in the NLSY, wage 1 is from 1987 to 1991 and wage 0 is from 1979 to 1986. All models include an intercept as well as Δage and year controls. The maternity leave variables refer to usage and coverage at the time of the most recent birth.

* = statistically significant (t–statistic > 1.96).

Table 4.8   Effects of Maternity Leave Coverage and Employment Continuity on Working Mothers' Wage Growth from Age 22 to Age 30: First-Difference Results Entering Early and Late Tenure Separately

	NLS-YW	NLSY
ΔExperience	0.0102	0.0163
	(0.0084)	(0.0096)
Tenure at age 30	0.0212*	0.0168*
	(0.0061)	(0.0048)
Tenure at age 22	−0.0794*	−0.0682*
	(0.0138)	(0.0104)
ΔCollege degree	0.2906*	0.3455*
	(0.0717)	(0.0498)
ΔSome college	0.1812*	0.0791
	(0.0580)	(0.0500)
ΔHigh school only	0.1048	0.0470
	(0.0616)	(0.0684)
ΔNumber of children	−0.0446	−0.0528*
	(0.0275)	(0.0207)
Returned postbirth	−0.0151	
	(0.0424)	
Covered and returned		0.0935*
		(0.0446)
Not covered but did return		0.0222
		(0.0516)
Covered but did not return		0.0539
		(0.0437)
Adj. R^2	.0979	.1027
Observations (N)	634	1,453

Notes: The dependent variable in all models is the difference in log hourly wage. In the NLS-YW, wage 1 is from 1975 to 1980 and wage 0 is from 1968 to 1978; in the NLSY, wage 1 is from 1987 to 1991 and wage 0 is from 1979 to 1986. All models include an intercept as well as Δage and year controls. The maternity leave variables refer to usage and coverage at the time of the most recent birth.

* = statistically significant (t–statistic > 1.96).

status, continue to be extremely important as well. Thus, as the gender gap was narrowing in the 1980s, the direct and indirect penalties associated with motherhood were becoming a larger share of the gap.

This study also provided some evidence to suggest that job-protected maternity leave could be an important remedy for the pay penalties associated with motherhood. In both cohorts, maintaining employment continuity over childbirth was associated with higher pay, reflecting higher starting wages but also higher levels of subsequent work experience and job tenure. In the later cohort, where data about formal maternity leave policies are available, there is a large wage premium associated with having been covered by a maternity leave policy at the time of the most recent birth. Women who were covered and returned to their original employer have higher subsequent wages, owing in part to pre-existing differences and in part to the higher levels of experience and tenure they accrue after childbirth. Even women who did not use the leave to return to their prior employer have higher wages, again reflecting heterogeneity as well as possibly the effects of their superior labor market position at the time of the birth.

Given the fact that some of the wage effects of maternity leave are due to pre-existing differences among women, and that heterogeneity among employers may also play a role (Waldfogel 1994b), the extent to which the positive effects of having maternity leave coverage and maintaining employment continuity will be observed for women covered by the maternity leave expansions occurring as a result of the FMLA is an open question. This is a promising direction for future research.

ACKNOWLEDGMENTS

I would like to thank Rebecca Blank, Francine Blau, Paula England, and Irv Garfinkel for very helpful comments and discussions. Alison Earl provided excellent research assistance. Funding was provided by the Malcolm Wiener Center for Social Policy at the Kennedy School of Government.

APPENDIX

Appendix Table 4.1   Means of Variables at Age 30

	NLS-YW Women (N = 2,255)	NLS-YM Men (N = 3,253)	NLSY Women (N = 2,934)	NLSY Men (N = 2,374)
Logwage	2.0835	2.5428	2.0783	2.2757
Age	29.5597	29.5692	29.5600	29.5692
Actual work experience	8.3776	11.8192	7.6671	8.1699
College degree	.2018	.2613	.2201	.1886
Some college	.1967	.2342	.2543	.3037
High school only	.4407	.3366	.3392	.2679
Less than high school	.1609	.1678	.1864	.2398
One child	.2178	.1688	.2367	.1882
Two children or more	.4441	.4491	.4003	.2748
Married	.6210	.7144	.5734	.5047
Divorced	.1210	.0741	.1124	.0874
Separated	.0651	.0510	.0561	.0453
Widowed	.0069	.0022	.0065	.0015
Never married	.1851	.1574	.2516	.3611
Part-time	.2239	.0375	.2417	.0840
African American	.3003	.2459	.2224	.2444
Hispanic	.0225	.0184	.1599	.1696
Parent	.6619	.6179	.6370	.4630

Appendix Table 4.2   Means of Variables for Working Mothers

	NLS-YW ($N = 634$)	NLSY ($N = 1,453$)
Variables at age 30		
Logwage	2.0824	2.0891
Age	29.7745	29.8500
Actual work experience	8.9688	8.4952
Job tenure	3.8449	3.7070
College degree	.1656	.1893
Some college	.2050	.2663
High school only	.5095	.3730
Less than high school	.1199	.1714
Number of children	2.0694	1.8527
Returned postbirth	.5599	.5279
Return data missing	.0662	(na)
Did not return postbirth	.3737	.4721
Covered by maternity leave policy	(na)	.6132
Not covered	(na)	.2849
Coverage missing	(na)	.1019
Covered and returned	(na)	.3613
Not covered but did return	(na)	.1274
Covered but did not return	(na)	.2519
Coverage missing, returned	(na)	.0392
Coverage missing, did not return	(na)	.0626
Not covered and did not return	(na)	.1576
African American	.3249	.2092
Hispanic	.0315	.1727
Variables at age 22		
Logwage	1.9051	1.8277
Age	21.9795	21.5829
Actual work experience	2.7367	2.6555
Job tenure	1.3106	1.5199
College degree	.1088	.1053
Some college	.1719	.2540
High school only	.5268	.4088
Less than high school	.1925	.2319
Number of children	.6262	.3613
Difference variables		
ΔLogwage	.1773	.2613
ΔAge	7.7950	8.2670
ΔActual work experience	6.2748	5.8398
ΔTenure	2.5343	2.1871
ΔCollege degree	.0599	.0840
ΔSome college	.0962	.0819
ΔHigh school only	.0836	.0420
ΔNumber of children	1.4432	1.4914

Note: Na = not applicable.

NOTES

1. One could define family status more broadly (for example, taking account of responsibility for elderly parents), but that would be beyond the scope of this paper.

2. Two recent studies also find positive effects of maternity leave usage on women's pay in Britain (Waldfogel 1995; Joshi, Paci, and Waldfogel 1996).

3. The reference group here is all men, without regard to family status. If mothers were compared with fathers only, the resulting gender gap would of course be even larger, as married men and men with children tend to be higher paid than other men. By the same reasoning, if non-mothers were compared with nonfathers only, the gap between them would be even smaller, and thus the contrast between mothers and nonmothers would be even greater.

4. Coverage information is not available in the NLS-YW until 1983, when many of the women in this cohort had already completed their childbearing. Nor can coverage be predicted for most cases before 1983, using prebirth job characteristics such as union status, as these job characteristics are recorded for only a small proportion of women at the job at which they were working when pregnant.

5. In both cohorts, I use the work history data to identify the job six months prior to the most recent birth and the job twelve months after the most recent birth. If a woman was working prior to the birth, she is coded as working when pregnant. If a woman was working when pregnant and is in the same job postbirth, she is coded as a "returner." If she was working when pregnant but is not at the same job after the birth, she is coded as a "nonreturner." Because the NLS-YW work histories are incomplete, some women (noted in table 4.4) have missing values for working when pregnant and returning to work postbirth.

6. This study addresses individual wage effects only. Waldfogel (1996) examines aggregate wage and employment effects pursuant to the maternity leave mandate in the FMLA.

7. In the absence of a policy, a good match might not be maintained owing to asymmetric information. It is costly for an employer to hold a job open unless a worker intends to return, but only the worker knows her intentions, and she cannot credibly signal them to her employer. A policy such as the short, unpaid leave mandated in the FMLA resolves the problem by requiring the employer to hold the job open, but for a limited amount of time and at minimal cost. The health insurance component (which workers are entitled to only if they are returning and which they must pay back if they do not) may also help by inducing workers to truthfully reveal their return intentions, but it is too soon to tell how this is working in practice.

8. I have argued elsewhere (Waldfogel 1994b) that one can think of women who lack maternity leave rights as displaced workers. Just as

displacement due to plant-closing has long-term wage effects, particularly for women, we might also expect displacement due to childbirth to have long-term negative effects.

9. Another possible explanation for high rates of apparent utilization among uncovered women is that coverage may be measured with error. If this is the case, the returns to coverage estimated here would be biased downwards.

10. This model, and the following ones, include controls for children because, although all the working mothers have at least one child, the number of children varies across women and may have an effect on wages. Alternative models, not shown here, were estimated excluding the number of children variable, and the other coefficients were in all cases very similar to those reported here.

11. Tenure in these models is current job tenure. In alternative models, not shown here, early job tenure (at the age 22 job) was never significant and had no effect on the other coefficients. Thus, it is unlikely that early tenure (at the prebirth job) accounts for the positive return to maintaining employment continuity or maternity leave coverage.

12. Another possibility, not explored here, is that the higher wages of covered workers reflect other attributes of their employers. If women who were covered worked for higher-wage firms and stayed at those firms over childbirth, their current higher wages might be due to current employer characteristics associated with both higher pay and with higher likelihood of coverage. Waldfogel (1994b) tested for this and found that current job characteristics (that is, firm size, union status, and maternity leave coverage) explained some but not all of the wage premium associated with having had maternity leave coverage at the time of the most recent birth.

13. In other models shown in table 4.8, I have experimented with entering the tenure terms separately rather than as differences so that the return to tenure on the current job (as opposed to tenure on the early job) can be explicitly estimated. The results suggest that they in fact do have different effects. As expected, current job tenure has a positive effect on wage growth and explains a good part of the maternity leave premium, although in this specification, the coefficient on covered and returned in the NLSY is still positive and significant. Early job tenure, on the other hand, has no positive effect on wage growth (in fact, it is strongly negative). This makes sense when one recalls that early job tenure had no effect on the wage level at age 30 and that the dependent variable in these models is wage growth from age 22 to age 30 (that is, since early tenure would be positively associated with wages at age 22 but has no effect on wages at age 30, the net effect of early job tenure on the difference between the two would be negative). There is no evidence here (or in the levels models) to support the idea that it might be early job tenure that accounts for the higher wages associated with employment continuity and maternity leave.

Commentary on Chapter 4

Rebecca M. Blank

Jane Waldfogel's paper looks at an increasingly important issue for women in the U.S. labor market: the impact of maternity leave coverage on their employment. Increases in female labor force participation in the 1960s and 1970s were heavily concentrated among women who returned to work when their children were school age or older. Over the last fifteen years, however, female labor force participation increases have been concentrated among mothers with preschoolers. More and more women are staying in the labor market continuously, taking only a short leave when their children are born.

In this situation, it is not surprising that more and more firms have established maternity leave policies, culminating in the passage of the Family and Medical Leave Act of 1993, which required all firms of fifty employees or more to provide up to twelve weeks of unpaid leave. Despite these policy changes, there is only limited evidence on the effects of leave policies on women's labor market involvement. Waldfogel's paper fills an important gap.

The primary result, according to Waldfogel, is that women who return to the same employer following the birth of a child receive higher wages at a later date. This effect appears to be concentrated among women whose firm offers them a maternity leave policy (as opposed to those who remain with the employer in the absence of any formal policy).

Of course, this result raises the inevitable questions about interpretation. One obvious interpretation is that maternity leave allows women to maintain tenure and experience on a job and may also make them more satisfied and productive employees. Strikingly, even after controlling for tenure and experience, there is still a positive effect of maternity leave on wages among the most recent cohort of women that Waldfogel analyzes (see column 7 of table 4.6).

The second obvious interpretation is that this effect is entirely due to selectivity. Women who are better, more productive, and more stable workers (along dimensions that are not well measured by aggregate education or experience variables) are more likely to be in a job that offers maternity leave. Or more successful firms that use their workers more productively are more likely to offer maternity leave. In either case, this would result in higher wages among women who had used maternity leave than among those who did not, but these higher wages would not be due to the availability of maternity leave.

Waldfogel addresses the question of selectivity by estimating wage growth among women between ages 22 and 30, rather than looking at wage levels at age 30, which should difference out individual fixed effects. The results indicate that maternity leave still has a significant effect among the most recent cohort. This effect is entirely explained by the differences in experience and tenure among those who use maternity leave and stay with the same job.

While Waldfogel's estimates provide an excellent first review of the relationship between maternity leave and wages, I am still not completely persuaded that these results show the impact of maternity leave, uncontaminated by other effects. Since women can have children any time in the seven-year window over which wage growth is calculated, it would be interesting to separate the effects of postbirth and prebirth tenure. It should be the *prebirth* tenure acquired by women who use maternity leave that matters the most, since women who go to work for another employer can have just as much postbirth tenure. Such a finding would reinforce the argument that it is the continued job tenure permitted by maternity leave that is driving these results.

Also, there is still a potential selectivity effect that the paper does not address, namely, a match-quality issue. It is possible that women who are in better matches are more likely to stay with their employer. If match quality affects not just wage levels but also wage growth, then the higher wage growth of those who use maternity leave may be partly due to the quality of the match and not to the availability of maternity leave, per se. The results in table 4.7 of the paper show that women who stayed with the same employer but had no maternity leave have no higher wage growth. This runs somewhat counter to the job match selectivity story, but suggests that there may be an interplay between "good jobs" with the potential for good match quality and the probability that a job offers maternity leave.

These are suggestions for the next round of research, however. In general, this paper goes a long way toward establishing a presumption that maternity leave *does* produce higher wages for those who utilize it. The burden of proof has shifted to researchers who want to question that conclusion.

Finally, it is worth noting that one of the important contributions of this paper is unrelated to the maternity leave question. The tabulations at the beginning of the paper indicate that "family issues"—marital status and the presence and age of children—explain almost half of the male-female wage gap. This result indicates that women's marriage and fertility choices continue to have a strong effect on their long-run earning power. This underscores the extent to which policies that predominantly influence the "domestic sphere"—from child care to divorce laws to child support enforcement—have major effects on women's involvement and returns from the "public sphere" of the labor market. In general, the research literature that studies the nature and magnitude of these effects is sparse. Waldfogel's paper is an excellent contribution to a field of research where too little is currently known.

Commentary on Chapter 4

Paula England

The past fifteen years have seen impressive reductions in the sex gap in pay; but the progress has been much greater among childless women than mothers. Waldfogel's paper has two important claims: (1) By 1980 penalties related to childbearing explained virtually all of the sex gap in pay among young cohorts in the United States, and (2) mothers who were covered by a formal maternity leave policy and returned to the same employer within a year after giving birth had higher wages, in large part because they continued to accumulate seniority. (Seniority refers to time working for one's current employer.) If these claims are true, then policy changes by employers (whether mandated by government or not) that allow parents to take time off at the birth of a child and return to a protected job and wage might be quite important in reducing the wage disadvantages of motherhood by allowing women to maintain their seniority after a birth. The Family and Medical Leave Act, passed in 1993, later than the data for this study, may have such an effect; it guarantees a postbirth (or adoption), unpaid, but job-protected leave of twelve weeks to mothers or fathers working for firms with fifty employees or more. My comments are designed to put Waldfogel's claims in perspective, as well as to evaluate them.

I want to register an objection to the convention, followed by Waldfogel, of using the terms "work" and "working" to distinguish women working for pay from those working in the household, where only the former group are labeled "working." This usage is inaccurate in its failure to acknowledge that those who care for children without pay are working. Our culture's glorification of work and devaluation of work associated with women are both deeply entrenched in our linguistic patterns. How better to devalue women's work than to deny it the label "work"? I think we should resist such sexist usages of language. Using a term such as "paid work" to distinguish between taking care of a child at home without pay and a paid job would increase accuracy, reduce sexism, and not be overly cumbersome. My comment does not imply that I want to encourage more mothers to stay home with children by linguistically valorizing their work. On the contrary, I favor less sex division of labor, and would like to see child care, paid and unpaid, done as often by men as women. I favor this for several reasons. Women who live with men have less bargaining power in their households when their earnings are lower relative to their male partners' (for a review of evidence and theory on this, see England and Kilbourne 1990), and assigning child-rearing to women reduces their earnings, as Waldfogel's evidence shows. Also, given high divorce rates, and the fact that divorce usually means low and badly enforced child support, full-time homemaking entails a risk of a drastic reduction in standard of living. Thus, anyone who wishes to see equal household bargaining power for women and equal economic risk-facing by men must see some disadvantage to the sex division of labor. However, none of this is reason to favor the sexism of denying value-laden terms such as "work" to kinds of work presently done largely by women. This is a criticism of Waldfogel's (and most writers') language, not her findings.

Let me turn to Waldfogel's findings. First, she claims that "direct (family status) and indirect (experience) effects of childbearing explain nearly all of the gender gap" in pay among young cohorts of workers in 1980 and 1991. She performs a decomposition in which a variable is taken to explain the gap to the extent that the pay gap is explained by the sex differences either in levels or in slopes or a combination. Using this procedure, when the combination of marital status, number of children, and experience largely explain the gap, she takes it to indicate that mothering is the key, since marriage often leads to mothering and mothering often leads to reductions in employment experience. This interpretation embodies assumptions. I find it reasonable to conjecture that most of the gap that results from differences in *levels* of experience between men and women result from women's childrearing work. What I question is Waldfogel's interpretation of sex differences in returns to experience. Consistent with her interpretation, it is possible that women have lower returns to experience because less of their experience is with their current employer—since Corcoran and Duncan (1979) and Wellington (1994) have shown seniority to have higher returns than experience with past employers—or because mothers seek promotions less than nonmothers. But it is also likely that sex differences in returns to experience result from employers' discrimination in assigning women to jobs with flat wage trajectories. And even when women chose their jobs voluntarily, there may be sex discrimination entailed in employers' choices to assigning low raises (returns to experience) to jobs numerically dominated by females. Fifty-two percent of the gap in 1980 and 43 percent in 1991 came from sex differences in returns to age and experience. If a good share of this results from discrimination, her conclusion that mothering explains most of the gap is false.

Let me move to a consideration of Waldfogel's finding on effects of leave coverage. The main question I have is what the variable is really tapping. The NLSY asks respondents whether they are covered by a formal maternity leave policy. Since the Pregnancy Discrimination Act of 1978, employers are required to give women medical leave for childbirth (or complications of pregnancy) *to the extent that* they allow leave for nonpregnancy-related medical conditions. Thus, a firm that has a policy permitting medical leave for, for example, a heart attack, in effect has a policy on pregnancy leave, or it is in violation of federal law. However, I question how often employees understand this. I can imagine many mothers simply knowing whether recently pregnant women had returned after a time, but not knowing whether this was per a formal policy or informally negotiated.

Let us look at the results from the first-difference models (table 4.7, equations 4–7), which are the most likely to reveal true causal effects because they adjust out effects of unmeasured but unchanging differences between individuals. Before controlling for seniority and experience, women who claimed to be covered by such a policy and who returned to work with the same employer within a year had significantly higher wages, by 12.9 percent, than those who were not covered and did not return. Most of this effect disappears when experience and seniority are added, leading to the interpretation that the effect of being covered and returning on wages is because the policy allows those women who return to work with the same employer to maintain seniority and the wage gains from it. But these same equations also imply that neither those who claimed to be covered but did not return nor those who returned but claimed not to be covered had significantly different wages than those who were not covered and did not return. It does not make sense that returning to the job without coverage was not as helpful as returning with coverage—indeed, was not helpful at all, even before controlling for seniority. Either should increase seniority, which the results show to be the main mechanism for the effect of "covered and returned." This makes me wonder what this variable is really tapping.

Might it be that higher-paying, more bureaucratic firms make official policies better known and that these firms also give steeper wage increases with seniority? It could be, then, that the interactive effects of "leave policies" are not really effects of the coverage interacted with returning, but of being in a more bureaucratic firm with more institutionalized guarantees for returns to seniority, interacted with returning (which is necessary to accumulate seniority). To put it another way, as the models are specified, fixed effects control for unmeasured heterogeneity in (unchanging) qualifications of *workers* between those who labeled their firms "covered" and those who did not, but they do not control for unmeasured differences between the *firms* that respondents labeled covered and those labeled not covered. Waldfogel explores this possibility in note 12, showing that unionization and firm size do not entirely explain the interactive effect of reported coverage. However, other firm characteristics, such as bureaucratization and internal labor markets, may be what is tapped by coverage (although one would think size would be a good proxy for these). I agree with Waldfogel that this issue as well as the effects of the FMLA are important directions for future research.

Chapter 5

Parental Leave Policies in Europe and North America

Christopher J. Ruhm and Jackqueline L. Teague

Despite widespread international implementation, limited information is currently available on the economic impact of mandated family leave policies. This paper increases our understanding of the nature and effects of parental leave entitlements in several ways. First, we provide a brief history of family leave legislation in Europe and North America and summarize arguments relating to the efficiency and incidence of mandated leave. Second, we have constructed a longitudinal data set detailing durations of job-protected leave in seventeen countries, during the 1960–1989 period and use this information to examine recent trends in the regulations. The data indicate that family leave durations grew rapidly during the decade of the 1970s, with more modest increases since that time. Third, we provide an exploratory investigation of the relationship between mandated leave policies and macroeconomic outcomes. The econometric estimates provide little support for the view that moderate periods of parental leave reduce economic efficiency but rather hint at a modest beneficial impact, particularly when considering paid time off work.

Attitudes toward women's roles at home and in the workplace have changed dramatically during the twentieth century. More women are presently employed than ever before and many no longer stop working when they have young children. Reflecting this trend, virtually all industrialized countries now provide entitlements to job-protected absences from employment during the period surrounding childbirth.[1] Frequently, fathers as well as mothers qualify for time off work and most countries provide income support during the leave period.

Until recently, the United States represented a notable exception. Prior to 1993, there was no federal legislation requiring U.S. employers to offer parental leave and only a few states had mandated job protection. This changed with the passage of the Family and Medical Leave Act (FMLA), which now requires medium-sized and large companies to supply twelve weeks of unpaid parental leave. Although the legislation is modest by international standards, since the leave is for a comparatively short duration and does not include payment, it represents an important change in U.S. policy and occurs at a time when many Europeans are questioning the wisdom of pervasive employment mandates.[2] Furthermore, advocates have argued for broadening the U.S. legislation. For instance, the Carnegie Task Force on Meeting the Needs of Young Children (1994) has recommended extending the law to cover smaller companies and favors providing at least some income assistance during the absence from work.

Despite the widespread international implementation, limited information is currently available on the economic impact of parental leave entitlements. One reason is that countries have typically passed or changed policies independently, making it difficult to ascertain trends. The absence of consistent longitudinal data also constrains the ability of researchers to examine whether family leave has positive or negative economic effects.[3]

This paper improves our understanding of family leave in three ways. First, we briefly describe the international development of parental leave policies and summarize arguments concerning the efficiency and incidence of this type of labor market intervention. Second, we have compiled a cross-country data set providing a fairly consistent time-series of parental leave regulations. Using these data, we report trends in leave entitlements for the thirty-year period from 1960 to 1989. Third, we supply a preliminary econometric analysis of the macroeconomic consequences of paid and unpaid leave.

PARENTAL LEAVE POLICIES IN EUROPE AND THE UNITED STATES

Legislated maternity leave has a long history in Europe. Germany adopted the first such law in 1883, followed by Sweden in 1891, and France in 1928. A 1919 meeting of the International Labor Organization led to an initial multinational recommendation regarding pregnant working women and advocated three fundamentals of maternity protection: a leave period, cash benefits, and job protection (Stoiber 1990).

Early legislation was typically paternalistic in its concern for the health of the child and mother. Prenatal and postnatal leave were compulsory and supplementary income support or job protection seldom provided. After World War II, the pronatalist rationale became quite explicit in social policies across Europe. Moeller (1993) notes that every country participating in World War II grappled with the status of females. Most nations had recruited women into occupations previously held exclusively by men, and following the hostilities many wished to return them to the home. The issues of family allowances, protective legislation, female participation in the wage labor force, and family-law reform predominated in West Germany as well as in other European countries. Often the motivation for the policies was to restore women to their "proper" role as mother and wife (Frank and Lipner 1988). Many nations (for example, Denmark, Finland, Greece, Japan, the Netherlands, and France) mandated compulsory pregnancy leave but failed to prohibit dismissal from jobs.

The late 1960s initiated two decades of change. During this period, the concept of maternity leave evolved from a prohibition on employing women during the period surrounding pregnancy to one of time off work to care for newborns and young children, combined with job security for the parents. Countries with compulsory leave added prohibitions against dismissal from employment. Portugal, Spain, Finland, and Canada instituted job-protected leave between 1969 and 1971; France and the Netherlands passed similar legislation in 1975 and 1976; Denmark, Ireland, and Greece ratified such laws between 1980 and 1984. Other nations, including Switzerland and the United Kingdom, inaugurated regulations that provided for job-protected maternity leave.

Despite these changes, vestiges of the previous protective legislation continue in many countries. For example, postnatal absences from employment remain compulsory rather than voluntary in Austria, Spain, Switzerland, Finland, France, and Norway (Brocas, Cailloux, and Oget 1990). Austria, France, and Italy also require prenatal leave. In some countries (for example, France), the motivations for parental leave legislation continue to be pronatalist and paternalistic in nature.

Income support is provided during the leave period in almost all industrialized countries. Wage replacement rates generally exceed 50 percent and often surpass 80 percent. The income maintenance is usually supplied through social insurance, although some nations (for example, Belgium, Germany, Italy, and the United Kingdom) require the employer to contribute part of the benefit. Several countries (for example, Canada, Denmark, Finland, France, Germany, Greece, Italy, Norway, Portugal, and Sweden) have made some or all of the leave available to either parent, but mothers continue to account for virtually all of the work absences in most countries.[4]

In addition to the policies of individual countries, the European Community (EC) Social Charter has recently established a minimum standard of fourteen weeks of maternity leave, to be paid at a level no less than the individual would have received if absent from work because of sickness (Addison and Siebert 1993). This represents a slight dilution of the original proposal, which would have required leave at full pay. On the other hand, the eligibility criteria for paid leave (twelve months of service) is less than the previous requirements in some countries.

In contrast to most other industrialized countries, the United States did not mandate entitlements to parental leave until passage of the Family and Medical Leave Act in 1993. The FMLA diverges from European policies in a variety of ways. Most important, the leave is unpaid; all EC countries provide income support during at least some of the absence from work.[5]

Also notable, the twelve weeks prescribed in the law is much shorter than the period of entitlement throughout most of Europe.[6]

Some U.S. workers did have rights to job-protected parental leave prior to passage of the FMLA. Although no state passed explicit maternity leave legislation before 1987, states providing temporary disability insurance (California, Connecticut, Hawaii, New Jersey, New York, and Rhode Island) were required to cover childbirth and pregnancy following the enactment of the 1978 Pregnancy Discrimination Act. The resulting leave ranged from four weeks to four months and the cash benefit was typically about half the wage of the average employee (Bookman 1991; Employment Benefits Research Institute 1995). Similarly, the Pregnancy Discrimination Act obliged employers offering short-term disability policies to provide leave for pregnancy and childbirth on the same terms as any other medical disability.[7]

Between 1987 and 1993, eleven states and the District of Columbia enacted maternity leave legislation (Klerman and Leibowitz this volume). Leave periods varied from four weeks in Hawaii to seventeen weeks in California. All the states exempted small firms and many excluded medium-sized firms. Several other states required maternity leave for government workers but not for private workers or provided limited job absences, without guaranteeing job security. Thus, by 1992, twenty-five states had enacted some form of parental leave (Trzcinski and Alpert 1994). The stricter provisions of the FMLA superseded most of these laws in 1993.

Notwithstanding these statutes, relatively few U.S. women were entitled to job-protected maternity leave, other than that provided through general disability or leave-of-absence policies, prior to the federal legislation. Trzcinski (1991) reports that only 13.9 percent of large Connecticut firms (500 employees or more) offered explicit infant care leave in 1988. Analysis of the 1991 Bureau of Labor Statistics Employee Benefits Survey indicates that 37 percent of full-time employees in medium-sized and large firms (100 workers or more) were covered by parental leave policies, with just 2 percent receiving paid leave (U.S. Department of Labor 1993). Since small firms supply nonwage benefits less frequently than larger ones, these figures overstate the overall entitlement to family leave in the United States.[8]

EFFICIENCY AND INCIDENCE OF MANDATED FAMILY LEAVE

Economists are generally wary of mandated benefits, such as parental leave, arguing that they interfere with the free operation of labor markets and so are likely to reduce welfare. Most simply, it is assumed that workers and firms will *voluntarily* agree to the provision of family leave if the expected benefits exceed the associated costs. Conversely, if costs surpass the benefits, workers will forgo the leave in exchange for receiving higher compensation. By eliminating this flexibility, an employer mandate may make one party or both worse off. Parental leave benefits could also increase occupational segregation, by raising the relative cost of employing women in some types of jobs, and lead to higher unemployment for the groups most likely to use it.[9]

Proponents of parental leave, by contrast, typically assert that time off work is necessary to protect the welfare of infants and emphasize the importance of placing women on an equal footing with men (Kamerman 1991a; Bravo 1991; Stoiber 1990; Gilliand 1989; Decker 1991). Unintended consequences of mandated leave are generally ignored or assumed to have relatively minor costs. The economic arguments that have been made favoring leave entitlements usually focus on retaining human capital or reducing unemployment. For instance, Trzcinski (1991) claims that the mandated benefit would improve the position of women by increasing job tenure, decreasing the unemployment that occurs when caregivers reenter the labor market, breaking down entry barriers that prevent women from entering highly paid occupations, and raising wages in female-dominated jobs.

Spalter-Roth and Hartmann (1990) calculate that the average benefits of parental leave are six times greater than the costs, mainly because of reduced unemployment and the preservation of job tenure. Dalto (1989) postulates that family leave raises productivity by allowing workers to continue in positions in which their sector-specific skills are best utilized. These contentions, however, generally do not identify sources of market failure that will be rectified by mandating entitlements to parental leave. For example, if Spalter-Roth and Hartmann are correct that the benefits of family leave far exceed the costs, in the absence of market failure, we would expect to observe widespread voluntary arrangements allowing job-protected absences from work.

In economic terms, entitlements to family leave could be desirable if the time off work provides a positive externality. For instance, young children might receive better care when at least one parent is away from employment and, as a result, be healthier and incur fewer medical costs. To the extent these expenses are not fully paid for by the family (for example, with universal health care), workers will undervalue the leave benefit and a mandate has the potential to improve efficiency. Although the presence of externalities is implicit in most arguments used to support mandatory parental leave rights, we know of no efforts to quantify their existence or importance.

Adverse selection under asymmetric information provides a second potential economic justification for mandated leave. It is reasonable to assume that workers have greater knowledge regarding the probability of having children (and so taking time off work) than their employers. As discussed by Summers (1989) and Krueger (1994), among others, individuals with high probabilities of using the leave will disproportionately choose to work for companies providing it, thereby increasing costs for these firms.[10] With competitive labor markets, the employers will need to compensate by decreasing wages, leading persons at low risk of taking time off work to shun these firms, in order to avoid the loss of earnings.[11] If the entitlement to parental leave were instead required by the government, the adverse selection problem would be avoided and all workers would receive coverage.[12]

Aghion and Hermalin (1990) have shown that, without a mandate, there are situations where socially desirable parental leave will not be provided to *any* workers. They point out that individuals with low probabilities of taking time off work will signal this to employers by accepting contracts with no (or very limited) provisions for leave. In some circumstances, high-risk workers do better by mimicking their counterparts (by accepting jobs with companies not offering the benefit) than by revealing information on their propensity to take time off work. As a result, too little parental leave will be provided and a mandate may increase welfare.

DATA

Our analysis uses a newly constructed data set covering seventeen industrialized nations over the 1960–1989 period. The countries included are Austria, Belgium, Canada, Denmark, Finland, France, Germany, Greece, Ireland, Italy, the Netherlands, Norway, Portugal, Spain, Sweden, Switzerland, and the United Kingdom.[13] Information on parental leave was obtained from the International Labour Office's *Legislative Series* and 1984 global survey on protection of working mothers, and from *Social Security Programs Throughout the World*, which has been published at approximately two year intervals by the U.S. Social Security Administration since 1958.

Assembling the data posed a variety of problems. First, it is difficult to compile comparable information on leave entitlements across countries. Our measures of parental leave refer to job-protected absences from work to care for infants or young children. Job protection means that dismissal is prohibited during pregnancy and reinstatement is guaranteed at the end of the leave period.[14] As mentioned, many European countries enacted compulsory "maternity protection" during the 1940s and 1950s but did not prohibit dismissals until much later. Job-protection provisions were added throughout much of Europe during the period covered by the data.

Second, there are ambiguities concerning how to treat partially paid absences from work and family allowances that are not tied to employment. In these data, paid leave refers to supplements that are directly related to the worker's previous earnings, as distinguished from social insurance payments available to individuals independent of their employment histories. Although we primarily focus on differentiating between unpaid and paid leave, information was also obtained on average wage replacement rates; and we constructed a measure of "full pay equivalent weeks," calculated as the average replacement rate multiplied by the number of weeks of paid leave. We do not distinguish between time off work that is available only to the mother and that which can be taken by either parent because, as noted above, almost all of the absences were accounted for by women during the time period analyzed.[15]

Third, countries differ in their qualification requirements for receiving parental leave. Since there was no obvious way to account for these disparities, the leave durations refer to workers who meet all qualifying conditions. This overstates the pervasiveness of compulsory leave but probably does not bias the analysis of time trends, since the conditions for receiving leave have not been modified in most countries during the sample period.[16] Changes that have occurred have generally been in the direction of making the leave easier to qualify for, by reducing the required number of hours or weeks of work. Thus, our data probably understate the increase in family leave entitlements occurring over time.

The dependent variables in the econometric analysis include per capita gross domestic products (GDP), employment-to-population (EP) ratios, civilian labor force participation rates (LFPR), and unemployment rates (UNRATE). Per capita GDP is measured in 1980 dollars and exchange rates, using a consistent series obtained for the 1960–1987 period from Organization for Economic Cooperation and Development (OECD) *National Accounts* data. The labor market outcomes were compiled over the 1968–1988 period, for women only and for males and females combined, using information from the OECD publication *Labour Force Statistics: 1968–1988.* Corresponding labor force data for the years prior to 1968 contain many gaps and breaks in series and so were not analyzed. Information on national populations (of civilians aged 15–64) was obtained from various issues of *Labour Force Statistics* and is used below to weight the data.[17]

TRENDS IN PARENTAL LEAVE

Widespread availability of job-protected parental leave is a relatively recent phenomenon. To illustrate, figures 5.1 and 5.2 summarize time trends in leave entitlements for the thirty-year period ending in 1989. Three types of absences are considered: total weeks of leave (LEAVE), weeks of paid leave (PAID), and full pay equivalent weeks (FULLPAY), defined as the average wage replacement rate multiplied by the number of weeks of paid leave. FULLPAY is calculated for the thirteen countries (excluding Germany, Norway, Switzerland, and the United Kingdom) providing workers on leave with a percentage of their previous pay, rather than a flat rate, throughout the observed period. The graphs differ in that figure 5.2 weights the observations by the size of the country's working-age population, whereas figure 5.1 treats all nations as having equal weight.

Figure 5.1   Average Weeks of Family Leave (Unweighted)

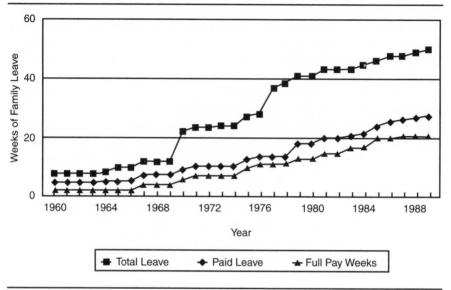

Figure 5.2   Average Weeks of Family Leave (Weighted)

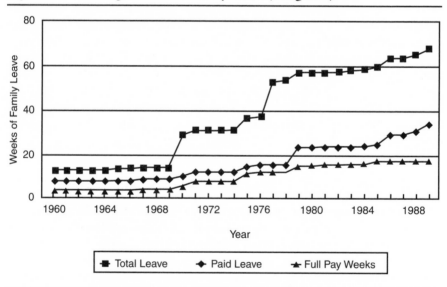

Durations of mandated leave remained at relatively low levels throughout most of the 1960s. The decade of the 1970s, however, was characterized by sharp increases in leave entitlements. For example, (weighted)
leave allowances rose from their 1969 averages of 14.3, 9.2, and 4.4 weeks
for LEAVE, PAID, and FULLPAY, respectively, to 57.4, 23.3, and 15.3

weeks in 1980. Job-protected time off work expanded still further during the 1980s, albeit at a slower rate: Weighted mean durations were 68.0, 33.4, and 17.3 weeks in 1989. The weighted averages (displayed in figure 5.2) are consistently higher than their unweighted counterparts (shown in figure 5.1) for total and paid leave, implying that large nations provided relatively generous benefits. Interestingly, the longer durations were not accompanied by higher wage replacement rates and so there is no corresponding country size pattern in full pay equivalent weeks.

Table 5.1 summarizes the parental leave provisions effective in 1989, the final year of our data. At that time, the seventeen countries offered a minimum of ten weeks of paid leave, with eleven nations mandating entitlements of between twelve and eighteen weeks and three countries (Finland, Germany, and Sweden) requiring companies to permit more than a year off work. Over half the nations allowed additional absences without pay, although in only four cases (Austria, France, Norway, and Spain) was the unpaid leave substantial. A portion of the leave could be taken by fathers in ten of the seventeen countries. Although the conditions required to qualify for the leave varied, persons with more than a year of service were usually covered.

Table 5.2 details the total and paid leave available in each country at approximately ten-year intervals beginning in 1960. As mentioned, job-protected family leave was only sporadically offered prior to 1970 but increased rapidly during the following decade. Some countries raised durations several times during the twenty-year period while others did so in a single increment. France and Spain are the most notable. France offered no job-protection until 1974 but provided sixteen weeks of paid leave and an additional two years of unpaid absence by 1979. Family leave was not required in Spain until 1970, at which point entitlements (largely unpaid) of up to three years were mandated.[18] It is important to reemphasize that our definition of parental leave is restricted to time off work with dismissal prohibited during pregnancy and job reinstatement guaranteed. Both France and Spain provided payment to mothers prior to 1969; however, neither supplied employment-protection until the 1970s.

Figure 5.3 plots parental leave against per capita GDP for 1960 and 1987. The area of the circle denoting each observation is proportional to the country's working-age population. For example, the highest entry on the top left plot indicates that Italy (a relatively large country) provided forty weeks of total leave in 1960. The smaller circle adjacent to it refers to Austria (with a much smaller population), which allowed absences of thirty-eight weeks during that year.

The figure shows that per capita GDP was unrelated to durations of either total or paid leave in 1960 but that a positive correlation had developed by 1987. It further suggests that large countries provided relatively lengthy absences from work, particularly during the early years of the data.

Table 5.1 Parental Leave Provisions in 1989

Country	Total Weeks of Leave	Weeks of Paid Leave	% of Pay	Weeks Available to Fathers	Qualification Conditions
Austria	67	16	100	None	10 months of social insurance coverage in last 2 years or 6 months coverage in last year
Belgium	14	14	71	None	6 months coverage preceding leave
Canada	24	15	60	24	15 hours per week employment for 20 weeks with same employer during last year
Denmark	28	28	90	12	6 months coverage and employment during previous year, including at least 40 hours of work during 4 weeks preceding leave
Finland	69	69	80	26	3 months employment, unless involuntarily unemployed
France	120	16	90	104	10 months of insurance prior to leave and at least 200 hours of work in 3 months preceding the pregnancy
Germany	83	14 / 69	100 / Flat rate	69	12 weeks of insurance or 6 months of employment
Greece	13	12	50	12	200 days of employment during last 2 years
Ireland	18	14	70	None	30 weeks of insurance contributions
Italy	46	46	52	26	Insured and employed at start of pregnancy
Netherlands	12	12	100	None	Insured and employed
Norway	52	18	90	40	Employed and insured at least 6 of the last 10 months
Portugal	12	12	100	8	Employed with 6 months of insurance
Spain	156	14	75	None	Insured 9 months, with 6 months of contributions
Sweden	78	72	90	60	Insured 8 months
Switzerland	14	10	Flat rate	None	Up to 9 months insurance (depending upon canton)
United Kingdom	40	18	Flat rate	None	6 months of insurance contributions during previous year and 2 years of work with same employer

Table 5.2   Parental Leave Durations in Selected Years

Country	Weeks of Leave				Weeks of Paid Leave			
	1960	1969	1979	1989	1960	1969	1979	1989
Austria	38	65	67	67	12	12	16	16
Belgium	4	14	14	14	4	14	14	14
Canada	0	0	17	24	0	0	15	15
Denmark	0	0	0	28	0	0	0	28
Finland	0	0	35	69	0	0	35	69
France	0	0	120	120	0	0	16	16
Germany	12	14	32	83	12	14	32	83
Greece	0	0	0	13	0	0	0	12
Ireland	0	0	0	18	0	0	0	14
Italy	40	40	46	46	14	14	46	46
Netherlands	0	0	12	12	0	0	12	12
Norway	12	12	52	52	12	12	18	18
Portugal	0	0	12	12	0	0	12	12
Spain	0	0	156	156	0	0	14	14
Sweden	12	36	78	78	12	36	54	72
Switzerland	0	8	14	14	0	8	10	10
United Kingdom	18	18	40	40	18	18	18	18

Figure 5.3   Relationship Between Family Leave and GDP, for Working-Age Population

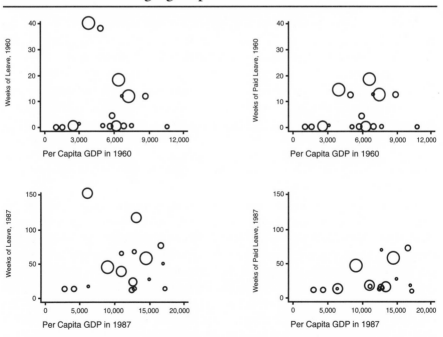

The three most populous nations (Germany, Italy, and the United Kingdom) offered at least twelve weeks of paid leave in 1960, whereas just three of the remaining fourteen countries did so. The entitlements continued to be positively correlated with size in 1987, although the relationship was quite weak when considering paid time off work.[19] Similar patterns are obtained for other years.

ECONOMETRIC ESTIMATES

Econometric techniques are used in this section to explore the relationships between parental leave and national incomes and labor market outcomes. If the opponents of compulsory leave are correct, longer durations may be associated with lower employment and incomes, whereas the reverse is possible if family leave increases economic efficiency. The outcomes analyzed are the natural log of per capita GDP (in $1980), the EP ratio, LFPR, and the UNRATE. The three labor market outcomes are specified for men and women together and also for women separately. The unemployment rate combines the effects of changes in employment and labor force participation. For example, lower unemployment could result from a rise in job-holding, a reduction in labor force participation, or some combination of the two.

In addition to controlling for parental leave, the regressions include vectors of country and year dummy variables. The country regressors account for characteristics specific to a single nation (for example, culture, resource endowments, and geography) that affect the dependent variables but do not change over time. The time-effect captures period-specific factors (for example, oil shocks) that have a common impact across countries.[20]

The econometric analysis is restricted to the 1968–1988 period (1968–1987 for GDP), rather than beginning with 1960, for two reasons. First, fairly consistent data on the outcomes are available for these years. By contrast, information is missing and there are breaks in series for many of the labor market variables prior to 1968. Second, leave durations were rising rapidly during this period, which makes it easier to identify the impact of changes in the entitlements and may reduce the importance of potential confounding factors.

Table 5.3 displays the results of econometric estimates examining the relationship between total leave entitlements and the four macroeconomic outcomes. Although year and country dummy variables are included in these and all subsequent regressions, the associated coefficients are not displayed in order to save space. LEAVE refers to total weeks of parental leave divided by 100. A quadratic specification is estimated in order to allow for nonlinearities in the effect of the leave entitlements. Reported p-values refer to the null hypothesis that the coefficients on LEAVE and LEAVE SQUARED are jointly equal to zero. The "maximum" effect occurs where the first derivative of the predicted leave impact is zero.[21]

Table 5.3   Econometric Estimates of the Relationship Between Parental Leave and Macroeconomic Outcomes

Regressor	Log of Gross Domestic Product	Employment-to-Population Ratio	Labor Force Participation Rate	Unemployment Rate
LEAVE	.1122 (2.45)	.4833 (3.85)	.3587 (3.52)	–.2889 (0.72)
LEAVE SQUARED	–.0008 (2.28)	–.0041 (4.42)	–.0031 (4.05)	.0043 (1.41)
P-Value	.0443	.0000	.0000	.0035
"Maximum" Leave Effect	74.0 weeks	59.4 weeks	59.4 weeks	33.4 weeks
Sample Size	340	344	343	337

Notes: Sample includes seventeen countries for 1968–1988 period (through 1987 for GDP). Country and year dummy variables are also included. LEAVE refers to the number of weeks of job-protected maternity leave divided by 100. Estimates in column 1 are obtained using weighted least squares (with observations weighted by the square root of the working-age population). Those in columns 2–4 are from grouped data logit models. Absolute values of t-statistics are shown in parentheses. The p-value refers to the total leave effect and is obtained by testing whether the coefficients on LEAVE and LEAVE SQUARED jointly differ from zero.

The estimates indicate that short to moderate durations of parental leave are positively and statistically significantly associated with per capita incomes, employment-to-population ratios, and labor force participation rates, while being negatively related to unemployment. The decrease in unemployment occurs because the increase in the percentage of the population employed more than offsets the higher rate of labor force participation. The coefficient on LEAVE SQUARED is negative and significant for all dependent variables, except the unemployment rate, implying diminishing marginal benefits of longer leave entitlements. Nonetheless, the beneficial effects are predicted to increase through at least seven months of leave rights for every outcome and, except for the unemployment rate, to increase for the entire first year of parental leave.[22]

These results suggest that short to moderate periods of family leave may increase economic efficiency, as measured by incomes and labor market status, while lengthy durations could reduce it. It is possible, however, that causation actually runs in the reverse direction—from economic outcomes to leave durations. For instance, there may be political pressure to raise the length of job-protected leave when the economy is depressed, in order to make it easier for new mothers to return to work. Alternatively, incomes and leave durations could be positively correlated, for example, if the latter are normal goods, even if the mandates do not affect incomes.

Although there is no way to definitively determine the direction of causation, useful information can be obtained by examining the relative timing of changes in leave entitlements and of the economic outcomes. Intuitively, if causation runs from parental leave to the macroeconomy, we expect that lagged values of the former will help to predict the latter. Conversely, if the direction of causation is reversed, lagged macroeconomic variables will help to predict leave durations.[23]

Results of the causality tests, which are summarized in appendix table 5.1, provide substantial support for the hypothesis that causation runs from family leave to labor market status, rather than in the opposite direction. This is seen by noting that LEAVE at time t-1 has a statistically significant impact on the EP ratio, LFPR, and UNRATE the following year (see the top panel of the table), whereas there is never a statistically significant relationship (at the .05 level) between lagged values of per capita incomes or of the three labor force variables on family leave durations.[24]

The impact of family leave could vary depending on whether or not payment is provided during the time away from work. For instance, the economic distortions might be larger for entitlements to paid absences than to unpaid absences, since the former are more costly to employers. Conversely, efficiency enhancements might be restricted to paid leave, if parents can afford to be away from the job only if they receive compensation. To investigate these issues, we next estimate models with paid and unpaid leave separately controlled for.

Short to moderate durations of either type of leave are associated with relatively high EP ratios and labor force participation rates (see table 5.4). The employment effect is more pronounced for paid time off work, whereas a stronger impact on participation is observed for unpaid absences. As a result, paid (unpaid) entitlements of intermediate length are associated with decreases (increases) in unemployment. The labor supply effects peak at around nine months for unpaid leave but grow through the longest observed rights to absences with pay. The first fifteen months of paid leave are also correlated with higher per capita incomes, but there is not a statistically significant relationship between unpaid leave and per capita GDP.

A mandated benefit that primarily affects an identifiable class of workers may (but need not) have a disproportionate impact on the employment of that group.[25] Since family leave is primarily used by females, even in countries where males share the entitlement, it is useful to examine whether stronger labor market effects are observed for women alone

Table 5.4   Econometric Estimates of the Relationship Between Unpaid
and Paid Parental Leave and Macroeconomic Outcomes

Regressor	Log of Gross Domestic Product	Employment-to-Population Ratio	Labor Force Participation Rate	Unemploy-ment Rate
UNPAID	−.0151	.2254	.2420	.6182
	(0.41)	(2.24)	(2.94)	(2.01)
UNPAID SQUARED	.0001	−.0028	−.0026	−.0026
	(0.27)	(3.06)	(3.57)	(0.86)
P-Value	.8462	.0006	.0005	.0001
"Maximum" Unpaid Leave Effect	86.3 weeks	40.7 weeks	46.0 weeks	119.3 weeks
PAID	.2386	.3436	.0808	−1.1896
	(3.23)	(1.43)	(0.41)	(1.77)
PAID SQUARED	−.0018	−.0005	.0002	.0089
	(1.85)	(0.17)	(0.09)	(1.05)
P-Value	.0006	.0035	.4246	.0484
"Maximum" Paid Leave Effect	66.3 weeks	319.9 weeks	no maximum	66.7 weeks

Notes: See notes on table 5.3. UNPAID and PAID, respectively, refer to the number of weeks of job-protected maternity leave, with and without pay, divided by 100.

than for men and women together. Toward this end, table 5.5 displays econometric findings for female employment-to-population ratios, labor force participation rates, and unemployment rates. The upper panel holds constant total weeks of leave. Unpaid and paid absences are separately controlled for in the lower panel.

The results are generally similar to those obtained for the entire labor force (see tables 5.3 and 5.4). In particular, moderate durations of leave are associated with statistically significant increases in the EP ratios of women, with a stronger relationship observed for paid than unpaid time off work. Female labor force participation rates are also positively correlated with leave entitlements, although the results are not as strong as for the full sample. Finally, unemployment rates are again positively (negatively) associated with unpaid (paid) leave of short to intermediate length.

Table 5.5 Econometric Estimates of the Relationship Between Parental Leave and Female Labor Force Outcomes

Regressor	Employment-to-Population Ratio	Labor Force Participation Rate	Unemployment Rate
LEAVE	.3836	.1669	.8561
	(2.29)	(0.94)	(1.68)
LEAVE SQUARED	−.0033	−.0017	−.0067
	(2.45)	(1.22)	(1.63)
P-Value	.0406	.1796	.2436
"Maximum" Leave Effect	58.1 weeks	48.2 weeks	63.9 weeks
UNPAID	.3330	.1959	1.930
	(2.41)	(1.37)	(4.96)
UNPAID SQUARED	−3.5E–5	−.0025	−.0195
	(2.51)	(1.68)	(4.79)
P-Value	.0437	.1477	.0000
"Maximum" Unpaid Leave Effect	46.7 weeks	39.5 weeks	49.4 weeks
PAID	−.0018	.0683	−.2508
	(0.01)	(0.24)	(0.34)
PAID SQUARED	.0018	−.0021	−.0014
	(0.55)	(0.60)	(0.15)
P-Value	.0035	.5833	.3632
"Maximum" Paid Leave Effect	no maximum	16.0 weeks	no maximum
Sample Size	330	325	323

Note: See notes on tables 5.3 and 5.4.

SIMULATIONS

To more clearly illustrate the effects of parental leave, table 5.6 displays predicted values of the dependent variables at specified durations of paid and unpaid leave. For instance, the first two entries in column 2 indicate that EP ratios would be expected to rise from 58.7 to 59.2 percent when a country moves from no mandated leave to entitling workers to ten weeks of unpaid time off work. If the ten weeks of leave were paid, the pro-

Table 5.6   Predicted Values of Outcome Variables at Different Durations of Unpaid and Paid Parental Leave

Duration and Type of Leave	Log of Per Capita GDP	Employment-to-Population Ratio	Labor Force Participation Rate	Unemployment Rate	Female Employment-to-Population Ratio	Female Labor Force Participation Rate	Female Unemployment Rate
No leave	9.069	58.7%	63.9%	6.8%	43.0%	47.3%	5.8%
Weeks of unpaid leave							
10	9.067	59.2	64.4	7.2	43.8	47.8	6.9
25	9.066	59.6	65.0	7.7	44.5	48.2	8.2
50	9.063	59.8	65.2	8.5	44.9	48.2	9.1
75	9.062	59.0	64.7	9.1	44.2	47.5	8.1
Weeks of paid leave							
10	9.091	59.5	64.1	6.1	43.1	47.5	5.7
25	9.117	60.7	64.4	5.4	43.3	47.4	5.5
50	9.143	62.5	65.0	4.8	44.1	46.9	5.0
75	9.146	64.1	65.6	4.7	45.5	45.6	4.5

Notes: The table shows predicted values of outcome variables at various durations of unpaid and paid leave. Estimates are based on the WLS and grouped data logit models summarized in tables 5.3–5.5, with variables other than maternity leave evaluated at their sample means.

portion of the population employed would be predicted to increase still further, to 59.5 percent (see row 6).[26]

The table highlights the generally stronger impact of paid leave over unpaid leave. For example, moving from 0 to 50 weeks of unpaid leave elevates expected per capita (log) GDP, employment-to-population ratios, and labor force participation rates by −.06, 1.79, and 1.98 percent, respectively. The predicted increases from instituting an equivalent amount of paid leave are .82, 6.44, and 1.65 percent. The most important disparity is the almost four times larger rise in employment for paid leave over unpaid leave.[27]

There is little evidence that the labor market impact of parental leave is concentrated among women. The responsiveness of employment to paid leave and of the LFPR to either paid or unpaid time off work is greater for the full sample than for women only. For instance, switching from no leave to 50 weeks with pay is predicted to increase the EP ratio by 6.4 percent (from 58.7 to 62.5 percent) and the participation rate by 1.7 percent (from 63.9 to 65.0 percent) for the full sample compared with 2.6 percent (43.0 to 44.1 percent) and −1.0 percent (47.3 to 46.9 percent) for women separately. Only when considering the relationship between unpaid leave and the employment-to-population ratio is the effect of a mandate larger for women alone than for the combined sample. In this case, increasing the entitlement from 0 to 50 weeks raises expected female employment rates by more than 4 percent versus a less than 2 percent rise in the overall EP ratio.

CONCLUSION

This paper increases our understanding of the nature and effects of parental leave policies in several ways. First, we provide a brief history of family leave mandates in Europe and North America and summarize arguments pertaining to the efficiency of this type of benefit. Second, having constructed a cross-country data set with information on parental leave in seventeen countries over the 1960–1989 period, we utilize these data to examine the evolution of leave regulations during a thirty-year period of rapidly increasing entitlement. Third, we provide an exploratory investigation of the relationship between family leave, per capita incomes, and several labor market outcomes.

It is worth reemphasizing the conceptual ambiguities that frequently surround discussions of parental leave. Our data collection and analysis have focused upon job-protected absences from work. By contrast, the first countries to institute maternity leave typically did so to "protect" mothers or to increase birth rates. Employment security did not become a concern until much later. Thus, the economic and employment consequences of early leave policies could be quite different from those currently implemented. Furthermore, many countries are switching from offering leave to mothers only to offering entitlements that can be used by either parent. It should be noted, however, that virtually all of the release time from work is presently taken by women. Thus, maternity leave and parental leave are currently roughly synonymous, although they may not be in the future.

Our research shows that job-protected parental leave grew rapidly in duration and frequency during the decade of the 1970s, with more modest increases since that time. Large countries are more likely to mandate entitlements to lengthy absences from work and the data provide some evidence that the parental leave is a normal good, increasing in duration as per capita incomes rise. The econometric investigation suggests that leave entitlements of moderate duration (especially when paid) operate to raise employment levels. Labor force participation rates are also higher in countries mandating short to intermediate durations of leave, although this increase is larger for unpaid leave than for paid leave. Worker rights to lengthy absences from jobs are associated with less favorable labor market outcomes.

These findings are preliminary and indicate the need for further investigation. For instance, it is important to understand why the employment effects of parental leave do not appear to be concentrated among women, even though they are the primary users of it. One possibility, suggested by Gruber's research (1994) on maternity benefits, is that changes in leave entitlements have a larger influence on the wages and work hours of women than on those of men, without disproportionately affecting their probabilities of holding jobs.

The issue of causation is also problematic. Although the causality tests undertaken suggest that changes in family leave precede corresponding movements in the macroeconomic variables, additional investigation of this issue would be desirable. One promising possibility is to consider men, who are likely to be affected by economy-wide shocks but relatively unaffected by changes in family leave legislation, as a natural control group. In this regard, the lack of evidence of disproportionate effects of leave mandates on female labor market outcomes raises the possibility that the preceding econometric analysis overstates the impact of the changes in family leave durations. Research using microdata would also be helpful, although such study would need to be carefully undertaken to minimize biases related to nonrandom selection into employment or job type.

Keeping these caveats in mind, the econometric results do suggest beneficial effects of short to moderate durations of parental leave and particularly of paid absences from work surrounding the birth of a child. It is reassuring that findings provide no evidence that harmful effects are likely to result from the recent enactment of the Family and Medical Leave Act in the United States. If anything, they suggest that the law may have modest benefits for the macroeconomy. Conversely, it is possible that the lengthy leave entitlements mandated in some European countries result in small reductions in the percentage of the population employed.

ACKNOWLEDGMENTS

We thank Rebecca Blank, Ronald Ehrenberg, Jonathan Gruber, and Marianne Ferber for helpful comments on earlier versions of this manuscript.

APPENDIX

Appendix Table 5.1   Granger Causality Tests

	Coefficient on Lagged Macroeconomic Variable (γ)	Coefficient on Lagged Family Leave (δ)
Model: $Y_{it} = \alpha_i + \beta_t + \gamma Y_{it-1} + \delta L_{it-1} + \varepsilon_{it}$		
Dependent variable (Y_{it})		
Log of gross domestic product	.835	−.0004
	(33.43)	(0.93)
Employment-to-population ratio	3.992	−.022
	(47.15)	(2.45)
Labor force participation rate	4.269	−.018
	(45.401)	(2.48)
Unemployment rate	8.384	.218
	(16.49)	(4.01)
Model: $L_{it} = \alpha_i + \beta_t + \gamma Y_{it-1} + \delta L_{it-1} + \varepsilon_{it}$		
Explanatory variable (Y_{it-1})		
Log of gross domestic product	.0852	.746
	(0.49)	(24.13)
Employment-to-population ratio	.333	.761
	(1.44)	(24.72)
Labor force participation rate	.296	.759
	(0.97)	(24.58)
Unemployment rate	−.597	.761
	(1.94)	(24.78)

Notes: See note on table 5.3. The dependent variables in the upper panel of the table are macroeconomic outcomes (Y). Weeks of parental leave (L) divided by 100 are the regressands in the lower panel.

NOTES

1. Kamerman (1988, 1991a) summarizes international parental leave entitlements.

2. One respect in which the U.S. law is relatively broad is that it extends job protection to persons caring for sick children and relatives.

3. By contrast, other types of employment mandates have been the subject of considerable research. For example, a proliferation of analysis followed passage of the 1988 Worker Retraining and Notification Act, which required some U.S. employers to provide advance notice of plant closings and mass layoffs (see Ehrenberg and Jakubson 1988; Lazear 1990; Swaim and Podgursky 1990; Addison and Portugal 1992; Ruhm 1992, 1994).

4. For example, according to the Organization for Economic Cooperation and Development (1995) mothers accounted for 93 percent of total family leave weeks in Sweden, in 1988, and over 98 percent of weeks in all other OECD countries for which information was available.

5. U.S. companies are responsible for continuing health insurance during the leave period.

6. U.S. leave need not be taken all at once, however, and the employee can work on a reduced schedule if it is certified as medically necessary.

7. Eighty-seven percent of full-time employees working in medium-sized and large private firms, in 1993, and 64 percent of those employed in small private establishments, in 1992, were covered by short-term disability plans (Employee Benefits Research Institute 1995).

8. In 1992, maternity leave was available to just 18 percent of persons working for small employers, with only 1 percent entitled to time off work with pay (U.S. Department of Labor 1994).

9. See Summers (1989) and Mitchell (1990) for detailed discussions of mandated benefits.

10. This result occurs after holding constant all characteristics observable to the employer (but not necessarily to the researcher). It is possible that women with superior observable characteristics, and so greater choice of jobs, will disproportionately work in positions providing leave benefits. If so, companies offering leave will employ relatively highly productive women and pay above-average compensation. We thank an anonymous referee for pointing out this possibility.

11. Consider the following example. "Type A" individuals constitute half the labor force and have an 80 percent probability of using parental leave. "Type B" persons account for the remaining 50 percent of the workforce and have a 20 percent probability of taking time off work. The cost to the employer of providing leave to any given worker is 1 and the benefit to employees using it is 2. The economy-wide expected benefits are therefore 1 ($[[(.5)(.8)(2) + (.5)(.2)(2)]$ and the associated costs are .5 $[(.5)(.8)(1) + (.5)(.2)(1)]$. A firm that reduced wages by

.5, in exchange for providing leave, would attract only type A individuals, since the expected benefit to the Bs (.4) is less than the wage reduction. The expected cost of providing leave to type A persons is .8, implying that the company would also lose money on these individuals. The employer could avoid a loss only by reducing wages by at least .8 (but less than 1.6). Thus, voluntarily provided leave would not be received by type B individuals.

12. Blank and Freeman (1994) make similar arguments in support of a variety of social insurance programs. They also point out that if there are work requirements for receiving the benefit, economic efficiency may be raised by encouraging employment. The inefficiency of privately negotiated labor market contracts, under asymmetric information, has been demonstrated in a variety of other contexts. For instance, McGuire and Ruhm (1993) indicate that excessive drug testing will occur, while Kuhn (1992) and Levine (1991), respectively, show that advance notice of job terminations and just-cause employment security regulations may be underprovided.

13. Japan and the United States are excluded because no leave was mandated during the sample period in the United States and the duration of leave was constant in Japan (at twelve weeks) from 1960 through the last quarter of 1987 (when it was increased to fourteen weeks).

14. We define leave entitlements as the *minimum* time the government requires employers to allow their employees to be off work. These will diverge from the actual absences if individuals choose to return sooner or if longer leave periods are voluntarily agreed upon.

15. A distinction is sometimes made (for example, by OECD 1995) between "maternity leave," which is granted only to mothers for a limited period around the time of childbirth, and "parental leave," which permits additional time off work to care for infants or young children. Both types of entitlements are included in the definition of parental leave used in this analysis.

16. There are large cross-country differences in the proportion of women on maternity leave at any point in time. For instance, 1.8 and 1.4 percent, respectively, of Danish and French working women were away from the job for this reason in 1988 compared with just 0.3 and 0.5 percent of their counterparts from Portugal and Greece (Commission of the European Communities 1990). It is not clear whether differences in eligibility criteria play any role in explaining these disparities.

17. Italy reports statistics for those aged 14–64. Some countries (for example, Austria, Greece, and Portugal) do not exclude the armed forces from these figures.

18. In Spain, reemployment is guaranteed for the first year of leave and the worker has preferential reinstatement rights during the next two years.

19. These findings are confirmed by regressions of leave durations on per capita GDP and the working-age population. The coefficients are positive for both variables in 1960, with associated t-statistics of .01 for GDP and 1.51 for population size, when total leave is the dependent

variable, and 1.01 and 2.16, respectively, for paid leave. The coefficients are also positive in 1987, with t-statistics of .29 and 1.65 (1.42 and .66) for total (paid) leave.

20. More precisely, the basic regression equation is a two-way fixed-effect model of the form:

$$Y_{it} = \alpha_i + \beta_t + L_{it}\gamma + \varepsilon_{it},$$

where Y_{it} is the outcome for country i at time t, α_1 is a country-specific (time-invariant) intercept, β_t is a time-specific (country-invariant) effect, L indicates a vector of parental leave variables, and ε is a disturbance term. The income equations are estimated by linear regression, with observations weighted by the square root of the working age population to correct for heteroscedasticity. Since the labor market variables are rates, restricted to the range zero through one, grouped data logit models are used for these outcomes. The dependent variable in logistic regression is the natural logarithm of the odds ratio; for instance, if Y_{it} is the participation rate, the regressand is $y_{it} = \ln[Y_{it}(1 - Y_{it})^{-1}]$. The error term is heteroscedastic, with variance $[Y_{it}(1 - Y_{it})n_{it}]^{-1}$, for n_{it} the working-age population of country i at time t. Efficiency is therefore maximized by using weighted least squares (WLS), with cell weights $[Y_{it}(1 - Y_{it})n_{it}]^{1/2}$.

21. If $Y = \gamma_1 L + \gamma_2 L^2$, where γ_1 and γ_2 are coefficient estimates with opposite signs, the "maximum" effect occurs at $-\gamma_1/2\gamma_2$ weeks of leave.

22. The models were also estimated with leave restricted to have a linear effect (that is, with LEAVE SQUARED excluded). When this was done, the coefficient on LEAVE was .0007, −.0603, −.0453, and .2954, for GDP, EP ratio, LFPR, and the UNRATE, respectively, with associated t-statistics of 1.05, 2.29, 2.13, and 3.08. The linear models were then run with the inclusion of lagged leave entitlements. The coefficient on LEAVE at year $t-1$ was larger than the contemporaneous coefficient for all three labor market variables, indicating that much of the parental leave effect occurred with a delay. Nonetheless, the sums of the parameter estimates at t and $t-1$ were virtually identical to those obtained for year t, when the lagged effect was excluded, indicating that little information is lost by deleting lags from the model.

23. More formally, we test for "Granger causality" (see Sims 1972) using the model:

$$Y_{it} = \alpha_{1i} + \beta_{1t} + \gamma_1 Y_{it-1} + \delta_1 L_{it-1} + \varepsilon_{1it} \quad \text{and}$$
$$L_{it} = \alpha_{2i} + \beta_{2t} + \gamma_2 Y_{it-1} + \delta_2 L_{it-1} + \varepsilon_{2it}.$$

The three labor market outcomes are estimated as grouped data logit models. WLS is used for GDP and for all estimates of the parental leave equations. Family leave "Granger causes" (is causally prior to) macroeconomic outcomes if the estimate for δ_1 differs statistically significantly from zero while that on γ_2 does not.

24. The lagged unemployment coefficient barely misses significance at the .05 level, however, and is significant at the .1 level. Coefficients on the lagged dependent variable are statistically significant in all eight equations, as would be expected, and there is little evidence that family leave either causes or is caused by national incomes. A concern with the Granger causality tests is that fixed-effect models induce serial correlation in the error term, leading to biased estimates of the lagged dependent variables (and possible inconsistency of the other coefficients). Nickell (1981) has shown that this bias diminishes as the length of the panel increases. As a crude method of avoiding this problem, Granger causality tests were implemented for models that excluded country fixed-effects. These results were qualitatively similar to the fixed-effect estimates. In particular, the lagged leave coefficients were statistically significant for the three labor market outcomes (with t-statistics ranging from −1.69 to −3.64), whereas those on all four lagged macroeconomic variables were insignificant in the parental leave equations (t-statistics ranged from −0.18 to −0.63).

25. See Gruber (1994) for a careful discussion of this issue.

26. Year and country variables are evaluated at their sample means in these calculations.

27. However, an important limitation of the *ceteris paribus* analysis is that, since unpaid leave is provided *subsequent to* an initial period of paid time off work in most countries, diminishing returns (to total leave durations) may have set in to a greater extent for unpaid than paid entitlements.

Commentary on Chapter 5

Jonathan Gruber

Christopher Ruhm and Jackqueline Teague have written a paper on a topic of considerable current policy interest: the effects of government mandated maternity leave on economic performance. The motivation of their paper is the dramatic increase in female labor force participation worldwide over the past forty years. In response to this trend, almost all industrialized nations have mandated that firms provide some form of job-protected leave for female, and in many cases male, workers. The United States is a relative latecomer to this club, having mandated leave only in 1993.

The paper begins by documenting the well-known arguments for and against mandated maternity leave. The major argument against such a mandate is that it distorts the design of compensation packages, and as such may impose efficiency costs on the economy, just as taxing firm payroll would. In the face of this criticism, there are three major arguments for having leave.

The first argument concerns adverse selection in the market for employee benefits such as maternity leave. While this is a compelling argument in theory, there is little empirical evidence that adverse selection in this market is an important problem in practice. Furthermore, the fact that 61 percent of firms with one hundred employees or more offered maternity leave voluntarily in the United States before 1993 suggests that adverse selection was not causing a complete market failure.[1]

A second, equity argument concerns improving the labor market prospects of female workers. A career in academia is an obvious example of one in which taking time off to have a child can potentially impede advancement. As a result, there should be some equalizing mechanism such as mandated leave to allow women an equal chance at such jobs. It is interesting to note, however, that the efficiency argument above may contradict this equity argument. If the government is correcting a market failure by mandating maternity leave, then women will pay for this valuable leave through lower wages. As a result, there will be no net redistribution toward women; they will be, in essence, buying the maternity leave. That

157

is, advocates of maternity leave cannot have it both ways; either the government is increasing efficiency or it is redistributing toward women.

Finally, there is the argument about positive externalities to children. Allowing mothers to take time off when their children are born can yield a long-term stream of benefits to the child that might not be internalized by either the mother or her employer. It is my sense that this is by far the dominant argument for having maternity leave; the benefits of even a small improvement in the lifetime prospects of a child would compensate for any productivity costs from having mothers away from work for one year. But, as with adverse selection, there remains no convincing evidence that there are benefits to children from having their mothers at home with them.

This paper makes two important contributions to the literature on the economic effects of maternity leave. The first is to carefully document the facts on leave policies worldwide. The data set that the authors have put together is a valuable tool for both this paper and for future research in this area. It involved extensive investigation across a variety of sources, with considerable cross-checking and detailed interpretation of legislative nuances.

The results of this analysis are presented in tables 5.1 and 5.2 and figures 5.1 and 5.2. As the figures show, there has been a dramatic upward trend in the availability of leave since 1968. Average weeks of leave across this sample of industrialized countries rose from 14.3 weeks in 1969 to 57.4 weeks in 1980, an increase of over 300 percent. And table 5.1 shows that leave is very generous by 1989: seven countries offer at least one year of unpaid leave, and three countries offer at least one year of paid leave! These are striking findings and provide a valuable baseline with which to compare the relatively meager twelve weeks of unpaid leave provided currently by the federal government.

That said, there are several potential problems with and questions about the construction of these data series. First, many of these countries had leave policies dating from much earlier than the 1960s, but they were not *job protected*, meaning that they did not guarantee reemployment in a comparable job after leave. Thus, in their measurement of changes over time, the authors are placing an enormous amount of weight on the concept of job protection. But how important is job protection in practice? It may be that the leave laws in place before the 1960s generally came with job protection, and the mandates from 1969 onwards simply codified this protection. Alternatively, it may be that the job protection guaranteed in the post-1968 laws is not as stringent as the authors suggest. It would be constructive for the paper to offer some information on how important job protection is now, especially relative to the past.

A related point is that the authors have no information on enforcement and coverage of leave policies more generally. Just because a law is on the books does not mean that it is binding. Furthermore, laws can apply to quite different segments of the workforce. For example, the recent U.S. regulations do not apply to many working mothers, such as those in firms with fewer than fifty workers. These types of holes in coverage could be quite important for their measures of leave generosity across countries. Countries with larger informal sectors that are not regulated by the government, such as some of the poorer countries in their sample, will have much lower effective leave than that which appears in the statutes. Thus, it would be valuable if the authors could incorporate data on enforcement and coverage.

The authors also do not use information on how long mothers must work to qualify for leave. This is obviously a critical restriction if countries are to avoid "churning." The defense of omitting this information from their model is that these restrictions are relatively constant over time, so that they will fall out of the analysis, which examines changes in laws within countries over time. But even if the work requirements themselves are constant over time, they *interact* with changes in leave generosity in an important way that could impact the later econometric estimates. Thus, in the econometric work, the authors could interact leave durations with service requirements and ask whether increasing leave duration matters differentially in countries with more or less stringent service requirements.

It would also be interesting to learn more about take-up of leave provisions. We know that men generally do not take paternity leave, even where they are eligible. What about women? The authors note that there was a much higher use of leave in Denmark and France in 1988 than in Greece and Portugal. This comparison of two of the higher-income countries in their sample with two of the lower-income ones suggests that time off from work may be a normal good. Even when leave is paid, there may be more implicit employer pressure on women to return to work in low-income countries than in higher-income ones. So it would be interesting to try to learn more about take-up and to incorporate this in the modeling.

The second contribution of the paper is to model the effect of leave on economic performance. The authors use several variables to measure performance: GDP, employment-population ratios, labor force participation rates, and unemployment rates. An additional variable that I would have found very interesting, but which may be tough to track down, is wages: Do the costs of these mandates get reflected in lower wages, particularly wages for women?

They estimate fixed-effects models, where performance is regressed on leave availability and a set of country-specific fixed effects, so that the effect of leave is identified only by variations in leave generosity over time. They find that it is important to model leave nonlinearly. That is, short leaves are found to have *beneficial* effects for national output, employment, and labor force participation. But this positive effect peaks at around fifty-nine weeks, and dissipates thereafter, so that very long leaves can depress economic performance. This is a quite striking finding and suggests serious consideration of the models that predict large productivity increases from maternity leave. The obvious concern with this result, however, would be that there is reverse causality: Countries that are performing well may be the ones that feel that they can afford to mandate maternity leave, causing a spurious positive coefficient on the leave variable.

The authors address this concern by using a Granger causality test: leave Granger causes output if δ_1 in their equation (2a) is significant and δ_2 in equation (2b) is not. This test runs into two problems, however. First, a positive shock that hits in year t could cause both the country's performance to improve and the implementation of leave. Second, there is a fundamental problem to carrying out a Granger causality test with fixed effects. Including country fixed effects in the model automatically induces serial correlation in the error term. As a result, the lagged dependent variable in each model will be correlated with the error term and its coefficient will be biased. For example, consider their model (2b). By this argument, their estimate of y_2 is biased, so that the coefficients on any variable correlated with L_{it-1} are biased. The point of the paper is to show that L_{it-1} will be correlated with Y_{it-1}. As a result, δ_2 is biased, which invalidates their test.

Given these problems, what else can the authors do? One solution is to look for a *within-country control group*. That is, they could find some group that should not be directly affected by leave and examine the effect of leave on their outcomes. If leave is having a causal impact on the labor market experience of women, then there should be no impact on this control group. But if leave is caused by some economy-wide shock, then we could see an effect on the controls.

In fact, there is an obvious choice for such a group: men. Of course, men may be somewhat affected by a mandate, for two reasons. First, many of the mandates do apply to men. But men rarely take leave, as noted earlier. Furthermore, it does not apply to men in all countries, and even when it does men often get less generous entitlement. Second, there may be complementarities of leisure. If women can get more time off, men may want some time off also. But I would imagine that this is a second-order effect. As a result, men should be a good control group.

In fact, the authors have data for men only, but they do not show us the result for that group. However, the fact that the results for the entire labor force are the same as for women only, which they show in the paper, leads one to suspect that there are effects on men also. At a minimum, the authors should compute the results for men, and it would be worrisome if the results were significant.

To summarize, then, I think that this paper is the first step in what could be a quite important research agenda. The authors have already done the hardest part of the work through their careful documentation of the legislative history across countries. The task before them now is to both complete their documentation of these legislative differences and perform tests that will allow them to more convincingly demonstrate the effects of these differences on economic performance.

NOTE

1. Interestingly, if there is a market failure, it is more likely to be occurring in small firms, only 21 percent of which offer maternity leave. Yet small firms are exempted from the 1993 federal legislation in the United States.

Commentary on Chapter 5

Marianne A. Ferber

The topic of this paper is especially timely today, when all forms of government mandates and government programs are under attack in the United States and increasingly in other countries as well. Parental leaves are useful because according to most experts in the field, children will do better when cared for in their own home at least for some months after they are born. This in turn is good for employers and for society in the long run, because children who get a better start are more likely to grow up to be productive workers and good citizens. Such leaves are also useful in the short run both for the parents, who are not confronted by a choice of having to find alternative care for their newborns or jeopardizing their job, and for employers, because they will be able to retain experienced workers who do not quit their job when their children are born. We know, however, that there are costs as well. Employers often find that temporarily absent workers are difficult to replace, and they incur additional costs to the extent that they provide pay and/or benefits to workers who are on leave. Parental leaves also may be a drain on the public purse to the extent that government provides some of the pay or benefits. This paper shows evidence that strongly suggests the benefits outweigh the costs in the short run, and this would presumably be true *a fortiori* in the long run.

The more technical parts of the paper have been very adequately addressed by the first discussant. Therefore, I will take this opportunity to expand upon several issues that deserve attention and that the authors have only mentioned briefly or not at all. The most important of these is perhaps the question of whether it is reasonable to have such leaves only for women, a practice that is still common in many countries. There are a number of reasons why such a policy is unacceptable. First, as long as only women take time off for childrearing, employers have one more incentive to prefer hiring men. In fact, it appears that the particularly generous leaves offered to mothers in some countries that are primarily interested in increasing the birth rate are even intended to reduce women's active participation in the labor market. Second, such practices tend to perpetuate stereotypical notions that only women are suited to the task of child-rearing. It is, of course, true that only women bear children. That is not, however, a very time-consuming activity. It is taking care of children that is, and should be, time-consuming, but there is little if any scientific evidence that men cannot do that just as well; only ex post, when women have taken care of children have they acquired an expertise not possessed by men who have not done so. Further, during a time when everyone bemoans the lack of many fathers' commitment to their children, we can ill afford policies that do not provide the same opportunity for early bonding with both parents.

It is often argued, and the authors appear to accept the argument, that even if child care leaves are offered to both parents, not many men will choose to take them. For the most part, the authors tend to accept this view, although they do mention at one point that this may change in the long run. There is no reason to be quite so tentative about that. Evidence from Sweden, the country that introduced paid leaves for fathers as well as mothers more than two decades ago, shows that over this period of time the behavior of fathers has changed substantially. Joseph Pleck (1990) reports that although "few fathers availed themselves of paternal leaves when they were first instituted, by the late 1980s about 85 percent took an average of 8.5 of the ten-day post-confinement benefit, 25 percent took an additional month during the child's first year, and 30 percent of fathers with children under age twelve took an average of five days' leave for child care per year."[1] Furthermore, should it turn out that American men are more resistant than Swedish men it is, at worst, harmless to offer them the opportunity to take parental leave.

The same cannot, however, be said of requiring women to take leave before and/or after childbirth, all the more so when their jobs are not protected. Insisting that a woman cannot work when she is pregnant is entirely inappropriate for all jobs except a very limited few that expose her or the fetus to physical risk. Insisting that she cannot work for an extended period after the child is born precludes a couple from choosing to share child care, or making alternative arrangements that have long been regarded as entirely satisfactory, such as having a grandparent or a trained nanny take care of the child. It is difficult to avoid the suspicion that such laws are often intended to keep women out of the labor force, either in order to restore the traditional family or, during times of high unemployment, to get them out of the labor market in order to have more jobs available for men.

Finally, before turning to another subject, it should also be noted that it would be worthwhile in future research to investigate the effect of parental, as opposed to maternal, leave on male and female employment separately. It would appear, *a priori*, that the effect on employment of women and men may well be somewhat different, depending on whether child care leaves are available to mothers only or to both parents.

Another issue deserves more attention than it receives in this paper: To the extent that leaves do impose some costs on particular employers, while some of the benefits accrue not only to them but to other employers and to society, these costs may be expected to be very much easier to bear when the leave is nationally mandated, so that everyone in the country is faced more nearly with the same situation. It is true that even such a mandate will not provide an entirely "level playing field" because some types of production are more labor-intensive than others, and some employers are more likely to employ people in the age group that is likely to have young children, but it may certainly be expected to be helpful. Further, in view of today's increasingly worldwide competition, it would be even better if international agreements on minimum standards would level the playing field as much as possible among different countries as well. Just as employers in the United States complain that they have trouble competing against countries with lower wages and less stringent environmental standards, so European employers have reason to complain that they find it difficult to compete against the United States, which has far less generous provisions for a variety of worker benefits.

It should also be noted, however, that in another respect this country is ahead of most others. The Family and Medical Leave Act of 1993 stipulates that leaves, albeit short and unpaid, may be used not merely to care for children, but for any family member. At a time when the number of children in families has declined considerably, but increasingly more adults have elderly parents in need of personal care, and these adults have increasingly fewer siblings to share that responsibility, this is clearly an issue that needs more attention than it has received to date.

Finally, it is somewhat puzzling why the authors assume that the costs of parental leaves would have to be offset by paying lower wages. A standard response of producers when their costs and the costs of all their competitors go up is, generally, to increase prices. It is difficult to see, therefore, why this would not also be the case when they have to pay for greater benefits. To the extent that workers are also consumers, they would of course bear some of the cost of higher prices, but so would consumers who receive nonwage income.

NOTE

1. Recently, Sweden has introduced ten days (twenty days for twins) of "daddy leave" to be used during the child's first sixty days, which can be taken only by fathers. It will be very interesting to see how many men avail themselves of this opportunity.

Chapter 6

Work Norms and Professional Labor Markets

Renee M. Landers, James B. Rebitzer, and Lowell J. Taylor

Women are entering previously male professions at an unprecedented rate. The new female entrants to these professions are likely to demand a different mix of hours and income than earlier cohorts. The same will likely be true for current cohorts of men. This paper presents a new framework for analyzing how firms respond to the demographic changes in the professions. We argue that in many professional settings, work norms produce a "rat race" equilibrium in which firms are unable to offer short hours in response to the growing proportion of professionals who want them.

Professional occupations are in the midst of an unprecedented demographic transition. The ratio of men to women in professional schools has declined from over 23 to 1 in 1962 to about 1.7 to 1 by 1988 (Goldin 1992). This influx of women is not limited to traditionally female occupations. In 1969 men constituted 77 percent of accountants and virtually all the engineers, lawyers and judges, and physicians. By 1991, men were 48 percent of accountants, 92 percent of engineers, 82 percent of lawyers and judges and 79 percent of physicians (see table 6.1).

These numbers probably understate the ultimate change in gender composition. For example, roughly 40 percent of students in law schools are female, a fact that led Sherwin Rosen to remark, "In many ways, the story of the legal profession (and, similarly, for the medical practice) in the 1970s and 1980s is the entry of women: the huge increase in women in both professions represents one of the largest demographic changes ever observed in American professions" (Rosen 1992, 222).

The entrance of women into previously male professions strains human resource systems designed for men with stay-at-home wives. Even when working full time, women spend considerably more time on home and child-related tasks than comparable men (Juster and Stafford 1991; Leete-Guy and Schor 1994). Thus, women entering male professions are likely to demand a different mix of hours and income than earlier cohorts. The same will be true of the current cohort of men. These men are

Table 6.1   Percentage Male in Selected Professions and Years

Occupation	1969[a]	1979[b]	1991[c]
Accountants	77%	69%	48%
Engineers	99	98	92
Lawyers and judges	99	92	82
Physicians and surgeons	90	93	79

[a]These are weighted averages for those currently employed (employment status recode 1 or 2) calculated using the May 1969 Current Population Survey. The following 1960 occupation codes were used: accountants, 0: engineers, 80–93; lawyers and judges, 105; physicians and surgeons, 162.

[b]These are weighted averages for those currently employed (employment status recode 1 or 2) calculated using the May 1979 Current Population Survey. The following 1970 occupation codes were used: accountants, 1; engineers, 6–23; lawyers and judges, 30–31; physicians and surgeons, 65.

[c]These are weighted averages for those currently employed (employment status recode 1 or 2) calculated using the outgoing rotation groups in the 1991 Current Population Surveys. The following 1990 occupation codes were used: accountants, 23; engineers, 44–59; lawyers and judges, 178–179; physicians and surgeons, 84.

increasingly married to women with strong labor market commitments and may, as a consequence, find themselves under pressure to spend more time meeting household responsibilities. Table 6.2 offers some insight into this aspect of the demographic shift in professions using data from a survey of lawyers in 1984. In the older cohort of married male attorneys (that is, those who had completed law school at least seven years prior to the survey), 26.4 percent had spouses who worked full time and 9.4 percent had spouses who were lawyers. For married men who graduated from law school in the six years prior to the survey, the comparable figures were 62.1 and 18.3 percent.[1]

The demographic transformation of the professional workforce should reward firms that use the promise of shorter hours to attract talent. There is, however, little evidence that short-hour jobs are appearing in professional firms. Indeed, aggregate statistics suggest that the work hours of college-educated employees have been trending steadily upwards since the 1940s (Coleman and Pencavel 1993a; 1993b).

This paper presents a new framework for analyzing how firms respond to the demographic changes in the professions. We argue that in many professional settings long work hours (or other performance measures that entail long hours) are used to screen for valuable yet hard-to-observe characteristics of employees, such as commitment or ambition. These work norms can lead to a "rat race" equilibrium in which firms are unable to offer short hours to the growing proportion of professionals who might want them.

Table 6.2 Working Status of Spouses for Lawyers in 1984

	Married Male Attorneys		Married Female Attorneys	
Year Since Law School Graduation	% with Spouse who Works Full Time	% with Spouse Who Is Lawyer	% with Spouse who Works Full Time	% with Spouse Who Is Lawyer
More than six years	26.1%[a]	9.4%[a]	87.5%	35.7%
Six years or fewer	62.1[a]	18.3[a]	89.2	40.0

Notes: Weighted averages calculated from the 1984 American Bar Association Survey of Career Satisfaction. Of the men who graduated from law school more than 6 years previously, 82 percent were married compared with 61 percent in the other experience group. For women, 59 percent of the women who graduated from law school more than six years previously were married, compared with 63 percent of the women with six years or fewer from graduation.

[a]Can reject hypothesis that experience is distributed independently of spouse's full-time status at the 1 percent confidence level. Pearson $\chi^2(1) = 146.31$.

The paper consists of four parts. In the first part, we present a model of stringent work norms in professional labor markets. In the second part, we present evidence for the existence of excessive hours norms. The third part analyzes the nature and extent of the policy interventions suggested by our analysis. The paper concludes with a discussion of unresolved research and policy issues.

ECONOMIC MODEL OF WORK NORMS

A RAT RACE MODEL OF WORK NORMS

This section considers how firms in professional labor markets will adjust to an increase in the number of employees who desire shorter and more flexible work hours. In textbook theory this issue is easily settled: The determination of work hours in labor markets is treated as an analog to the determination of product characteristics in consumer goods markets. Just as automobile makers match car colors to consumer preferences to attract buyers, employers will match work hours to the hours preferences of the workforce in order to attract talent. It follows that if a sufficiently large number of professionals want shorter or more flexible hours, self-interested employers will provide jobs with these features.

The textbook account of the determination of work hours abstracts from an important feature of professional labor markets: Professionals often work together in firms or partnerships to exploit gains from cooperation. These partnerships are different from other firms in that the professionals typically share the surplus generated by their activities.[2] If all professionals were equally productive, sharing rules would have no economic significance. When some professionals produce more surplus than others, however, these distributional rules become important. In particular, professionals who produce lots of surplus by virtue of working long hours will end up subsidizing their less hard-working colleagues.

If the work propensities and work activities of every professional were easy to track, then the best any individual could do would be to form a firm with others who are similarly motivated (Farrell and Scotchmer 1988). It is quite different, however, when work propensities and activities are *not* directly observable. In this setting the market for work hours resembles less the market for car colors than the market for health insurance.

When health status is hard to observe directly, employers may refrain from offering generous health insurance policies because they fear attracting a disproportionate number of sick (and therefore expensive) employees. A similar adverse selection problem appears with work hours. Members of partnerships (or other teams of professionals characterized by sharing rules) will refrain from offering short-hour jobs for fear of attracting too many employees wishing to work short hours. Indeed, as we demonstrate below, partnerships may respond to the presence of short-hour employees in the workforce by imposing a stringent hours requirement (or work norm) on themselves as a means of screening out short-hour employees.

To analyze the problem of adverse selection in work hours, we present a model of the job market for attorneys.[3] For simplicity we imagine that there are two types of attorneys, "short-hour attorneys" and "long-hour attorneys," who differ only in their preferences for work hours. Because these attorneys have identical ability, one might expect that employers of legal talent would be indifferent as to which type they hired. However, in our model some law firms are partnerships characterized by revenue sharing among the partners. Partners in such firms always prefer to be partnered with other attorneys who are inclined to work long hours, and they thus adopt work norms that discourage short-hour attorneys from accepting positions with the firm.

Three interesting outcomes emerge from our model. First, there can be a "rat race" equilibrium in which attorneys are overworked. Second, all firms could potentially be better off if they were to simultaneously abandon the excessive work norms, but these firms nonetheless are individually disinclined to alter their own work hours policy. Third, an increase in the number of attorneys who wish to work short hours will not induce firms to adjust hours downward.[4]

In our model, attorneys provide legal services over the course of a two-period work life. All attorneys are presumed to be identical in ability, but different with regard to their preference for nonmarket activities. Let c indicate consumption and h be hours worked in a period. Long-hour (LH) attorneys differ from short-hour (SH) attorneys by having a lower weight on the disutility they place on hours worked. For instance, they might have the following utility functions:

$$u_{LH}(c,h) = c - b_{LH}h^2$$

and   (1)

$$u_{SH}(c,h) = c - b_{SH}h^2,$$

where b_{LH} and b_{SH} are (positive) parameters determining the disutility of work hours, and $b_{SH} > b_{LH}$.

We suppose that legal services can be produced in two distinct ways. First, attorneys can work in a spot market for attorneys (for example, as solo practitioners) and receive a wage equal to their productivity. Clearly, in this market each type of attorney will work optimal hours, with short-hour attorneys adopting shorter work days than their long-hour counterparts. If productivity in the solo practitioner market is m_1, then the hours of short- and long-hour workers with preferences described in equation 1 will be maximizing their utility when they choose $h_{SH} = m_1/4b_{SH}$ and $h_{LH} = m_1/4b_{LH} > h_{SH}$, respectively.

The second way that legal services are produced is in partnerships. It is helpful (and realistic) to think of these partnerships as enterprises in which associates and partners provide complex, client-specific legal services (Rebitzer and Taylor 1995b). Associates are paid a wage equal to the value of their hourly productivity, m_1. Partners, in contrast, have acquired sufficient client-specific expertise so that they can together produce $m_2 > m_1$ for each hour worked. Since acquiring client-specific knowledge takes time, partnership positions are reserved for senior attorneys working in their second (and last) period. At the end of this period, partners retire and "sell" their partnership stake to an incoming cohort of experienced attorneys.[5] Since the relevant expertise is client-specific, outgoing partners always sell the firm to some of the firm's current associates.[6]

For our purposes, the key institutional feature of partnerships are the sharing rules that divide the surplus among the individual partners. These sharing rules create the previously noted complication: Each partner's compensation will depend on the work propensities of the other members of the partnership.

We express the interdependence among partners formally by considering the simplest case—a partnership composed of two experienced attorneys. If each partner has preferences as given in (1), then it is easy to show that the utility a partner of type i gains from being in a partnership with a partner of type j (net of utility received in the spot market) is

$$m_2^2 \left[\frac{1}{16b_i} + \frac{1}{8b_j} \right] - \frac{w_1^2}{4b_i}.$$ (2)

Given that $b_{SH} > b_{LH}$, it is clear that both long- and short-hour attorneys would like to be in a partnership with a long-hour attorney. In what follows, we consider the implications that equation 2 has for the determination of the work hours of associates.

Suppose first that work propensities were directly observable so that associates and partners alike can easily distinguish short- from long-hour attorneys. Then the partners will be indifferent over which type of associate they hire. Both short- and long-hour attorneys will be paid a wage, w_1, which is equal to their productivity, m_1. The short-hour attorneys would work optimal hours, h_{SR}^*, and the long-hour attorneys would work h_{LR}^*.

Figure 6.1 illustrates this outcome. The line coming from the origin is a "budget constraint" showing combinations of hours and income that are attainable by any attorney. Because income equals $w_1 h$, this budget constraint has slope w_1. An attorney who maximizes utility chooses the point on this constraint that puts her on the highest possible "indifference curve." (The indifference curve represents various combinations of income and hours that give the individual the same level of utility.) Notice that for both a short-hour attorney, whose indifference curve is labeled U_{SH}, and a long-hour attorney, whose indifference curve is labeled U_{LH}, utility maximization is characterized by points of tangency; these attorneys are on their highest possible indifference curve when this curve just touches the budget constraint.

Although partners would be indifferent to which type of attorney they employ as associates, they would have, at the same time, a financial interest in keeping short-hour attorneys out of the partnership. This financial interest arises because the salaries of incoming partners (and therefore the price incoming partners are willing to pay for the firm) is greatest when it is common knowledge that all the new partners are willing to work long hours.

When work propensities are *not* directly observable, partners need to take actions to discourage short-hour attorneys from entering the partnership. Since all incoming partners are drawn from the ranks of last period's associates, a natural way to screen out short-hour partners is to require that associates work "too many" hours.

We can build intuition for this result by asking what would happen if firms simply offered attorneys the market wage, $w_1 = m_1$, and gave individuals the choice of selecting optimal hours h_{SR}^* or h_{LR}^*, as illustrated in figure 6.1. The current partners could then decide to keep out of the partnership any associates working h_{SR}^*. In anticipation of this screening rule, some short-hour attorneys might try to disguise themselves as long-hour attorneys h_{LR}^*. By working these overly long hours a short-hour attorney reduces his current level of utility, but he also earns the opportunity to bid for future ownership of the firm. As a short-hour attorney paired with long-hour attorneys, this attorney would then earn large future returns that may be more than enough to compensate for the loss in utility suffered in the first period of his career.

A single firm can prevent this sort of camouflage by requiring that all associates work just slightly in excess of h_{LR}^*. This hours norm makes the

**Figure 6.1   Hours for Short-Hour and Long-Hour Associates in
The Full Information Equilibrium**

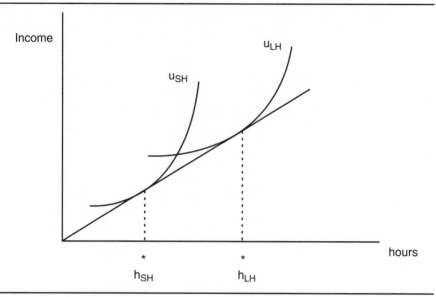

firm particularly unattractive to short-hour attorneys. Of course, a firm imposing an hours norm must boost associate wages so that long-hour attorneys will accept employment at the firm. But the necessary wage increase is small (that is, second-order) relative to the benefits from keeping short-hour attorneys out of the partnership. The benefits a firm gets from increasing work hours are dissipated, however, when competing firms also raise hours to discourage additional short-hour attorneys. Each subsequent increase in work norms is negated until all firms have increased hours to a level such that short-hour attorneys no longer find it attractive to pretend to be long-hour attorneys.

Figure 6.2 depicts the resulting rat race equilibrium. In this equilibrium all firms offer attorneys the wage-hours package marked A. Long-hour attorneys are willing to accept this wage-hours package because it provides them the same level of utility they can achieve on the market, working $\tilde{h}_{LR}^*$ at the market wage. The posted hours, $\tilde{h}_{LH}$, are set just high enough that the loss in utility to a short-hour attorney pretending to be a long-hour attorney is sufficient to offset any potential gain from being viewed as a long-hour attorney. (In figure 6.2 the dollar value of the loss of utility to a short-hour attorney accepting the wage-hours package A is $I_1 - I_2$.)[7]

Figure 6.2 shows that in the rat race equilibrium long-hour attorneys are working very long hours. They are willing to do this because they are paid a wage rate that exceeds the market wage (point A lies above the bud-

Figure 6.2   Hours for Attorneys in The "Rat Race" Equilibrium

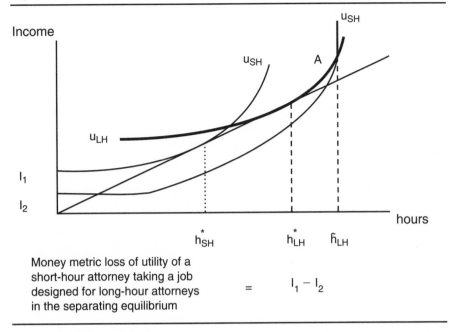

Money metric loss of utility of a
short-hour attorney taking a job
designed for long-hour attorneys   = $I_1 - I_2$
in the separating equilibrium

get constraint). However, these attorneys would be better off if they
could work fewer hours at this higher wage rate. In particular, if the firm
were to allow attorneys to choose their own hours given this higher wage
rate, attorneys would then be choosing hours on a new budget constraint
coming from the origin and passing through point A. The attorneys
would be able to adjust hours downward until they arrived at a new tangency point, on an indifference curve higher than U_{LH}.

There are three important characteristics of this equilibrium that we wish
to emphasize: First, as just demonstrated, associates working in these firms
will consider themselves to be "overworked." Given current hourly wage,
associates would prefer to work fewer hours. In contrast to the textbook
model, however, firms will not have an incentive to reduce hours because
doing so would allow short-hour workers to enter the partnership.

Second, the rat race equilibrium need not be efficient. To see this, consider the case where there is a modest number of short-hour attorneys.
Any one firm offering shorter hours (that is, h_{LR}^*) to its associates would
immediately be flooded by these short-hour attorneys. The value of the
firm would decline. However, if *all* firms were to offer these shorter hours,
short-hour attorneys would be allocated among all firms and would have
only a small effect on each firm's value. Furthermore, all of these firms
would be able to reduce wages paid to associates, which in turn would

result in higher profits and firm value. Thus, we can have a situation in which all firms would benefit from a change in the hours norm, but no individual firm has the incentive to relax its hours requirements.

Third, an increase in the number of short-hour attorneys in the market can have the perverse effect of *increasing* hours that firms require from their associates. Suppose that there were a substantial growth in the number of short-hour attorneys. This supply shift reduces the wage in the spot market for attorneys, making these positions less attractive relative to the positions being offered associates. To keep short-hour attorneys from accepting associate positions, firms must increase hours requirements still further.

Consequences of the Rat Race for Income and Welfare

In the textbook model, heterogeneity in preferences over work hours will result in disparity in earnings even if there are no differences in productivity. Short-hour employees will work shorter hours than long-hour employees and will therefore have lower incomes. These income differentials are innocuous, however, because they result from the fact that each employee is selecting utility-maximizing work hours conditional on a common wage level.

The consequences of a rat race equilibrium for income and welfare are slightly more complicated than the textbook model. Short-hour attorneys are, as we have seen, restricted to the spot market. Long-hour attorneys working as associates in partnerships earn more money than their counterparts in the spot market, but this increase in income simply compensates for the disutility resulting from extra long hours. Partners in our model (and in the actual labor market) may earn very high salaries, but these high salaries could in principle be merely compensating the partners for the long hours they endured as associates, as well as other costs associated with having achieved partnership (for example, the purchase price of their equity stake). Indeed, it is easy to specify a model in which the implicit price of the partnership adjusts so that the net utility of partnership for long-hour attorneys exactly equals the utility of employment in the spot market (Landers, Rebitzer, and Taylor 1996). Thus, although a rat race equilibrium increases observed income disparity, it does not necessarily alter the distribution of welfare across employees with different hours preferences.[8]

More generally, the welfare consequences of a rat race depend on whether employment in the partnership sector brings with it "ex ante employment rents." We would expect young attorneys to evaluate, at the beginning of their careers, the expected (that is, ex ante) rewards of various positions. Partnerships carry an "employment rent" if entry-level attorneys view partner-track associate positions in law firms as more attractive than other available jobs. If we allow for the possibility of such ex ante employment rents in partnerships, then stringent work norms can have the effect of eliminating short-hour attorneys from consideration for "good jobs" even though these workers are as talented and capable as their long-hour counterparts.[9] Alternatively, we might imagine that there is heterogeneity not only in hours preferences but also in talent, assuming that neither is perfectly observable. If the returns to talent are higher in partnerships than in the spot market, a rat race results in talented short-hour attorneys being shut out of the market where they would receive the highest returns on their ability.

EVIDENCE OF STRINGENT WORK NORMS: THE CASE OF LARGE LAW FIRMS

RESULTS FROM A SURVEY OF LARGE LAW FIRMS

Law firms are a natural place to look for evidence of work norms because virtually all these firms are structured as partnerships in which each partner shares in the revenues generated by other partners.[10] These sharing rules, once in place, are typically difficult to adjust in response to differences in the contributions made by each partner. Thus, partners working long hours will want to exclude from the partnership those who produce less. Stringent work norms are a natural way to screen out partners who may want to work shorter hours.

In this section we focus our attention on associates in large law firms. These firms typically occupy a privileged position in the market for legal services (Galanter and Palay 1991). Partners in such firms will often have a large stake in preserving their profitable organizational structure. As a result, these firms can be expected to devote more resources to screening out associates not inclined to work long hours.

Large law firms employ only two classes of attorneys: associates and partners.[11] Associates are hired for a fixed period—usually between six and ten years—and then promoted to partner or fired. Virtually all partners in large firms are promoted from the ranks of their associates. If stringent work norms are used to keep short-hour attorneys out of the partnership, we ought to find evidence of "excessive" hours among associates.[12]

The defining feature of work norms is that individuals are required to work *more* hours than they would otherwise desire at the going wage. It should therefore be possible to identify work norms by asking associates whether they would like to change their hours given their current wage. In practice, however, implementing this empirical strategy is problematic. When stringent work norms are present, a question about hours reduction at the current wage requires respondents to consider an option that was not available to them in the past. Since the respondents could not anticipate the opportunity to reduce hours, they may have made consumption plans on the basis of the high incomes associated with their excessive hours. These consumption plans may entail financial commitments (for example, mortgage payments, car loans, and school tuition payments for children) that preclude a downward adjustment in work hours at the current wage.

For these reasons we adopted an alternative approach to identifying overwork. Rather than asking how associates would adjust hours given their current wage, we asked how they would prefer to adjust to a small wage increase. Specifically, we asked associates to pick from three choices: (1) decrease hours by 5 percent with no change in accompanying income over the coming year, (2) keep hours the same over the coming year with a 5 percent increase in income, or (3) increase hours by 5 percent over the coming year with a 10 percent increase in income.[13]

We collected the data for this study in a survey of associates and partners at two major law firms in a large northeastern city. The surveys asked all associates on a partnership track about their work hours, billable hours, and attitudes toward work hours. A total of 216 surveys were distributed and 133 were returned, for a response rate of 62 percent. A simultaneous survey questioned the partners at these firms about the decision to promote associates to partners. We distributed 188 surveys and received responses from 64.4 percent of the partners in our sample.

The results of our work hours question are reported in table 6.3. We found that 25.56 percent of respondents wanted to keep their hours unchanged and enjoy a 5 percent increase in income. Nearly two thirds (65.41 percent) of the associates indicated that they would prefer to *reduce* work hours and to keep income unchanged over the coming year. This pattern is what we would expect if associates are working under the sort of stringent work norms predicted by our rat race model.

Table 6.4 presents descriptive statistics for associates who want to reduce, keep the same, or increase hours of work. Associates who wanted to reduce hours and those who wanted to keep the same hours looked very similar and in no case were the differences in the means across these groups statistically significant. Particularly noteworthy is the finding that the annual salaries across these two groups were the same. This is important because the magnitude of the income change implicit in the work hours questions was likely to be the same across groups.

Associates who wanted to increase hours were a little different from the others. In general they tended to have less legal experience prior to joining the current firm and therefore slightly lower average salaries. It is possible that associates in this group were trying to "catch up" to other associates in the firm by accumulating more experience. In any case, there were only nine associates in the "increase hours" group.

If the high incidence of overwork recorded in table 6.3 is indeed the result of the processes described by our screening model, we should also find that work hours are an important indicator in the promotion to partnership decision. To address this issue we asked each attorney in the firm to indicate the importance of billable hours and other factors in determining promo-

**Table 6.3   How Associates Would Choose to Use a Hypothetical
5 Percent Wage Increase**

Choice	% of Associates	N of Associates
Reduce billable and non-billable work hours by **5% with no change** in annual salary.	65.41	87
Continue working **the same number** of hours with a **5% increase** in annual salary.	25.56	34
Increase billable and non-billable work hours by **5%** with a **10% increase** in annual salary.	9.02	12

Note: These data are taken from a survey of two large law firms in a northeastern city.

tion to partnership. We then asked each attorney the importance of hours billed as an *indicator* of qualities that the firm might look for in partners.

Factors Important in Promotion: Respondents were asked to evaluate the importance of twelve different factors that were likely to play a role in the promotion process in these law firms. Importance was measured using a 5-point scale where 1 was not important, 2 was slightly important, 3 was moderately important, 4 was very important, and 5 was of the utmost importance. Table 6.5 lists the percentage of respondents who claimed that a factor had an importance of 4 or 5. Column 1 presents the results for associates and column 2 presents the results for partners.

It is clear from inspection that associates and partners had similar views about which factors were important in the promotion process. The correlation coefficient between the two columns in table 6.5 is 0.99. The vast majority of associates (90 percent) and partners (99 percent) viewed the quality of work product as important in promotion decisions. Willingness to work long hours was also considered important by large numbers of associates (96 percent) and partners (89 percent). In contrast, the number of hours billed to clients was seen to be important by a much smaller proportion of associates (68 percent) and partners (52 percent). Indeed, billable hours ranked 7th in importance for both associates and partners.

Hours as an Indicator: Quite a different picture emerges when attorneys are asked about the importance of billable hours as an *indicator* of other traits and achievements relevant to the partnership decision. Respondents were asked to evaluate the importance of billable hours as an indicator for five of the twelve factors listed in table 6.5 (and one additional factor). Attorneys who believed that billable hours are an important indicator and who also believed that the factor itself was important in promotion were assigned a value of 1; otherwise a value of 0 was assigned.[14] Thus, 46 percent of associ-

Table 6.4   Characteristics of Associates by Hours Preferences

	Associate Would Choose to Use 5% Wage Increase to		
	Reduce Hours 5%	Keep Current Hours	Increase Hours 5%
Percentage male	52.9%	64.7%	66.7%
Mean year graduated from law school	1989	1989	1990**
Mean age (years)	32	31.8	29.8*
Mean tenure (years)	3.1	3.0	2.2
Percentage married	73.6%	58.8%	83.3%
Percentage with children	30.2%	38.2%	33.3%
Mean annual salary	$80,264	$80,053	$72,645**
Mean hours worked per month	198	199	204
Mean hours billed per month	164	160	169
Percentage working part time	5.8%	8.8%	8.3%
Weekend days worked: average week	0.5 days	0.4 days	0.6 days
Weekend days worked: busy week	1.3 days	1.3 days	1.4 days

Note: These data are taken from a survey of two large law firms in a northeastern city.
*Difference from column 1 significant at 10 percent level.
**Difference from column 1 significant at 5 percent level.

ates reported that ambition was very important in promotion decisions *and* that partners assigned much importance to billable hours as an indicator of ambition. The comparable figure for partners was 39 percent. Inspection of columns 1 and 2 in table 6.6 reveals that similar proportions of associates and partners viewed billable hours as an important indicator of underlying associate abilities and accomplishments. The correlation coefficient between rows one to six of columns 1 and 2 is 0.94. Consistent with our model of income sharing among partners, a large majority of associates (92 percent) and partners (78 percent) viewed billable hours as an important indicator of a willingness to work long hours when required. The signaling value of work hours was *not* limited, however, to work propensities. In our sample of associates, the median number of important factors for which billable hours was also an important indicator was three. The median for partners was two.

The importance of work hours as a signal in promotion is also reflected in a nationally representative survey of attorneys conducted by the American Bar Association. In this survey 59.3 percent of respondents believed that reduced-hour or part-time employment limited opportunities for advancement including partnership (American Bar Association 1990, 27).

Table 6.5   Fraction of Associates and Partners Who Consider the Following Factors Very Important for Promotion to Partnership

Factor in the Promotion Decision	Associates	Partners
Quality of work product	0.90	0.99
Number of hours billed to clients	0.68	0.52
Mastery of an important area of specialization	0.67	0.75
Contribution to administration or recruitment	0.08	0.01
Development of good working relationships or mentoring relationships with senior lawyers in the firm	0.68	0.51
Development of a good working relationship with clients and peers	0.76	0.81
Potential for bringing new clients and business to the firm	0.75	0.69
Demonstrated ability to bring new clients and business to the firm	0.48	0.19
Willingness to work long hours when required	0.96	0.89
Loyalty to the firm	0.69	0.71
Willingness to pursue the interests of clients aggressively	0.76	0.76
Ambition for success and respect in the legal profession	0.67	0.51
Total Observations	130	118

Notes: These data are taken from a survey of two large law firms in a northeastern city. Respondents were asked to rate factors on the following 5 point scale: 1 = not important; 2 = slightly important; 3 = moderately important; 4 = very important; and 5 = of the utmost importance. The table lists the proportion of respondents who rated the factor 4 or 5.

ALTERNATIVE INTERPRETATIONS OF THE SURVEY RESULTS

Can Respondents Be Working Optimal Hours?

The results in table 6.3 can be reconciled with conventional theory if individuals always work their preferred level of work hours and their preferred level of work hours falls sharply when wages rise. In particular, economic theory suggests two competing responses to an increase in one's wage: On the one hand, the reward for an additional hour of work has risen, which gives the worker incentive to accept an additional hour of work. This is the "substitution effect." On the other hand, for any given number of work hours, the individual's income has increased. This "income effect" would typically induce an individual to take on fewer hours of work. Thus, is it conceivable that our associates simply have sharply backward-bending labor supply curves; that is, the income effect dominates the substitution effect.

In each of the firms we study, however, wages increase with job tenure, but we find no evidence that work hours change with tenure. The plausibility of a backward-bending labor supply curve explanation is also called into question by the magnitude of the desired reduction in hours. The

Table 6.6 **Fraction of Associates and Partners Who Considered Billable Hours an Important Indicator of a Factor Viewed as Important for Promotion**

Factor in the Promotion Decision	Associates	Partners
Ambition for success and respect in the legal profession	0.46	0.39
Willingness to pursue the interests of clients aggressively	0.48	0.37
Willingness to work long hours when required	0.92	0.78
Loyalty to the firm	0.5	0.28
Ability to produce high-quality work product	0.32	0.32
Demonstrated ability to bring new clients and business to the firm	0.16	0.20
Median number of important factors for which hours are an important indicator	3	2
Total Observations	130	117

Notes: These data are taken from a survey of two large law firms in a northeastern city. Respondents were asked to rate the importance of billable hours as an indicator for six different factors in the promotion process. A 5-point scale was used to record responses: 1 = not important; 2 = slightly important; 3 = moderately important; 4 = very important; 5 = of the utmost importance. Billable hours were seen as an important indicator when two conditions held. First, respondents gave billable hours a score of 4 or 5 as an indicator. Second, the factor that was being indicated by billable hours was given an importance rating of 4 or 5 in the previous table.

response of preferred hours to a 5 percent wage increase is much larger than has been observed in other empirical studies of the effect of wages on work hours. The respondents in row 1 of table 6.3 indicated that they would reduce work hours 5 percent in response to a 5 percent increase in wages. This choice implies an elasticity of hours with respect to wages of −1. This elasticity is roughly ten times that usually reported in the literature (Pencavel 1986).[15]

Fixed Employment Costs
The results of table 6.3 could be consistent with the conventional economic model of work hours if there are substantial fixed employment costs. Consider, for example, a firm that spends a large amount of money to train associates. With the same training, a part-time associate would cost the firm much more per hour than an associate working sixty hours per week. Since firms pay the fixed employment costs, they will require hours that seem excessive to employees. This might produce the results in table 6.3. The fixed employment cost explanation is harder to reconcile with tables 6.5 and 6.6. The presence of fixed employment costs alone should not lead firms to use work hours as an indicator of important, but hard-to-observe, characteristics.[16]

In order to further investigate the possible importance of fixed employment costs, we surveyed thirty-six attorneys working at a large public agency. Attorneys in this agency were typically young and they received formal and informal training and supervision. Unlike the large law firms we studied, however, the structure of the agency was flat—with very few internal promotion possibilities. Neither managers nor individual attorneys kept track of their hours and only 19.4 percent of these public-sector attorneys believed that hours played an important role in promotion decisions. In contrast, 68 percent of the associates in large law firms believed that hours were important in promotion decisions.

In the law firms we observed 65 percent of the associates wanted to reduce hours in response to a 5 percent wage increase. If fixed employment costs, rather than promotion incentives, were driving these results, we should expect a similar pattern of responses from our sample of attorneys working in the public agency.[17] Instead, we find that only 14 percent of the public-sector attorneys wanted to use the 5 percent wage increase to reduce hours. Similarly, 54 percent of the public-sector attorneys wanted to keep their current hours, and 31 percent wanted to increase hours.[18]

Long Hours as a Commitment Device

Our discussion has so far assumed that firms demand long work hours to screen out associates who have predetermined work propensities. An alternative explanation is that firms require long hours from associates in order to *commit* associates to long hours.

One possible commitment mechanism is discussed in social psychology as the "oversufficient justification effect" (Fiske and Taylor 1991). This term refers to a process in which individuals attribute to themselves motivation for behavior that cannot be the result of external pressures. Performing a task for insufficient external rewards leads individuals to conclude that they must be motivated by intrinsic interest. In the context of law firms, subjecting associates to hours longer than they otherwise would choose produces a reaction like: "I couldn't have done it for the money, so I must have done it because it was important to me" (Fiske and Taylor 1991, 46). The result is that associates will come to place a greater value on their work than would otherwise be the case.

Cognitive dissonance is a closely related psychological process that might also produce a commitment to excess hours. The term "cognitive dissonance" refers to the conflict or anxiety resulting from an inconsistency between beliefs and actions. To reduce anxiety, individuals may revise their beliefs and resolve the inconsistency. In economics, cognitive dissonance has been applied to analyzing workplace safety. Workers who are exposed to dangerous situations learn to cope by revising their assessment of risk (Akerlof and Dickens 1982). Similarly, professionals subjected to stringent work norms may adjust their hours preferences in order to reduce the inconsistency between actions and beliefs.

The keys to applying both the oversufficient justification and the cognitive dissonance mechanisms to overwork are the twin assumptions that preferences or beliefs (1) are malleable at some early state and (2) are persistent at some later state. An alternative mechanism for creating a commitment to long hours focuses on hard-to-reverse investments in the infrastructure required to support long hours. An associate who has spent six to ten years working evenings and weekends invests in numerous adaptations to long hours. For example, the associate may have married someone who likes having a spouse who works long hours and earns a large income. Once made, these accommodations may be hard to undo. The result is that the associates who enter a firm with one set of behaviors emerge years later with another set of behaviors that simply are not going to change.[19]

Commitment mechanisms might also be important for explaining the long hours that associates work. The data we have, however, do not offer much support for models in which associates adapt to long hours as a result of their experience with strict work norms. If individuals acclimatize to long hours over the course of the employment relationship, we should find that hours are the same across tenure groups, but that the degree of satisfaction with hours increases with job tenure. In our data, work hours do not change with increased job tenure but neither do the preferred hours of associates. This can be seen in table 6.4, where the average tenure of associates who want to reduce hours is the same as the average tenure of associates who want to keep their current level of work hours.

DISTRIBUTION OF ASSOCIATE WORK HOURS ACROSS LAW FIRMS OF DIFFERENT SIZES

Our model of work norms in professional firms requires that partners in the firm not be able to fully adjust sharing rules in response to differences in the contributions made by each professional. We suspect that this crucial condition will tend to hold with greater force in large law firms than in small firms. There are three reasons to expect that renegotiation would be more difficult in large firms than in small firms. First, it is more difficult for partners in large firms to directly observe the productive activities of their colleagues. Second, the problem of negotiating changes to an existing sharing arrangement is likely to be more difficult the larger the number of parties affected by the negotiation.

The final reason to expect difficulties in adjusting sharing rules in large firms has to do with the economic role these rules may play in partnerships. Legal scholars have noted that the sharing rules in partnerships make it possible for risk-averse attorneys to diversify their investments in human capital

(Gilson and Mnookin 1985). Bankruptcy attorneys may do very well in hard times and, with sharing rules in place, they will subsidize their colleagues in commercial litigation who might suffer if business activity slows. The reverse may be true in times of economic growth. Large firms offer their partners a more diversified human capital investment portfolio, and investing in income insurance via sharing rules is therefore more likely to take place in large firms. (See Lang and Gordon, 1995, for a formal demonstration of this point.) Thus, it will be hard for large firms to adjust sharing rules for individuals without threatening the credibility of the insurance function of the partnership. As an empirical matter, there is some evidence that sharing rules are more prevalent in large firms than in small law firms (Lang and Gordon, 1995).

If rigid sharing rules are more common in large firms than in small firms, then the problem of screening associates for their work propensities would be more important in large firms. The value of screening would be further enhanced if, as we have already suggested, partnership positions in large firms offer significant employment rents. Our rat race model would, on this basis, predict that stringent work norms ought to be more prevalent among associates in large firms. Data required to directly test this hypothesis (that is, the sort of data we collected from our survey of two large law firms) is not available for a cross section of firms. We can, however, learn something about the incidence of work norms across firms of different sizes by examining more conventional data on work hours. In particular, if work norms are more prevalent in large firms, we should find that associates in large firms work longer hours than associates in small firms.

Table 6.7 compares the work hours of a nationally representative sample of associates from law firms of various sizes.[20] Columns 1 and 2 present the results of a regression in which monthly hours are regressed on dummy variables for each of the firm-size categories in the data. Column 1 reports results for a regression that conditions on age, marital status, number of children, gender, years since law school graduation, tenure with the firm, and whether the firm is located in a legal center (that is, in Boston, Chicago, Los Angeles, New York, San Francisco, or Washington, DC). After controlling for these variables, we find that associates in large firms (in firm-size categories of more than thirty lawyers) work significantly more hours than associates in smaller firms.

The size difference in work hours that we observe in column 1 of table 6.7 may reflect differences in the types of practice or types of activities that associates in different firms engage in. Column 2 reports results from a regression that includes variables measuring the amount of time that associates spend in fifteen different practice areas and eleven different types of legal activities. Including these additional twenty-six variables, we find virtually no change in the relationship between firm size and associate work hours. In both regressions, coefficients do not differ significantly from

Table 6.7 Comparison of Work Hours and Satisfaction Measures for Associates, by Firm Size

Number of Lawyers in Firm (mean of hours)	Ordinary Least Squares (t-statistics)		Ordered Probits (z-statistics)		Ordered Probits (z-statistics)	
	Monthly Hours (1)	Monthly Hours (2)	Enough Time for Yourself? (3)	Enough Time for Yourself? (4)	Enough Time with Family? (5)	Enough Time with Family? (6)
4–9	10.013	11.315	0.148	0.141	0.280	0.284
(192.5)	(1.401)	(1.543)	(0.699)	(0.654)	(1.311)	(1.303)
10–20	9.462	10.136	0.149	0.074	0.262	0.202
(190.5)	(1.225)	(1.251)	(0.653)	(0.319)	(1.137)	(0.859)
21–30	–1.425	1.430	0.336	0.201	0.496	0.355
(181.7)	(–0.151)	(0.144)	(1.198)	(0.690)	(1.745)	(1.203)
31–60	19.404◊	17.413◊	0.553◊	0.565◊	0.760◊	0.774◊
(201.9)	(2.242)	(1.844)	(2.156)	(2.141)	(2.949)	(2.923)
61–90	26.235◊	31.041◊	0.666◊	0.547◊	0.781◊	0.635◊
(206.2)	(2.753)	(3.073)	(2.342)	(1.858)	(2.658)	(2.084)
90+	13.635◊	17.306◊	0.572◊	0.544◊	0.752◊	0.684◊
(195.25)	(1.744)	(2.039)	(2.451)	(2.267)	(3.164)	(2.818)
Controls 1	yes	yes	yes		yes	yes
Controls 2		yes		yes		yes
Controls 3						yes
	$R^2 = 0.058$	$R^2 = 0.116$	$\chi^2 = 29.28*$	$\chi^2 = 39.28*$	$\chi^2 = 30.37*$	$\chi^2 = 35.76*$
N	364	364	365	351	350	337

Notes: For columns 3–6, responses to the statements "I have enough time for myself" and "I have enough time to spend with my family" ranged from 1 (very descriptive) to 5 (just the opposite).

(*Notes for table 6.7 continued on p. 185.*)

(*Notes for table 6.7 continued from p. 184.*)

The sample was restricted to associates in private practice and not in solo practice in 1984. The distribution of associates over the firm-size categories were: 4–9 lawyers, 9.6 percent; 10–20 lawyers, 29.7 percent; 21–30 lawyers, 17.9 percent; 31–60 lawyers, 7.1 percent; 61–90 lawyers, 11 percent; 90+ lawyers, 17.6 percent. Firms with 2 or 3 attorneys were omitted; lawyers in these firms were 9.6 percent of the sample. The mean hours for these firms was 181.8.

Controls 1: Variables measuring age, marital status, number of children, gender, years since law school graduation, tenure with firm, and a dummy variable indicating whether or not respondent worked in a legal center (Boston, Chicago, Los Angeles, New York, San Francisco, or Washington, DC).

Controls 2: Proportion of time spent in the following fifteen practice areas and eleven activities. Practice areas: antitrust, corporation/business, criminal, civil rights, family, labor/employment, municipal, natural resources, patent, poverty, probates and trust, public utility, real estate, taxation, torts and insurance. Activities: client contact, research/memo writing, negotiation, depositions, trials/court appearances, client development, miscellaneous personal contact, internal administration, drafting instruments, non–law-related work, clerical work.

Controls 3: Two dummy variables indicating, respectively, whether over the previous twelve months a respondent experienced an extremely stressful event in his/her personal life (death of a spouse, divorce, family problems) or business life (firm split up, lost major case, and so on). In addition, we include the depression subscale of the Hopkins Symptom Check List. This is a widely used measure of stress.

^{0}Cannot reject hypothesis that coefficients on firm sizes 31–60, 61–90, and 91+ are identical; can reject the hypothesis (at 5 percent level) that these coefficients are jointly different from zero. Replacing the three dummy variables indicating employment in a firm with 31+ variables with a single dummy variable yields the following coefficients (t– or z–statistics): column 1, 18.06 (25.53); column 2, 20.5 (2.643); column 3, 0.587 (2.777); column 4, 0.551 (2.543); column 5, 0.752 (3.164); and column 6, 0.684 (2.818).

*Reject hypothesis that $\chi^2 = 0$ at 5 percent confidence level or better.

zero for the smallest three firm sizes, but are economically and statistically significant for the larger firm sizes.

The firm size–hours correlations reported in table 6.7 are consistent with the predictions of our work norm model, but can also be explained by more conventional sorting processes. It could be that large law firms specialize in tasks entailing long hours and therefore select lawyers who better tolerate long hours or whose family responsibilities are such that they could spend more time at work.[21] If, for example, we discover that the typical associate in a large law firm finds hours no more onerous than associates at small firms (who work on average fewer hours) we could reject our work norm explanation of long hours in large firms in favor of a conventional sorting mechanism.[22]

We examine the disutility of hours across firm sizes in columns 3–6 of table 6.7 using data on employee attitudes toward hours. Associates were asked whether the statement "I have enough time for myself" is descriptive of their current job. The answers to this question are analyzed in column 3 of table 6.7. We find that associates in firms with more than thirty attorneys are more likely to report not having enough time for themselves than other associates.

Before concluding that the correlation between firm size and dissatisfaction with "time for oneself" reflect the disutility of long hours, it is worth investigating other psychological explanations—particularly those related to stress and depression. Consider, for example, the possibility that the higher stakes involved in legal practice in large firms increase the level of stress associated with normal business failures. If so, then associates in large firms may be dissatisfied with time for themselves because they are experiencing a higher level of stress at work. High levels of stress at work can also increase an individual's vulnerability to depression. Depression may make individuals less able to experience satisfaction—leading to a correlation between firm size and hours dissatisfaction that is not the result of the disutility of hours per se.

Depression may also be important if the personality types best suited to sustain very long hours are those with some degree of depression. If depression impairs an individual's ability to experience pleasure from family and leisure activities, then mild amounts of depression may encourage long hours by reducing the psychological opportunity cost of work. These mechanisms would produce the paradoxical result that low satisfaction scores reflect a personality that helps associates who choose to work long hours. This view of the relationship between depression and work hours was nicely summed up by an MIT professor's explanation for the heavy work loads and miserable expressions she observed among undergraduates: "They're not happy unless they are unhappy."

To analyze the contribution that stress and depression play in the relationship between firm size and hours dissatisfaction, we re-estimate the satisfaction equation in column 3 and include direct indicators of stress and depression. The stress measures are dummy variables equal to one if the respondent reported an extremely stressful event in personal or business life over the last year. The measure of depression is the Depression Subscale of the Hopkins Symptom Check List, a widely used measure of distress based on respondents' indication of the frequency they experience various physical and emotional symptoms of depression and stress. Although we find (in unreported results) that higher levels of distress correlate with higher levels of dissatisfaction with work hours, including these additional variables does not alter the magnitude or statistical significance of the relationship between firm size and dissatisfaction with hours (see column 4 of table 6.7).

We have so far only considered associates' assessments of the time they have for themselves. Work norms, however, have implications for gender equity because of the different roles that men and women play in child and elder care. In the same survey, respondents were asked to consider the statement, "I have enough time to spend with my family." The results, presented in columns 5 and 6 of table 6.7 parallel those in columns 3 and 4. On average, associates in large firms are more likely to report that they do not have enough time for their families than associates in smaller firms.

Satisfaction measures of the sort we have analyzed are likely to be influenced by the expectations that individual attorneys bring to the job. It may be that the sort of people recruited to large firms (often high achievers from elite schools) simply have higher expectations for job satisfaction than their counterparts in smaller firms. This would produce a positive correlation between firm size and dissatisfaction with hours—even if the disutility of hours themselves were no different for associates in different firm-size categories. If higher expectations were driving the results in columns 3–6 of table 6.7, we would expect to see the correlation between firm size and dissatisfaction to persist when individuals were asked how satisfied they were with their job overall. Table 6.8 presents an analysis of similarly worded satisfaction questions. Columns 1 and 2 concern answers to the question of how satisfied associates were with the time they had for themselves. Columns 3 and 4 concern satisfaction with time with family. Columns 5 and 6 presents an analysis of associate responses to the question, "In thinking about your current job, *overall* how satisfied are you or do you feel neutral?" The pattern of responses to the job satisfaction question are quite different from the pattern observed when associates were asked about satisfaction with hours. There does not appear to be any association between firm size and overall job satisfaction. This finding suggests that it is unlikely that our earlier results were driven by generically higher expectations among associates in large firms.

POLICY IMPLICATIONS

In this section of the paper, we consider the policy implications of our analysis of work norms in professional labor markets. As discussed earlier, the effect of work norms on income and welfare distribution hinges criti-

Table 6.8 Satisfaction Measures for Associates, by Firm Size

Number of Lawyers in Firm	Ordered Probits (z-statistics)		Ordered Probits (z-statistics)		Ordered Probits (z-statistics)	
	Satisfied with Time for Yourself? (1)	Satisfied with Time for Yourself? (2)	Satisfied with Time with Family? (3)	Satisfied with Time with Family? (4)	Overall Job Satisfaction (5)	Overall Job Satisfaction (6)
4–9	0.369	0.382	0.458	0.478	−0.308	−0.282
	(1.640)	(1.656)	(1.994)	(2.029)	(−1.446)	(−1.299)
10–20	0.359	0.308	0.506	0.452	−0.133	−0.133
	(1.484)	(1.242)	(2.050)	(1.791)	(−0.581)	(−0.565)
21–30	0.454	0.369	0.529	0.404	−0.617	−0.578
	(1.508)	(1.179)	(1.755)◊	(1.291)	(−2.157)	(−1.948)
31–60	0.708◊	0.737◊	1.027◊	1.060	−0.483	−0.371
	(2.540)	(2.562)	(3.585)	(3.585)	(−1.864)	(−1.397)
61–90	0.680◊	0.565◊	0.810◊	0.650	−0.214	0.064
	(2.218)	(1.787)	(2.529)	(1.966)	(−0.760)	(0.220)
90+	0.637◊	0.660◊	1.038	0.995	−0.026	−0.045
	(2.544)	(2.554)	(3.956)	(3.696)	(−0.113)	(−0.189)
Controls 1	yes	yes	yes	yes	yes	yes
Controls 2			yes	yes		yes
χ^2	17.44	27.18**	34.77*	42.83*	31.70*	47.35*
N	364	350	354	341	364	350

Notes: For columns 1–4, responses to questions about satisfaction with time for self and family ranged from 1 (satisfied) to 3 (not satisfied); for columns 5 and 6, responses ranged from 1 (very satisfied) to 5 (very dissatisfied).

(Notes for table 6.8 continued on p. 189.)

(*Notes for table 6.8 continued from p. 188.*)

The sample was restricted to associates in private practice and not in solo practice in 1984. The distribution of associates over the firm size categories were: 4–9 lawyers, 9.6 percent; 10–20 lawyers, 29.7 percent; 21–30 lawyers, 17.9 percent; 31–60 lawyers, 7.1 percent; 61–90 lawyers, 11 percent; 90+ lawyers, 17.6 percent. Firms with 2 or 3 attorneys were omitted; lawyers in these firms were 9.6 percent of the sample.

Controls 2: Variables measuring age, marital status, number of children, gender, years since law school graduation, tenure with firm, and a dummy variable indicating whether or not respondent worked in a legal center (Boston, Chicago, Los Angeles, New York, San Francisco, or Washington, DC).

Controls 3: Two dummy variables indicating, respectively, whether over the previous twelve months a respondent experienced an extremely stressful event in his/her personal life (death of a spouse, divorce, family problems) or business life (firm split up, lost major case, and so on). In addition, we include the depression subscale of the Hopkins Symptom Check List. This is a widely used measure of stress.

[a]Cannot reject hypothesis that coefficients on firm sizes 31–60, 61–90, and 91+ are identical; can reject the hypothesis (at 5 percent level) that these coefficients are jointly different from zero. Replacing the three dummy variables indicating employment in a firm with 31+ variables with a single dummy variable yields the following coefficients (t– or z–statistics): column 1, 0.661 (2.875); column 2, 0.668 (2.961); column 3, 0.85 (4.223); column 4, 0.941 (3.933).

*Reject hypothesis that $\chi^2 = 0$ at 5 percent confidence level or better.

**Reject hypothesis that $\chi^2 = 0$ at 10 percent confidence level or better.

cally on whether jobs for which these norms pertain offer employment rents. That is, does the rat race typically emerge in firms that offer the "best jobs"? We begin by considering this issue for the case of law firms. We then discuss the sorts of policy interventions that our analysis suggests.

ARE THERE EX ANTE RENTS IN THE RAT RACE SECTOR?

Earlier we argued that differences in work propensities generally produce inequalities in income even among otherwise identical workers, but also that the policy significance of these inequalities depends upon the nature of the labor market. In settings where fully rational actors operate in frictionless markets, an employee's current job will have the same ex ante utility as the next best alternative. The concentration of short-hour employees into lower-wage jobs will in this context be the result of an efficient sorting process in a market offering equality of opportunity to all participants. In contrast, if work norms prevail in sectors characterized by ex ante employment rents, short-hour employees will experience a reduction in economic opportunities relative to those of long-hour employees. The ex post inequalities in labor market outcomes cannot, in this setting, be presumed to be the result of efficient sorting, and policy interventions may be able to improve economic efficiency while, at the same time, reducing inequality.

Although our model of rat race equilibria does not offer an explanation for ex ante employment rents, the theory does suggest that stringent work norms are more likely to appear in settings where such rents exist. Firms paying premium wages will, all else equal, be more attractive to short-hour employees than other firms. These desirable firms will, therefore, need to devote more resources to screening out undesired employees. In terms of our model, these extra expenditures take the form of compensating long-hour professionals for the even longer hours required to keep short-hour professionals out of unusually desirable jobs.

To examine empirically the relationship between rat race equilibria and ex ante employment rents, we return to the job market for attorneys. Historical accounts of the origins of large law firms suggest that these firms reached their current size because they occupy (by virtue of their reputation and connections) a privileged position in the market for legal services (Galanter and Palay 1991). Until recently, however, data did not exist that allowed for a systematic comparison of the economic returns from positions in large and small firms.

Rebitzer and Taylor (1995b) used the American Bar Association (ABA) 1984 survey to compare the earnings of partners in large and small firms. Table 6.9 presents the basic results. Column 1 provides estimates of the log of income as a linear function of the log of firm size and usual hours.[23] On average, an increase in firm size of 0.1 log points is associated with an increases in partner earnings of 0.024 log points. This is a large effect when

Table 6.9   Effect of Firm Size on Earnings of Partners, 1984

Dependent Variable	Earnings 1983	Earnings 1983
Log of firm size	0.24	0.16
	(11.92)	(5.50)
Usual hours	−0.0001	0.001
	(−0.13)	(1.25)
Male		0.36
		(1.89)
Age		0.02
		(4.65)
Tenure of 4–9 years		0.18
		(2.03)
Tenure of 10+ years		0.39
		(3.63)
Very prestigious law school		0.14
		(1.26)
Somewhat prestigious law school		0.12
		(1.50)
Law review		0.09
		(1.14)
Legal center		0.13
		(1.10)
Law school class top quartile		0.18
		(1.51)
Law school class second quartile		0.17
		(1.46)
Population > 1 million		−0.002
		(−0.017)
Population 250,000 to 1 million		−0.012
		(−0.155)
Additional variables:		
Legal practices and tasks	no	yes
Satisfaction with practices and tasks	no	yes
Pre–law school preparation	no	yes
Log likelihood:	−695.28	−436.411
N	403	298

Notes: Numbers in parentheses are t-statistics. See table 6.11 for variable definitions.

one considers the wide variation in law firm size. According to our estimates, a lawyer moving from a firm of 15 attorneys to one with 200 attorneys would experience a 0.6 log point increase in earnings. Since the average earnings of partners in 15-person firms was roughly $90,000 in 1983 dollars, the move to the larger firm would entail an increase in annual salary of $77,000. Column 2 of table 6.9 introduces a wide variety of variables to control for other factors that determine salary levels: demographics, ability, quality of education, legal experience location, and type of practice. The firm size coefficient, although smaller, remains statistically significant and large in magnitude. *Ceteris paribus*, moving from a firm with 15 attorneys to a firm with 200 attorneys increases partner salaries by 0.4 log points. This translates into an annual salary increase of $46,000. Similar results hold in fixed-effect models that eliminate the influence of time-invariant characteristics of attorneys (see Rebitzer and Taylor 1995b).

The reward for winning the contest for promotion to partner in a large firm may be great, but if the odds of victory are small, then the opportunity to work as an associate in a large firm may be no more valuable than the opportunity to work as an associate in a smaller firm.[24] We can infer something about the expected value of entering the promotion tournaments in large and small firms by comparing the earnings of *associates* in large and small law firms. In order to interpret these comparisons, it is first necessary to consider the economics of promotion tournaments in more detail.

Promotion tournaments are structured to create work incentives for associates. In order for the associates to be properly motivated, the firm must, at the margin, set the expected reward from working hard and winning the tournament equal to the cost to the associate of working hard. For similar attorneys doing similar work, the rewards from working hard in the associate period must be the same.[25] This means that the *expected value* of promotion to partnership must be the same in a large firm as in a small firms. If the expected value of promotion to partnership is the same at both firms, then a finding that similar associates doing similar work are paid more in the larger firm would be proof that the positions in the large firm have a greater ex ante value than analogous positions in the small firm.[26]

Estimates of the firm size effect on associate wages are presented in table 6.10. The results in column 1 mean that if an associate moved from a firm of 15 attorneys to one with 200 attorneys annual salary would increase by about 37 percent. Column 2 presents analogous estimates after the vector of control variables for demographic factors, human capital, practice type, and location were introduced. The coefficient on firm size falls in magnitude, but it remains substantial and statistically significant. All else equal, associates moving from a firm of 15 to 200 attorneys would experience an increase in annual salary of roughly 20 percent. Similar results hold in fixed-effects models (see Rebitzer and Taylor 1995b).

POLICY INTERVENTIONS

Our analysis of rat race equilibria suggests that excessive hours may be the result of a coordination failure in labor markets. A *single* firm that abandons a stringent work norm will be inundated with short-hour employees. If all firms simultaneously abandoned their hours norm, the short-hour employees would be distributed over many firms. For this reason, the private costs of innovation exceed the social costs. The result of the wedge between private and social costs is that stringent norms

Table 6.10   Effect of Firm Size on Earnings of Associates, 1984

Dependent Variable	Earnings 1983	Earnings 1983
Log of firm size	0.12	0.07
	(8.23)	(3.87)
Usual hours	0.002	0.002
	(4.33)	(2.60)
Male		0.06
		(1.12)
Age		0.02
		(4.82)
Tenure of 4–9 years		0.24
		(4.95)
Tenure of 10+ years		0.58
		(2.68)
Very prestigious law school		0.16
		(2.60)
Somewhat prestigious law school		0.15
		(3.05)
Law review		0.10
		(1.76)
Legal center		0.10
		(1.53)
Law school class top quartile		−0.02
		(−0.41)
Law school class second quartile		−0.05
		(−0.80)
Population > 1 million		0.18
		(2.85)
Population 250,000 to 1 million		0.08
		(1.58)
Additional variables:		
Legal practices and tasks	no	yes
Satisfaction with practices and tasks	no	yes
Pre–law school preparation	no	yes
Log likelihood:	−538.551	−399.513
N	388	357

Notes: Numbers in parentheses are t-statistics. See table 6.11 for variable definitions.

may persist even if they are not justified on the basis of economic efficiency. It follows that policy interventions that correct the coordination failure can, in some circumstances, enhance both equality and efficiency.

Maximum-Hours Laws

The instinctive policy prescription for labor markets that generate persistent excessive hours is to impose a maximum-hours rule. Such a rule has two virtues. First, if the law were carefully enforced and the hours maximum was set correctly, it would be impossible for firms to screen on work hours. Second, by forcing all firms to abandon their hours screens at the same time, a maximum-hours law spreads the costs of shorter hours across all firms. In this way, labor markets would be able to achieve shorter work hours than would otherwise be possible.

The great disadvantage of a maximum-hours rule in a professional setting is that it is a blunt policy instrument capable of producing unintended effects on the quality or cost of service delivered. The complexity of even the most commonsensical maximum-hours rule can be seen in the recent effort by the state of New York to limit the hours worked by residents and interns in hospitals.[27] In 1984, the daughter of a *New York Times* journalist died while under the care of residents and interns working the late night shift at a New York hospital. Investigation of this death led to concerns about substandard care and, in 1989, New York implemented regulations limiting doctor hours and requiring a minimum level of supervision by experienced physicians (French 1989). The new rules limited shifts to 24 hours (as opposed to the former 36 hours) and work weeks to 80 hours. Hospitals and insurers resisted this law on the grounds that it increased costs. Perhaps more surprising were the concerns, expressed by professors and interns, that the quality of care and medical education would deteriorate as a result of the change. Some doctors were worried that the increase in expenditures on physicians would lead to a deterioration of already inadequate support services. Others were troubled about miscues in the "handing off" of recently admitted patients when interns and residents reached the end of their 12-hour shift.

Making Long Hours Less Costly to Workers

The same adverse selection problems that cause a collapse of the market for short-hour jobs will also cause a collapse in the market for benefits valued most by short-hour employees. One way to level the playing field might therefore be for the government to require that employers provide benefits that reduce the cost of long hours for employees otherwise likely to work short hours. An example of this sort of mandate is contained in the recently passed Family and Medical Leave Act (FMLA).

The twelve weeks of unpaid leave mandated by the FMLA is clearly inadequate to induce a single mother to work as many hours as an equivalent woman with no children, and more costly employer mandates are likely to face fierce political resistance. An alternative approach to reducing the cost of long hours might be to offer employers or employees substantial tax breaks for the purchase of child care and elder care services. Our rat race model, however, suggests caution in pursuing this strategy. As long as firms remain committed to sorting on the basis of work propensities, interventions that increases the hours of short-hour employees may cause firms to make the prevailing work norm more stringent. A partial intervention may, in this sense, be worse than no policy intervention at all. Also, if work norms are most prevalent in high-wage professions, it is not clear that such subsidies are warranted on equity grounds.

Reasonable Accommodation

An alternative to finding the "right number" of maximum hours or to "subsidizing" the right mix of benefits might be to adopt the regulatory framework developed for handling gender and race discrimination in the workplace. In particular, it might make sense to mirror the Americans With Disabilities Act and require all employers to make a "reasonable accommodation" to employees wanting to work shorter hours for reasons of child or elder care. The great advantage of this framework is also its great disadvantage: The key concept "reasonable accommodation" is not explicitly defined. The ambiguity of the term allows employers and employees a great deal of latitude in responding to the legislative mandate and allows for the development of rich case law to guide employer decisions. This same ambiguity can, however, lead to a law that is either ineffective or excessively restrictive.

Flexibility in the notion of "reasonable accommodation" is important because the effectiveness of various actions is likely to depend on the specifics of the employment practice in question. To see this, consider the case of promotion decisions in academic departments of research universities. In these departments, each faculty member is affected by the reputation of the department and therefore by the research activities of his or her colleagues. Since research productivity is often hard to directly assess, academic departments may come to rely on indicators. One plausible indicator is the number of publications an assistant professor has in top-ranked journals. If published articles are an increasing function of work time, a "publications" norm will have many of the same consequences as norms that are specified in terms of work hours.

Accepting for the moment this sketch of the workings of academic departments, what would constitute a "reasonable accommodation" for family and elder care? One low-cost accommodation might be to limit the number of articles that could be considered in the promotion decision. Such a restriction, if generally applied, would shift emphasis from quantity to quality and therefore possibly reduce the distortions in work hours created by competition for promotion to tenured professor. On the other hand, if members of the department and outside referees knew, even in rough form, the full vitae of the candidate, restricting the number of papers considered may be entirely ineffective in breaking down a rat race in publications.

In Canada, there has recently been some discussion of the use of antidiscrimination laws to regulate work hours. Interestingly, this discussion has involved the legal profession. In 1994 a task force of the Canadian Bar Association released a report on gender equality in the legal profession. The report concluded that the legal profession regularly discriminates against

Table 6.11   Variable Definitions

Variable	Definition
Earnings 1983	Gross income from legal job (eight categories)
Log of firm size	Natural log of firm size (this variable was constructed by setting firm size equal to the midpoint of the size category; respondents in the top size category were assigned the expected value of firm size in this category; the expected firm size was calculated under the assumption that the size of firms followed a log-normal distribution)
Usual hours	Number of hours worked per month
Male	Gender of respondent equal to 1 if male
Age	Age of respondent
Tenure of 4–9 years	Dummy variable equal to 1 if respondent worked at the firm 4–9 years
Tenure of 10+ years	Dummy variable equal to 1 if respondent worked at the firm 10 years or more
Very prestigious law school	Dummy variable equal to 1 if respondent viewed his/her law school as "very prestigious."
Somewhat prestigious law school	Dummy variable equal to 1 if respondent viewed his/her law school as "somewhat prestigious"
Law review	Dummy variable equal to 1 if respondent was on a law review in law school
Law school class top quartile	Dummy variable equal to 1 if respondent was in the top quartile of his/her law school class
Law school class second quartile	Dummy variable equal to 1 if respondent was in the second quartile of his/her law school class
Legal center	Dummy variable equal to 1 if respondent lived in a city that is a legal center (New York, Washington, Boston, Chicago, Los Angeles, or San Francisco)
Population > 1 million	Dummy variable equal to 1 if respondent lived in a city with more than 1 million people
Population 250,000 to 1 million	Dummy variable equal to 1 if respondent lived in a city with more than 250,000 and less than 1 million people
Log of 1989 income	Gross income from legal job in 1989 (in 2–7th earnings categories, respondent was assigned an income equal to the log of the midpoint of the category: in the top and bottom categories, respondents were assigned the expected value of earnings under the assumption that earnings followed a log-normal distribution)
Log of 1989 firm size	Log of firm size in 1989 (see log of firm size above)
Partner in 1989	Dummy variable equal to 1 if respondent became a partner in a law firm in 1989

Table 6.11 *Continued*

Variable	Definition
Promoted to partner in 1984 firm	Dummy variable equal to 1 if respondent became a partner at the same firm that employed him/her in 1989
Additional variables	
Legal practices and tasks	Vector of fifteen dummy variables indicating the proportion of time that respondent spends on different areas of law (for example, antitrust, taxation, torts and insurance) and a vector of eleven dummy variables indicating the proportion of time spent on various legal tasks (for example, client contact, negotiations, research/memo writing, depositions)
Satisfaction with practice and tasks	Vector of four dummy variables indicating whether the respondent found his/her mix of legal practices and tasks "attractive" or "neutral"; the omitted category is "unattractive"
Pre–law school preparation	Vector of variables indicating the prestige of respondent's undergraduate college; whether or not the respondent was regularly on the dean's list; and the respondent's LSAT score

women. One of the report's most controversial suggestions was the idea that firms "set realistic targets of billable hours for women with child rearing responsibilities pursuant to their legal duty to accommodate."

The same year, a similar approach was suggested in a debate on the rules of professional conduct in the Law Society of Upper Canada. The society circulated Rule 28, which declared that engaging in various sorts of discrimination constituted misconduct. The definition of discrimination was quite broad and included actions whose effects were both inadvertent and unintended. One discriminatory practice listed in the rule was "requiring billable hours or workload expectations which effectively exclude those who have child care responsibilities and adversely impacting such persons on the basis of family status or sex."

Neither of these proposals was adopted by the respective bar associations in their original form.[28] The debate about these proposals, however, highlights a feature of our view of work norms that is typically absent in economic analysis: The sociology of professions can fundamentally alter the operation of professional labor markets. As we have stated, rat race equilibria persist because of the inability of markets to effectively coordinate innovations in the human resource policies of firms. Professional associations might in this case improve labor market efficiency by persuading a block of employers to simultaneously relax work norms. The ability of professional associations to undertake this task depends, of course, on the actions taken by influential and powerful members. In the case of law firms, partners in large firms have considerable influence over the activities of bar associations, but the work norms we have analyzed suggest that access to these influential positions are limited to those willing to tolerate excessive work hours early in their careers. This selection process may give leadership positions to those individuals who are personally least well equipped to understand and react to the shifting demographics of the legal profession. This selection pressure may have important consequences for the ability of firms and professions to adjust work norms in the face of continued change in the demographics of the work force.

CONCLUSION

This paper reports the results of a series of theoretical and empirical investigations into the origins and significance of work norms in professional labor markets. Throughout this research we have focused on law firms and the job market for lawyers. Idiosyncratic features of the partnership system in law firms make them a convenient vehicle for the study of work norms. These same idiosyncrasies, however, require that we proceed cautiously in generalizing our findings to other professional settings.

Our theoretical analysis suggests that rat race equilibria need not be limited to law firms or the legal profession. Indeed, we would expect stringent work norms in any co-equal grouping of professionals where (1) the members of the group benefit from the productive activity of other group members, (2) the output of the group can be significantly influenced by the work effort of individual members, and (3) the productive contributions of individuals are hard to observe directly. Casual empiricism suggests that these conditions are often met in elite business consultancies, academic departments, and product development teams.[29] Are the long hours observed in these settings the result of stringent work norms of the sort we describe in law firms? The answer to this question may tell us much about the interplay of gender and family issues in the professions.

NOTES

1. Differences in the work patterns of the spouses of the new cohorts of men that we observe in the cross section are unlikely to be the result of life-cycle differences in the number of children in the household. A linear probability model that regresses full-time status for spouse against an attorney's age, and a full set of dummy variables for the number of children, still finds that men with six years or fewer in the profession are

9.5 percentage points more likely to be married to a women working full time (with a t-statistic of 2.52).

2. There are a number of reasons why professional firms would adopt sharing rules, including the difficulty in monitoring the contributions of team members, the difficulty of writing complete ex ante contracts, risk sharing, and status concerns. For a discussion of these issues see Rebitzer and Taylor (1995b), Lang and Gordon (forthcoming), and Frank (1985).

3. The idea that adverse selection in work hours can lead to stringent work norms first appeared in a paper entitled "The Economics of Caste and of the Rat Race and Other Woeful Tales" (Akerlof 1976). Akerlof made his case for the existence of rat race equilibria in a self-consciously unrealistic numerical example. We develop Akerlof's argument in the context of a model of professional partnerships.

4. We provide a sketch of the model in the remainder of this section. Some readers may wish to proceed to the next section. Readers who would like to see *more* technical detail are referred to Landers, Rebitzer, and Taylor (1996).

5. The device of having partners "sell" the firm to incoming associates is a convenient means for describing the incentives that current partners have to preserve the future value of the partnership. In many law firms incoming partners do directly purchase an equity stake in the enterprise. However, this purchase need not take the form of an exchange of equity for cash. Purchases might also take the form of upward-sloping wage profiles.

6. Rebitzer and Taylor (1996) describe how complementarities among partners together with client-specific knowledge can produce the "up-or-out" partnership system that characterizes virtually every large law firm. For the analysis presented below, it does not matter whether the associates who are not promoted stay with the firm or leave.

7. This equilibrium corresponds to the separating equilibrium described by Rothschild and Stiglitz (1976) in an insurance market, and is derived explicitly for our case in Landers, Rebitzer, and Taylor (1996).

8. The model presented in Landers, Rebitzer, and Taylor (1996) describes a rat race equilibrium in which all the employment rents associated with partnership are absorbed in the sales price of the partnership. In this setup, there are no differences in welfare between short- and long-hour workers that are attributable to the rat race.

9. Rebitzer and Taylor (1995a) present a model in which efficiency wage incentives in the primary labor market lead to persistent ex ante employment rents. In this setup, we demonstrate that adverse selection reduces the ex ante welfare of short-hour employees relative to long-hour employees.

10. The results discussed in this section are taken from Landers, Rebitzer, and Taylor (1996).

11. Some law firms hire a small number of so-called permanent associates. Typically these attorneys have important technical skills but lack the full complement of skills required to succeed as partners.

12. For an analysis of the relationship between firm size and the "up-or-out" partnership system, see Rebitzer and Taylor (1996).

13. The surveys also included a table describing what a 5 percent change in work hours would mean for associates working different hours. For example, an associate working two hundred hours per month would learn from the table that a 5 percent change in hours would imply an increase or decrease of one eight-hour day per month or twelve eight-hour days per year.

14. The importance of hours as an indicator was measured by the same 5-point scale described in the previous paragraph. Hours were classified as an important indicator whenever the respondent indicated that they were *very important* (4) or *of the utmost importance* (5).

15. Kahn and Lang (1991) find that the elasticity of actual hours with respect to wages is nearly identical to the elasticity of desired hours with respect to the wage.

16. We present more evidence on the importance of work hours in promotion decisions in Landers, Rebitzer, and Taylor (1996).

17. The public-sector attorneys we surveyed made, on average, a little less than half the mean salary of our associates from the big law firms. While this salary differential is no doubt important for attracting and retaining attorneys, it should not alter the expected effect of fixed employment costs. Regardless of salary levels, cost-minimizing employers who have fixed employment costs should expect more hours from employees than employees should want to deliver at their average wage.

18. The public-sector attorneys reported working an average of forty-three hours in the week prior to the survey. This suggests that the average public attorney worked seven fewer hours per week than the average associate in a big firm. This result is consistent with the impression conveyed by the public-sector attorneys we interviewed that they work fewer hours than their counterparts in large law firms. We believe, however, that these figures *understate* the magnitude of the hours differentials between associates and public-sector attorneys. First, the public-sector attorneys we surveyed were not a random sample of the agency. Management restricted our survey to attorneys in particular groups, which may have been more likely to exhibit longer work hours. Second, both management and individual attorneys we interviewed were sensitive to the perception that public employees do not work as hard as their private-sector counterparts. This may have led some respondents to inflate their estimates of weekly hours worked. Finally, many of the attorneys we interviewed stated that although their pay was considerably lower, they were able to do work that was more responsible, more diverse, and more intrinsically valuable than their counterparts in big commercial firms. This suggests that if we could control for

the type of legal practice and tasks across public and private employers, the hours differential would be larger than that we observed.

19. We are grateful to Claudia Goldin for raising this issue in a personal communication.

20. Lawyers in this study were surveyed in 1984. For a complete description of the data, see American Bar Association (1990).

21. Farrell and Scotchmer (1988) demonstrate that in settings where work propensities are directly observable, equilibrium will be characterized by homogeneous firms—with some specializing in long hours and others in short hours.

22. It is important to note, however, that the converse is *not* true. A finding that hours were more of a burden in large firms than small firms would not be grounds for rejecting conventional sorting. If wages were identical across all firms, fully rational actors in a frictionless labor market would have the same marginal disutility of hours in all firms—even if associates were working more hours in large firms. If large firms pay higher wages than small firms, however, we might observe that associates in these firms work longer hours and that the marginal disutility of hours would, in equilibrium, be higher in large firms.

23. The ABA survey collected salary data in eight categories: less than $15,000, $15,000–24,999, $25,000–39,999, $40,000–54,999, $55,000–74,999, $75,000–99,999, $100,000–199,999, and $200,000 or more. To accommodate this data, we estimated tables 6.9 and 6.10 as ordered probits with known cutoffs. In this framework, the model parameters have the same interpretation as in a conventional earnings regression. The description of the likelihood function is presented in Data Appendix II of Rebitzer and Taylor (1995b). The restrictions implied in the log-linear firm-size variable could not be rejected at conventional significance level. We obtained very similar results if we substituted firm-size dummies for the log of firm size.

24. A recent *Wall Street Journal* report indicates that the probability an associate hired in the classes of 1981, 1982, or 1983 would have made partner by 1992 was 0.10 at the thirty largest New York firms. This is likely to be a lower bound promotion probability. First, promotion rates in 1992 were depressed by the cyclical downturn in the legal services industry (Woo 1992). Second, these thirty New York firms have the reputation of being among the most difficult firms to make partner in the whole country.

25. If the marginal returns to similar effort were different, one of these firms is either offering an insufficient work incentive or an excessively generous work incentive.

26. Rebitzer and Taylor (1995b) demonstrate that this conclusion holds under very general assumptions. Specifically, Rebitzer and Taylor show that in a promotion tournament where the expected utility of employment is the same across firms, then the salaries of similarly skilled associates

should be the same across firms. Higher associate salaries in large firms are, in this context, indicators of ex ante employment rents in large firms.

27. We use the example of interns to illustrate the unexpected ramifications of maximum-hours laws. We do not, however, claim that the long hours worked by residents and interns represent a rat race equilibrium.

28. In each case, the bar associations affirmed their opposition to discrimination in the profession but backed away from extending the notion of discriminatory practices to include long work hours.

29. For discussion of a case study of work norms in a large business consultancy see Landers, Rebitzer, and Taylor (forthcoming). A notable difference between the consulting firm we studied and law firms was the importance of travel. Travel is generally more important in the career of a business traveler than a lawyer. Long trips out of town are, if anything, more disruptive of family life than long and irregular hours. If consulting firms use willingness to travel as an indicator of underlying work propensities, then the travel component of jobs may be excessive in the same sense that work hours can be excessive.

Commentary on Chapter 6

Michael Waldman

During the past few decades, there has been a significant increase both in the number of two-income households and in the representation of women in professional labor markets. Both changes suggest that workers in professional labor markets should now have a stronger desire for shorter work hours. The puzzle that Landers, Rebitzer, and Taylor address is that work hours in these markets have in fact not decreased; rather, if there has been any change, it is toward increased work hours.

The authors begin their paper by constructing a theoretical model that explains long work hours in professional labor markets. Their argument is that there is adverse selection concerning work hours. In particular, in their model the population of potential workers consists of some workers with a low disutility for work hours and some workers with a high disutility. Because firms prefer to employ workers with a low disutility, the firms set overly long work hours for entry-level workers in order to discourage high disutility workers from applying for employment.

After developing the theory described above, the authors proceed to provide evidence for the theory and then discuss some of the alternative explanations for why there are long work hours in professional labor markets. They end with a discussion of public policy implications, which I found particularly interesting. The authors argue that, if their theory is correct, a number of policies that have been put forth to address the long hours issue may be counterproductive. In particular, policies designed to make it easier for high disutility workers to work long hours may, in fact, reduce welfare. The reason is that if firms continue to try to discourage high disutility workers from applying for employment, such a policy could actually cause firms to increase the work hours norm.

My reaction to the paper is that it identifies an interesting puzzle and provides and develops a plausible explanation. That is, for reasons discussed by the authors, it is quite clear that traditional labor market theory is an inadequate explanation for long work hours in professional labor markets. Further, adverse selection, which is a fundamental idea in the application of information economics to labor markets, does provide a plausible explanation for the puzzle. My only criticism is that the authors do not rule out at least one other plausible explanation that has significantly different public policy implications.

Another fundamental idea in the application of information economics to labor markets is that of labor market tournaments. In a labor market tournament, the firm offers prizes to successful workers, and each worker exerts great effort in an attempt to win one of the prizes. Not surprisingly, the theory finds that, as the size of the prizes increases, workers will increase their levels of effort in an attempt to win the tournament.

The theory of labor market tournaments provides a potential alternative explanation for long hours in professional labor markets. The logic here is simple. One way that workers can exert effort in a labor market tournament is by working long hours. Hence, a potential alternative explanation for the puzzle considered by Landers, Rebitzer, and Taylor is that professional labor markets are characterized by labor market tournaments, and the prizes in these tournaments are sufficiently large that the workers respond by working very long hours.

In fact, in their discussion of empirical evidence concerning professional labor markets, the authors discuss some evidence that is at least as consistent with labor market tournaments as it is with adverse selection. For example, the authors find that work hours are longer in large law firms than in small law firms. Since the average salary of partners is also larger in large firms than in small firms, this piece of evidence is consistent with the theory of labor market tournaments.

Another interesting piece of evidence is the authors' finding that in large law firms number of hours worked is an important factor in the promotion decision. If these firms are characterized by labor market tournaments, and number of hours worked is one of the factors determining who wins the prizes, then, as discussed earlier, overly long work hours is a likely outcome. Hence, the finding that number of hours worked matters in the promotion decision is perfectly consistent with long hours being the result of labor market tournaments.

One interesting aspect of this alternative explanation for long work hours in professional labor markets concerns public policy implications. As discussed earlier, the adverse selection explanation suggests that policies that make it easier for high disutility workers to work long hours may in fact be counterproductive. The reason put forth was that, according to adverse selection, the imposition of such a policy could easily result in firms increasing the required number of work hours for entry-level workers.

In contrast, in terms of this type of policy, the labor market tournament explanation for long work hours in professional labor markets has significantly different implications. In the labor market tournament explanation, long work hours are the result of workers competing for prizes, and not the result of a work hours norm imposed by the firm to discourage high disutility workers from applying. Given this, suppose that professional labor markets were characterized by labor market tournaments and that a policy that makes it easier for high disutility workers to work long hours was imposed. The main result would be a leveling of the playing field. That is, rather than work hours increasing for everyone in a significant fashion, the result would be a capability for all workers to compete for the important prizes on an equal footing. In other words, if the driving force for long work hours is labor market tournaments, then these policies would likely work in a fashion that closely matches their intended effect.

Overall, the authors have identified an interesting issue, and their analysis clearly advances our understanding of how professional labor markets operate. I hope, however, that in future work the authors will expand their focus and include in their investigation the labor market tournament explanation for the long work hours phenomenon.

Commentary on Chapter 6

Janice Fanning Madden

In their paper, Landers, Rebitzer, and Taylor argue that the work hours of lawyers in large firms are inefficiently high and that these excess work requirements reduce employment opportunities for women lawyers. They argue that the long work hours are not based on the production needs of the law firm, but are used to protect law partnerships from an adverse selection of lawyers who will not perform their share of work when they become partners. Because excess work hours in this sense represent a market failure, the authors consider various policy interventions that would reduce the adverse selection effects for law firms that allow associates to work fewer hours.

The model of the rat race is interesting and provocative. When the assumptions are met, it follows that a market failure occurs for which an appropriate policy intervention (one that allows firms to reduce the hours of workers without risking an adverse selection that would occur if a firm, acting alone, reduced work hours) would increase the welfare of firms and workers, and in all likelihood create greater welfare gains for women than for men. So, are the assumptions of the model applicable in real labor markets? The authors propose that the model applies to large law firms. I am not fully convinced that is the case. It appears to me that academe is, in fact, a more likely venue for the rat race. I ask, then, two questions of this paper: Does the evidence clearly show that protection from an adverse selection of future partners accounts for the longer work hours in large law firms? Are other labor markets more appropriate for the model? If there are other relevant labor markets, then the case for policy intervention remains, but the target shifts.

To establish that adverse selection, and not productivity, accounts for the long hours worked by associates in large law firms, it is necessary to present empirical evidence that is consistent with the selection explanation but not the productivity explanation. The empirical evidence presented by the authors includes the following: Associates would prefer a shorter work week to a higher salary, and long hours are at least an indirect, and probably a direct, factor considered in the promotion of associates to partnership.

Landers, Rebitzer, and Taylor attempt to dismiss one alternate explanation—substantial fixed costs motivate firms to use labor more intensely to increase profits—by considering the case of training costs. While their arguments and evidence that training costs cannot account for longer hours are convincing, they have failed to consider a more important fixed cost: office rental. The authors argue that training costs cannot explain why lawyers in public agencies work substantially fewer hours and are far more willing to work longer hours for higher wages than lawyers in large private firms. While training costs are arguably similar for lawyers in public and private practice, other types of fixed costs are not. Office space costs, in particular, differ from training costs because office space plays a different role in the production decisions of lawyers in public versus private practice. Public agencies do not market their services to their clients and, therefore, do not use expensive office space to show competence or importance. Private firms do. The response to office costs would, therefore, differ for public agencies and private firms. The differences in the leisure-income trade-off documented by the authors for public and private lawyers cannot dismiss the role of office rental costs in accounting for longer hours in private firms. Furthermore, larger private law firms are located more centrally within metropolitan areas than smaller firms and the larger the law firm, the more likely it is to be in a more populous metropolitan area. Both of these spatial characteristics are highly correlated with the square foot price of office space. New York City law firms may have the longest hours because they are in the highest cost office rental market. In order to minimize office rental costs, lawyers in large private firms would work longer than lawyers in smaller firms or those in private practice. In this case, the longer hours of lawyers in larger firms is based on productivity, not selectivity.

Another way that longer hours may be productive (or profit-maximizing for partners) and not selective arises in the case of specialization. It is possible that longer work hours are more productive when teams (law firms) are larger. As team size increases, workers become more specialized. The marginal product of additional hours per lawyer may not decrease as quickly as in the case of smaller teams. Larger teams have greater productivity because they allow greater specialization relative to the client's needs. Furthermore, because specialization reduces the substitutability between lawyers, there are greater efficiency losses when one team member substitutes for another. The gains to specialization increase with team size and specialization increases with work hours. Specialization, then, leads to longer hours in larger firms. The greater productivity from specialization provides the means to compensate lawyers for their dissatisfaction with longer hours. (The trade-off between hours and wages cannot be evaluated at the marginal work hour, however, but must be measured with respect to discrete packages of compensation and hours.)

The selectivity explanation also fails if it is possible to adjust earnings to productivity in the second period. There is reason to question the authors' assertion that "partners in the firm [are] not . . . able to fully adjust sharing rules in response to differences in the contributions made by each professional" or that large firms are less able to make these adjustments than small firms. There are numerous ways that law firms can adjust pay in the second period (that is, during the partnership) to create incentives. The share of profits that accrue to each partner can be adjusted each year, reflecting the partner's value to the firm in terms of both billable hours and business generated. The latter component is of central importance to firms (see table 6.5) and is not necessarily associated with long hours or with traits observed during service as an associate. Hours billed is easily and directly observed for partners. There is no need to rely on information from when a partner was an associate to select or to compensate partners. In large firms, compensation decisions are usually made annually by an executive committee of the firm that is elected by the membership. Because the executive committee is concerned with maximizing profits, and in very large firms has looser social connections with other partners, it is easier to tie returns to contributions in larger firms than in smaller firms. Longer hours in larger firms, in this case, are productivity-based because there is simply no reason to use such criteria to protect against adverse selection of associates into partnership.

Finally, there is a more credible reason than either optimal productivity or selection for partners to encourage longer hours from associates. The partnership redistributes from associates to partners. Associates are paid a flat wage regardless of hours. If associates bill more hours, profits increase, increasing the share going to partners. Associates take wages lower than their marginal product because they have less "power" in the sense that the team has value so their productivity with the team is greater than in sole practice and they have attached an expected value of becoming a partner. Furthermore, the amount of compensation redistributed is such that a "short-hour" associate cannot compensate the partnership for shorter hours by taking a lower salary. Consider the case of an associate billing 2,000 hours per year. If the time is billed at $150 per hour, the associate generates $300,000 for the firm. An associate who bills half that amount brings in $150,000. Because the associate is not paid $150,000, he or she does not have sufficient salary to compensate the partnership for shorter hours through a salary reduction.

While I am not convinced that the rat race model explains long hours as a screening device in law firms, the model is nonetheless an intriguing one. I believe it is more appropriate to academe. The reported work hours for faculty are similar to the long hours that Landers, Rebitzer, and Taylor cite for large law firms: 51.6 hours per week in research universities (50.1 in liberal arts colleges, 48.7 in doctoral universities, and 47.7 in comprehensive universities). While the distribution of work load across teaching and research changes with age, the total time does not, at least in research universities.[1]

The authors acknowledge that there are sharing issues for faculty in research universities because the reputation of the department and the university is shared by all. But what makes the case more convincing for academe is that there is much less ability to adjust salary (at least in periods of low inflation and slow salary growth) after tenure for faculty than is the case for lawyers. In addition, academic productivity is not as easily measured by objective measures such as annual hours billed or clients brought in. Academic productivity is assessed by other scholars in indirect ways (such as citations), often years after the work hours are exerted. The salaries of tenured faculty members cannot be reduced except in extreme and rare situations. There are no constraints on lawyers in this regard. Furthermore, colleagues must work more as the percentage of slackers, or "dead wood," in the department increases and administrative and teaching duties are shared by a smaller group.

The authors discuss maximum-hours laws, requirements that employers provide benefits that reduce the costs of long hours for workers, and a requirement that employers make "reasonable accommodations" to employees who prefer shorter work hours to care for family. This discussion is discouraging because it illustrates the difficulty of designing an appropriate policy intervention, even if long hours are clearly inefficient.

One encouraging possibility may be that the changing gender composition of the work force may render long hours a less-effective screen. Are long hours as effective in screening against adverse selection for women as for men? Surely, hours on the job during childbearing and childrearing years are less predictive of hours and effort invested in the job in middle age for women than for men. Firms (and universities) that use such screens will make worse decisions about women workers than those that create policies more compatible with the life work cycles of women.

NOTE

1. See Singell, Lillydahl, and Singell forthcoming.

Chapter 7

Early Career Supervisor Gender and the Labor Market Outcomes of Young Workers

Donna S. Rothstein

This study evaluates whether the gender match between supervisors and employees has an influence on employees' early career labor market attainments. Three simple theories are posited to help explain why supervisor gender might affect employees' labor market outcomes. These theories include employee preferences toward a certain supervisor gender, differential productivity effects of supervisors on their employees, and the role of supervisors in providing on-the-job training and promotion opportunities for their employees. From these theories, empirically testable implications regarding current wages, perceived likelihood of promotion, and wage profiles are obtained; they are tested using data from the National Longitudinal Survey of Youth. The empirical results suggest that for both male and female employees there is a negative impact on current wages associated with working for a female supervisor. Supervisor gender is found to have no effect on individuals' perceived likelihood of promotion and minimal positive effects on employee wage growth. Taken together, the empirical results do not provide strong, clear-cut support for any of the three theories. In addition, it cannot be ruled out that supervisor gender is serving as a proxy for the "type" of job held.

Most employed individuals, particularly early in their careers, have a supervisor who may take on a number of different roles. These roles may include monitoring their work, providing them with on-the-job training and promotion opportunities, and preparing them for the next stage in their careers. Given all of these possible roles for supervisors, it seems that who supervises whom might be important; this could especially be true early in individuals' careers, when supervisors may have the biggest impact on their future labor market experiences.

This study focuses on a particular characteristic of supervisors—their gender—and asks what effect the gender match between supervisors and employees has on male and female employees' early career labor market attainments. Three simple theories are posited to help explain why supervisor gender might affect employees' labor market outcomes; the expected empirical impacts of different supervisor and employee matches are derived under each model. These theories include employee preferences toward a certain supervisor gender, differential productivity effects of supervisors on their employees, and the role of supervisors in providing on-the-job training and promotion opportunities for their employees. From these theories, empirically testable implications regarding current wages, perceived likelihood of promotion, and wage profiles are obtained. They are tested using a panel of data from the National Longitudinal Survey of Youth (NLSY); the NLSY contains extensive data on labor market experiences of young workers, including information on their early career supervisor.

The outline of this paper is as follows: The first section contains a review of the past research on the influence of supervisors and also establishes some "facts," using Census of Population data, regarding who supervises whom. The second section outlines three theories that describe why supervisor gender might have an impact on employees' labor market experiences. (Appendix 7.1 gives a more detailed development of the theories.) The third and fourth sections discuss the data used in the analysis and show the empirical results. The final section concludes the paper.

REVIEW OF PAST RESEARCH

In the economics literature, the presence of a supervisor has generally been analyzed in the context of a monitoring framework (for example, Groshen and Krueger 1990; Leonard 1987). In this type of literature the influence of "intensity of supervision" on employees' wages is often explored, although the role of gender of supervisor is not addressed.[1] However, in other disciplines, such as personnel and human resources, psychology, and sociology, a number of studies analyze employee preferences toward gender of supervisor (many of them are case studies) as well as the influence of supervisor gender on employee performance evaluations. For example, Ferber, Huber, and Spitze (1979) and Cannings and Montmarquette (1991) find that male employees tend to have a preference toward working for a male supervisor, whereas Bretz, Milkovich, and Read (1990), in a review of the literature on supervisor and employee evaluations, do not find a clear-cut consensus regarding whether supervisor and employee gender matches influence ratings.

Two studies have looked at the influence of supervisor gender on employee earnings. The first of these studies appears in a series of papers—Ferber and Spaeth (1984); Ferber, Green, and Spaeth (1986); and Ferber and Green (1991). They utilize a sample of individuals from Illinois collected (by the authors) in 1982. In the 1991 paper the data set is augmented through collection of data on the individuals' supervisors (and their supervisors' supervisors, and so on). The major purpose of these papers is to look at the role of different work characteristics in explaining the earnings gap between men and women, with one of these work characteristics being gender of supervisor. Their early sample (1986) indicates that most men work for male supervisors, while women are fairly evenly divided between working for male and female supervisors (about 56 percent work for male supervisors). In the augmented sample (Ferber and Green 1991), which includes a number of men and women in higher management positions, the pattern remains the same for men, although the percentage of women with male supervisors is higher at nearly 64 percent.

In Ferber and Green (1991), the results (excluding individuals in the topmost management positions) indicate that working for a male supervisor has a large, positive, and statistically significant effect on annual earnings for female employees. For male employees the effect is smaller, although positive and marginally significant. Gender of supervisor does not appear to matter for those in top management positions. The authors suggest that the finding of a supervisor gender effect for women may be due to the variable proxying for the sex-type of the job, although they do control for percentage female in the occupation. This implies that the variable might be picking up the results of a "crowding effect" (Bergmann 1986). In other words, the supply of women to certain occupations (in what becomes the "female-dominated" sector) is larger than it would be otherwise owing to barriers to entry into other occupations (in the "male-dominated" sector); this large supply drives down wages in the female-dominated sector relative to what could be earned in the other sector.

The second study that examines the effect of supervisor gender is by Ragan and Tremblay (1988). The major purpose of their paper is to test for the existence of employee discrimination by race and gender; this includes discrimination due to the racial and gender composition of coworkers, as well as supervisor race and gender. The data utilized in their analysis are from the National Longitudinal Survey of Youth (NLSY) 1980 interview. The authors estimate hourly earnings equations for full-time workers aged 15–23. The results suggest that working for a female supervisor has a negative, statistically significant effect on wages for white women, but no effect for men or black or Hispanic women. However, being employed in a workplace with a high percentage of female coworkers appears to have a negative impact on wages for both genders.

The direction of the impact of supervisor gender in the Ragan and Tremblay (1988) study, when statistically significant, appears to be similar to that in Ferber and Green (1991). That is, working for a female supervisor has a negative effect on wages. And, in both studies, the authors do not find support for the hypothesis that employee discrimination is causing the supervisor gender effect.[2] However, the two studies do not resolve the question of why supervisor gender appears to have an effect on employee wages.[3] In the paper presented here, a number of competing explanations and their testable implications are developed to try to explain why the gender match between supervisors and employees might influence employees' labor market outcomes. These include employee discrimination (as in the other two papers), possible productivity effects of supervisors on their employees, and the training and promotion opportunities that supervisors may provide for their employees.

Before moving to the theoretical section, in which three theories of supervisor gender effects are presented, a glance at some aggregate statistics on the gender composition of supervisors and employees from the 1980 Census of Population might provide some insights into the issue being addressed in this study.[4] Although these data do not match up individuals with their supervisors, they do give a general picture of whether the gender composition of supervisors in certain occupation groups differs from the gender composition of employees. They also give a rough picture of who supervises whom.

The presence of sex-segregated occupations is evident in table 7.1. Perhaps even more interesting is that in some of the more heavily female-dominated occupations depicted (such as computer equipment operators and financial records processing) the proportion of supervisors who are female is much lower than the proportion of employees who are female.[5] In fact, none of the occupations in table 7.1 has a higher percentage of female supervisors than employees. (This could occur for a number of reasons, including that, on average, men tend to have spent relatively more years in the labor market and thus would be expected to hold more supervisory positions.)

THEORETICAL FRAMEWORK

In this section, three simple theories of the possible influence of supervisor gender are outlined along with their labor market implications. (A more detailed development of the theories appears in the chapter appendix) The main goal is to see whether there are empirically testable implications that differentiate the theories. The theories propose three different avenues for the effect of supervisor gender on employees: (1) employee preferences—male employees, for example, prefer not to work for female supervisors; (2) productivity effects—all male employees who are matched with female supervisors become less productive; and (3) training effectiveness—when male employees are matched with female supervisors training is more costly. The theories provide implications involving patterns of gender matches between employees and their supervisors, supervisory wages, and employees' wages, wage growth, and promotion likelihoods. The NLSY data set contains information on employees and their matching supervisors' gender (but not their supervisors' wages) and thus allows the labor market implications relating to employees to be analyzed empirically.

Table 7.1   Percentage of Female Supervisors and Female Employees in Selected Occupations: 1980 Census of the Population

Occupation	Supervisors	Employees
Computer equipment operators	.30	.59
Financial records processing	.49	.88
Police and detectives	.03	.08
Food preparation and service	.57	.66
Cleaning and building service (excluding private household)	.28	.35
Farm workers	.17	.22
Motor vehicle operators	.06	.09

Source: Author's calculations from the U.S. Bureau of the Census, 1980 Census of Population, "Detailed Occupation and Years of School Completed by Age for the Civilian Labor Force by Sex, Race, and Spanish Origin: 1980" (Table 1), series PC80-S1-8.

THEORY 1: EMPLOYEE DISCRIMINATION

One reason found in the literature on supervision that relates to why the gender match between employees and supervisors might matter is employee preferences. For example, men might prefer not to work with female supervisors (Cannings and Montmarquette 1991; Ferber, Huber, and Spitze 1979). In order to examine the types of labor market implications that would arise in a situation like this, a simple model in which male employees discriminate against female supervisors is outlined below; the model is an extension of Becker's classic theory (1971) of employee discrimination.

To begin, competitive firms are assumed to hire male and female employees and supervisors to fill work groups of an equal size (one supervisor is matched with a number of employees). In the absence of discrimination, firms are assumed to view both male and female employees and supervisors as equally well qualified and productive. Now suppose, for example, that male employees do not like to work for female supervisors. They express this discriminatory "taste" by demanding a higher wage when working for a female supervisor (Becker 1971). As a consequence, all cost-minimizing firms will systematically match male employees with male supervisors. If the proportion of male supervisors relative to male employees in the labor force accommodates this matching situation, then no wage differential will arise. In other words, all employees will be paid the same wage, as will all supervisors, but there will be segregation in the form of male employees matched only with male supervisors.

On the other hand, if some male employees are matched with female supervisors, it suggests that female employees relative to male employees are in short supply, as are male supervisors relative to female supervisors. Otherwise, male employees would never be matched with female supervisors owing to the wage premium that those male employees demand. Before discussing what the wages for each gender supervisor and employee will be, a simple example of this occurrence might be useful. Assume the following: One employee is matched with one supervisor, the supply of male employees is fifty, the supply of male supervisors is forty-nine, the supply of female employees is one, and the supply of female supervisors is two. Here, given the matching scheme of pairing male employees with male supervisors, female employees *relative* to male employees are in short supply, as are male supervisors relative to female supervisors. In addition, as the example illustrates, if any male employees are matched with female supervisors, then there will be *no* female employees matched with male supervisors.

To continue, recall that male employees who work with a female supervisor require a higher wage. As a consequence, female employees are worth more to firms—the wage of the relatively scarce female employees will be bid up to the wage level of those male employees who work for a female supervisor. Male supervisors will be worth more to firms, too, since they are relatively scarce, thus causing their wage to be higher than that of female supervisors. As shown in appendix 7.1, the resulting supervisor and employee wages cause firms' costs to be equalized for each type of work group (male employees with a female supervisor, male employees with a male supervisor, and female employees with a female supervisor); no reallocation of workers would allow a less expensive work group to be obtained.

In summary, the model described above implies the following: (1) Male employees are expected to be supervised by male supervisors and (2) if there is a female supervising male employees, those male employees will receive a wage premium; (2) is a key testable implication. If (2) holds, then (3) all female employees will receive a wage equal to that of the male employees who work for a female supervisor, (4) female employees will not be supervised by male supervisors, and (5) all male supervisors will have a higher wage than all female supervisors.[6]

THEORY 2: PRODUCTIVITY

The gender match between employees and supervisors may affect employee productivity. Blau and Ferber (1992) discuss the prospect of male employees having lower productivity when working for a female supervisor (one could, perhaps, think of this as a morale issue). Alternatively, Tannen (1994) and Lang (1986) consider the possibility of differences in communication styles between "types" of individuals. A model in which male employees have lower productivity when working for female supervisors is sketched below.

Assume, as in the model above, that competitive firms hire (equally well-qualified/productive) male and female employees and supervisors to fill work groups of an equal size. Now suppose, for example, that working for a female supervisor decreases male employee productivity by a fixed amount. As a result, all competitive firms will systematically match male employees with male supervisors. If the labor force is such that any male employees are matched with female supervisors then, as in the model above, the following work groups will exist: male employees with a female supervisor, male employees with a male supervisor, and female employees with a female supervisor. Male employees who work with a female supervisor have lower productivity, which has implications for the wages of female employees. At the margin, female employees are worth relatively more to firms.[7] Thus, all female employees will receive a higher wage than *all* male employees (in the amount of the productivity differential). Male supervisors, who are also relatively scarce, will be worth more to firms, too; all male supervisors will receive a higher wage than all female supervisors. The resulting supervisor and employee wages will be such that the cost (for a given level of output) to the competitive firms for each type of work group will be equal.

To summarize, the model described above implies that (1) male employees are expected to be supervised by male supervisors. However, in the extreme case where some male employees are supervised by females, the following occur: (2) All female employees will receive a higher wage than all male employees, (3) female employees will not be supervised by male supervisors, and (4) all male supervisors will receive a higher wage than all female supervisors. What should be noted at this point is that one major implication that is in the discrimination effects model does not occur here. Here, male employees do not receive a different wage when working with a female supervisor; this can be tested using the NLSY data set.

THEORY 3: HUMAN CAPITAL

A third reason why the gender match between supervisors and employees may be important involves on-the-job training that supervisors provide to their employees. If certain gender matches imply relatively more training opportunities for those employees, it can have considerable longer-run effects on employees' promotion opportunities and wage growth (see, for example, literature on workplace mentoring by Hunt and Michael 1983, and Johnson and Scandura 1994). A simple model in which male employees' training costs are higher with female supervisors is outlined below.

As in the two models above, assume that competitive firms hire male and female employees and supervisors to fill work groups of an equal size. Now suppose that within a job there are two possible tracks for employees: the "training track," or fast track, and the "no-training track." (Employees can be either high cost or low cost to train; low-training-cost employees are placed on the training track and high-training-cost employees are placed on the no-training track.) As the names of the tracks indicate, what happens to employees on each track with respect to training is not the same. On the training track, employees are trained in period 1 by their supervisor (causing decreased employee productivity during training). In period 2, the employees' training pays off in higher productivity, and training track employees are also rewarded with a promotion.[8] The training track employees' wages are assumed to be lower in period 1 (owing to the productivity decrease during training) and higher in period 2 (when the benefits from training are reaped). On the no-training track, however, employees receive no training and their productivity is assumed to be constant over time; employees' wages for this track are assumed to be constant over time, equal to the value of what the employee produces.[9]

As long as employees' training costs are not affected by supervisor type, there is no systematic matching of employees and supervisors by gender, for either track. Now suppose that if a male employee on the training track is matched with a female supervisor his training cost is increased by a certain fixed amount. This has implications for who is matched with whom on the training track; male employees on the training track will be systematically matched with male supervisors, owing to the lower training cost. As will be discussed below, this causes male employees matched with male supervisors, on average, to have different wages and promotion probabilities than male employees matched with female supervisors.

In summary, the labor market implications of the model are as follows: (1) Employees on the training track are expected to have steeper wage profiles than those on the no-training track (this involves a *lower* wage than otherwise in period 1 and a *higher* wage than otherwise in period 2); (2) individuals on the training track are expected to receive a promotion following the period of on-the-job training; and (3) male employees on the training track are expected to be systematically matched with male supervisors.[10] Putting (1) through (3) together, male employees who work with male supervisors are expected, on average (because they are more likely to be on the training track), to have higher wage growth, as well as higher promotion probabilities than male employees with female supervisors. In addition, if the model were extended so that female employees' training costs were also affected by the gender of their supervisor, then additional systematic matching of employee and supervisor gender on the training track would occur with the types of implications listed above.

TESTABLE IMPLICATIONS OF THE THREE THEORIES

Table 7.2 outlines some of the major implications of the three theories sketched above that are testable with the NLSY data set. These include employee wage differentials (each period), wage growth, and promotion

Table 7.2 **Some Implications of the Three Models Assuming That Same-Gender Matches Are "More Productive"**

	Discrimination	Productivity	Human Capital
Example 1: Female supervisor and male employee			
Employee wage in period 1	positive	no effect	positive
Employee wage in period 2	no prediction	no prediction	negative
Employee wage growth	no prediction	no prediction	negative
Promotion probability	no prediction	no prediction	negative
Example 2: Female supervisor and female employee			
Employee wage in period 1	negative	no effect	negative
Employee wage in period 2	no prediction	no prediction	positive
Employee wage growth	no prediction	no prediction	positive
Promotion probability	no prediction	no prediction	positive

Note: If opposite-gender matches are assumed to be "more productive," then the signs in the table are reversed.

probabilities. Two separate examples are shown in table 7.2. First, the example used throughout this section, involving a male employee matched with a female supervisor, is depicted; all effects are relative to that of a male employee matched with a male supervisor. In this example, a male employee prefers not to work for a female supervisor (and thus receives a wage premium) (theory 1); a male employee has lower productivity with a female supervisor than otherwise (theory 2); and, finally, a male employee is *less* likely to be on the training track if he is matched with a female supervisor (theory 3). Thus, for male employees who work with female supervisors, both the discrimination and human capital models predict a higher wage in period 1, but only the human capital model predicts a lower wage in period 2, as well as lower wage growth and a lower promotion probability.

An (independent) example involving a female employee matched with a female supervisor is also shown in table 7.2; all effects are relative to the match of a female employee and a male supervisor. In this example, a female employee is assumed to prefer to work for a female supervisor (theory 1); a female employee has relatively higher productivity with a female supervisor than otherwise (theory 2); and, finally, a female employee is *more* likely to be on the training track if she is matched with a female supervisor (theory 3). That is, female employees who work with female supervisors earn a lower wage in period 1 according to the discrimination and human capital models, but the human capital model also predicts a higher wage in period 2, higher wage growth, and a higher promotion probability.

The two examples shown in table 7.2 assume that own-gender matches (that is, male employees with male supervisors and female employees with female supervisors) are preferable. However, clearly this need not be so, and if the reverse assumption were made, the signs in table 7.2 would simply be reversed. Note that although the discrimination and human capital models predict a wage effect in period 1 associated with supervisor gender, only the human capital model suggests that there will be a systematic supervisor gender effect on employee wages in period 2, wage growth, and promotion probabilities.

DATA AND VARIABLES

The theories described in the previous section generate predictions regarding employees' current (period 1) wages, promotion probabilities, and wage profiles. In this section, the data and variables used to test the competing predictions empirically are discussed.

The main data source used for this study is the National Longitudinal Survey of Youth (NLSY). In 1979, the base year, 12,686 individuals between ages 14 and 22 were surveyed; follow-ups of these individuals are available through 1994. Of the 12,686 individuals in the NLSY, 6,111 constitute a representative cross-sectional sample; 1,280 are part of a military subsample; and 5,295 are from a supplementary subsample of Hispanic, black, and economically disadvantaged individuals. In order to account for this sampling scheme, the empirical analyses in this study will condition upon "presence" in a particular supplementary subsample—that is, dummy variables that indicate whether the individual is a member of a particular subsample will be used in the estimations.

The NLSY data set is especially suited for a study like this; it contains extensive longitudinal information on individuals' work experiences and personal backgrounds. In addition, in both the 1980 and 1982 interviews questions regarding gender of supervisor were asked. However, owing to the young age of the individuals, the 1982 information regarding supervisor gender (when the individuals are aged 17–25) has been focused upon here. Information on individuals' work experiences through the 1984 interview is used to construct wage profiles.[11]

The subsample of individuals from the NLSY used for the empirical analyses in this paper consists of 1,980 women and 2,319 men who are employed at least thirty hours per week, have fewer than three years of tenure with their employer, have hourly wages between $2 and $50, are not in the military, are not in school full time, and are not self-employed or working without pay at the current/most recent job at the 1982 interview.[12]

Variable definitions are presented in table 7.3; the variables are time-varying (1982–1984) unless indicated in the definition. The 1982 hourly wage will be used to test the predictions of the three theories regarding the effect of supervisor gender on current wages, as outlined in table 7.2. In conjunction with the 1982 hourly wage, the 1983–1984 hourly wages will be utilized to test the predictions of the training theory regarding wage paths and wage growth. The promotion and learning on the job variables will also be used to test the implications of the training theory regarding the possible effect of supervisor gender.[13]

Most of the "individual and job characteristics" variables (which will be used as independent variables in the analyses) are similar to those found in standard wage equations. The educational variables were constructed through tracing degree information from the 1979 interview forward. The female sector variable was created by obtaining the percentage female from the 1980 Census of Population at the three-digit census occupation code level (U.S. Bureau of the Census 1983). This was then matched to the individual's three-digit census occupation code. However, since the NLSY data contain 1970 occupation codes (rather than 1980), the 1980 information was first mapped into the 1970 codes using an occupational code conversion chart provided by the U.S. Bureau of the Census (1989).[14] The female sector variable will be included as a control in some estimations to try to ensure that the female supervisor variable is not proxying for the sex-type of the job; the same is true for the industry and occupation variables.

Descriptive statistics of selected variables are presented in tables 7.4 (for women) and 7.5 (for men); they are broken down by gender of supervisor. All monetary variables are in real 1982–1984 dollars (deflated using the CPI, 1982–1984 = 100). It is interesting to note that about 47 percent of the women in the sample worked for a female supervisor in 1982, while only 9 percent of the men did. In addition, while women were only slightly more likely to work for a female supervisor if they worked in an occupational sector with at least 60 percent women, men were about three times more likely. Women who worked for a male supervisor had a 1982 hourly wage that was about 30 cents higher than those who worked for a female supervisor; for men this differential was about 90 cents. The magnitude of these differentials falls for both men and women between 1982 and

(*Text continues on p. 224.*)

Table 7.3   Variable Definitions

Variable	Definition
Labor market outcomes	
Hourly wage	Real hourly wage
Perceived likelihood of promotion 1982	Ordered response variable for perceived likelihood of promotion, ranging from 1 (not likely) to 4 (very likely) in 1982
Perceived level of learning on the job 1982	Ordered response variable for perceived level of learning on the job, ranging from 1 (lowest) to 4 (highest) in 1982
Individual and job characteristics	
Female supervisor	Dummy variable that equals 1 if the individual worked for a female supervisor in 1982
Female sector	Dummy variable that equals 1 if the individual worked in an occupational sector with at least 60 percent women
Occupational dummy variables	Dummy variables that describe sixteen broad census occupational categories
Industry dummy variables	Dummy variables that describe eleven broad census industry categories
Experience, experience squared	Age − actual years of completed education − 6, squared
Tenure, tenure squared	Actual number of weeks with current employer/52, squared
Less than high school	Dummy variable that equals 1 if the individual has less than a high school diploma
Some college	Dummy variable that equals 1 if the individual has some college education
Bachelor's degree	Dummy variable that equals 1 if the individual has a bachelor's degree or higher
Black	Dummy variable that equals 1 if the individual is black
Hispanic	Dummy variable that equals 1 if the individual is Hispanic
Northeast, South, West	Dummy variables that equal 1 if the individual resides in the Northeast, South, or West, respectively

Table 7.4   Descriptive Statistics of Selected Variables (Women)

	All	Female Supervisor	Male Supervisor
Labor market outcomes			
Hourly wage 1982	4.975	4.826	5.107
	(1.851)	(1.678)	(1.983)
Hourly wage 1983	5.314	5.238	5.381
	(2.147)	(2.074)	(2.208)
Hourly wage 1984	5.496	5.387	5.593
	(2.228)	(2.096)	(2.337)
Highest perceived likeli-	.251	.248	.252
hood of promotion (1982)	(.433)	(.432)	(.435)
Highest perceived level of	.463	.486	.443
learning on the job (1982)	(.499)	(.500)	(.497)
Individual and job characteristics (1982)			
Female supervisor	.470	1.000	0.000
	(.499)		
Female sector	.600	.639	.566
	(.490)	(.481)	(.496)
Experience	3.037	3.029	3.044
	(2.078)	(2.054)	(2.100)
Experience squared	13.538	13.390	13.669
	(16.356)	(16.522)	(16.215)
Tenure	1.025	1.038	1.013
	(.819)	(.813)	(.825)
Tenure squared	1.721	1.737	1.706
	(2.276)	(2.240)	(2.308)
Less than high school	.153	.151	.155
	(.360)	(.358)	(.362)
Some college	.215	.218	.211
	(.411)	(.413)	(.409)
Bachelor's degree	.099	.087	.110
	(.299)	(.282)	(.312)
Black	.191	.223	.164
	(.394)	(.416)	(.370)
Hispanic	.152	.148	.155
	(.359)	(.356)	(.362)
South	.394	.394	.394
	(.489)	(.489)	(.489)
N(1982)	1,980	930	1,050
N(1983)	1,672	785	887
N(1984)	1,590	752	838

Note: Standard deviations are in parentheses.

Table 7.5   Descriptive Statistics of Selected Variables (Men)

	All	Female Supervisor	Male Supervisor
Labor market outcomes			
Hourly wage 1982	5.975	5.152	6.058
	(2.662)	(2.259)	(2.685)
Hourly wage 1983	6.263	5.839	6.306
	(3.063)	(3.438)	(3.020)
Hourly wage 1984	6.569	6.311	6.594
	(3.257)	(3.203)	(3.262)
Highest perceived likeli-	.298	.264	.302
hood of promotion (1982)	(.458)	(.442)	(.459)
Highest perceived level of	.441	.370	.448
learning on the job (1982)	(.497)	(.484)	(.497)
Individual and job characteristics (1982)			
Female supervisor	.091	1.000	0.000
	(.288)		
Female sector	.141	.354	.119
	(.348)	(.479)	(.324)
Experience	3.703	3.406	3.733
	(2.210)	(2.150)	(2.214)
Experience squared	18.593	16.198	18.834
	(19.593)	(18.593)	(19.679)
Tenure	.923	.812	.934
	(.788)	(.733)	(.793)
Tenure squared	1.472	1.195	1.500
	(2.119)	(1.919)	(2.137)
Less than high school	.293	.278	.294
	(.455)	(.449)	(.456)
Some college	.134	.212	.126
	(.340)	(.410)	(.332)
Bachelor's degree	.061	.080	.059
	(.240)	(.272)	(.236)
Black	.213	.259	.208
	(.409)	(.439)	(.406)
Hispanic	.161	.203	.157
	(.368)	(.403)	(.364)
South	.401	.321	.409
	(.490)	(.468)	(.492)
N (1982)	2,319	212	2,107
N (1983)	2,052	186	1,866
N (1984)	1,993	181	1,812

Note: Standard deviations are in parenthesis.

1983.[15] In addition, both males and females who work for a male supervisor are slightly more likely to believe that their likelihood of a promotion is high. The empirical results in the next section will help to determine whether these differential effects (of supervisor gender) remain once individual characteristics are held constant.

EMPIRICAL RESULTS

This section presents empirical findings regarding the impact of supervisor gender on employees' current wages, perceived likelihood of promotion, wage profiles, and wage growth. The results will be related to the predictions of the three theories presented earlier, as well as to other possible explanations.

CURRENT WAGES

The models described in the second section suggest that supervisor gender might be associated with current employee wages owing to either employee discrimination or on-the-job training differences. The empirical results from a number of different specifications of log of 1982 hourly wage equations are presented in tables 7.6 (for women) and 7.7 (for men). Working for a female supervisor is associated with between about a –3.4 to –4.3 percentage wage differential for women, depending upon the specification chosen.[16] The female sector variable also has a negative effect for women (at about 2.5 percent), although it becomes nonsignificant when industry controls are added. An interesting result occurs when female supervisor and female sector are interacted. Column 2 of table 7.6 shows that conditional on being in a "male" sector the supervisor gender differential is about –6.4 percent for women working for a female supervisor, but conditional on being in a "female" sector the differential is only about –1.5 percent. Thus, there appears to be a "larger" negative effect associated with working for a female supervisor in a "male" sector.

For men, the female supervisor effect (shown in table 7.7) is between about –8.3 and –11.1 percent, depending upon the specification chosen. The female sector variable also has a negative impact on wages, but the effect greatly diminishes when industry controls are added. Column 2 shows that conditional on being in a "male" sector the wage differential is –13.8 percent for men working for a female supervisor, but conditional on being in a "female" sector the differential is only about –5 percent for men working for a female supervisor. This suggests that the supervisor gender effect may vary by sector. Most of the other explanatory variables have the expected effects; experience, tenure, and higher education levels are positively related to male and female employees' wages.

Attempts were made to treat supervisor gender as endogenous. It is difficult to think of characteristics that are correlated with the female super-

Table 7.6 Ordinary Least Squares Log of 1982 Hourly Wage Equation Estimates (Women)

	(1)	(2)	(3)	(4)	(5)	(6)
Intercept	1.371	1.384	1.229	1.238	1.431	1.288
	(.027)	(.028)	(.051)	(.051)	(.035)	(.072)
Female	−.035	−.066	−.044	−.078	−.035	−.041
supervisor	(.013)	(.020)	(.013)	(.020)	(.013)	(.013)
Female sector	−.025	−.048	−.009	−.035	—	—
	(.013)	(.018)	(.014)	(.018)	—	—
Female super-	—	.051	—	.058	—	—
visor * female	—	(.026)	—	(.026)	—	—
sector						
Experience	.040	.039	.038	.037	.039	.037
	(.009)	(.009)	(.009)	(.009)	(.009)	(.009)
Experience	−.003	−.003	−.003	−.003	−.003	−.002
squared	(.001)	(.001)	(.001)	(.001)	(.001)	(.001)
Tenure	.131	.131	.125	.126	.118	.116
	(.028)	(.028)	(.028)	(.028)	(.028)	(.028)
Tenure	−.028	−.028	−.027	−.027	−.025	−.025
squared	(.010)	(.010)	(.010)	(.010)	(.010)	(.010)
Less than high	−.135	−.134	−.116	−.116	−.118	−.110
school	(.020)	(.020)	(.019)	(.019)	(.020)	(.019)
Some college	.171	.171	.167	.167	.160	.157
	(.017)	(.017)	(.016)	(.016)	(.017)	(.016)
Bachelor's degree	.350	.349	.343	.343	.317	.302
	(.024)	(.024)	(.024)	(.024)	(.026)	(.026)
Black	−.027	−.027	−.037	−.036	−.021	−.027
	(.018)	(.018)	(.018)	(.018)	(.018)	(.017)
Hispanic	.006	.005	−.001	−.002	.000	−.003
	(.020)	(.020)	(.019)	(.019)	(.020)	(.019)
South	−.042	−.040	−.043	−.041	−.047	−.046
	(.018)	(.018)	(.017)	(.017)	(.018)	(.017)
Industry dummy	no	no	yes	yes	no	yes
variables						
Occupation	no	no	no	no	yes	yes
dummy variables						
Adj. R^2	.219	.220	.262	.263	.233	.272
N	1,980	1,980	1,980	1,980	1,980	1,980

Notes: Standard errors are in parentheses. Also included in equations are two additional regional dummy variables as well as two dummy variables for presence in a supplementary sample of the NLSY.

visor variable, but not with the disturbance terms in the outcome equations. Ferber, Huber, and Spitze (1979) find that individuals who have worked for or associated with a female boss or professional are more likely to be accepting of a female supervisor. Thus, characteristics of the individual's mother, such as her education level, were used as instruments. The instruments were not able to identify empirically the supervisor gender

Table 7.7 Ordinary Least Squares Log of 1982 Hourly Wage Equation Estimates (Men)

	(1)	(2)	(3)	(4)	(5)	(6)
Intercept	1.490	1.494	1.334	1.335	1.588	1.508
	(.030)	(.030)	(.042)	(.042)	(.045)	(.062)
Female supervisor	−.118	−.148	−.094	−.102	−.096	−.087
	(.025)	(.031)	(.025)	(.029)	(.026)	(.025)
Female sector	−.110	−.128	−.041	−.046	—	—
	(.022)	(.024)	(.021)	(.023)	—	—
Female super- visor * female sector	—	.097	—	.028	—	—
	—	(.055)	—	(.052)	—	—
Experience	.051	.050	.038	.038	.045	.037
	(.011)	(.011)	(.010)	(.010)	(.011)	(.010)
Experience squared	−.002	−.002	−.001	−.001	−.002	−.001
	(.001)	(.001)	(.001)	(.001)	(.001)	(.001)
Tenure	.198	.198	.181	.181	.191	.174
	(.032)	(.032)	(.030)	(.030)	(.032)	(.030)
Tenure squared	−.042	−.042	−.037	−.037	−.040	−.035
	(.012)	(.012)	(.011)	(.011)	(.012)	(.011)
Less than high school	−.162	−.162	−.151	−.151	−.148	−.141
	(.019)	(.019)	(.018)	(.018)	(.018)	(.018)
Some college	.148	.146	.155	.154	.153	.144
	(.022)	(.022)	(.021)	(.021)	(.022)	(.022)
Bachelor's degree	.416	.418	.390	.391	.371	.336
	(.033)	(.033)	(.032)	(.032)	(.036)	(.034)
Black	−.095	−.095	−.073	−.073	−.073	−.061
	(.020)	(.020)	(.019)	(.019)	(.020)	(.019)
Hispanic	−.012	−.012	−.003	−.003	−.009	−.002
	(.022)	(.022)	(.021)	(.021)	(.022)	(.021)
South	−.023	−.024	−.048	−.048	−.025	−.051
	(.020)	(.020)	(.019)	(.019)	(.019)	(.019)
Industry dummy variables	no	no	yes	yes	no	yes
Occupation dummy variables	no	no	no	no	yes	yes
Adj. R^2	.206	.206	.299	.299	.236	.306
N	2,319	2,319	2,319	2,319	2,319	2,319

Notes: Standard errors are in parentheses. Also included in equations are two additional regional dummy variables as well as two dummy variables for presence in a supplementary sample of the NLSY.

effect though; the standard errors on the supervisor gender coefficient were large, and the coefficient estimate was very sensitive to the model specification. However, reduced form probit estimates of the probability of working for a female supervisor are interesting in their own right; they are shown in tables 7.8 (for women) and 7.9 (for men).[17]

Table 7.8   Probit Estimates of the Probability of Working for a Female Supervisor (Women)

	(1)	(2)	(3)	(4)
Intercept	−.306	−.931	.087	−.544
	(.128)	(.265)	(.166)	(.355)
Female sector	.213	.076	—	—
	(.059)	(.066)	—	—
Experience	.013	.003	.009	.005
	(.042)	(.043)	(.043)	(.044)
Experience squared	−.002	−.001	−.001	−.002
	(.005)	(.005)	(.005)	(.005)
Tenure	.170	.098	.150	.107
	(.128)	(.131)	(.131)	(.133)
Tenure squared	−.056	−.036	−.050	−.038
	(.046)	(.047)	(.047)	(.047)
Less than high school	−.025	.066	.030	.066
	(.089)	(.092)	(.092)	(.093)
Some college	−.073	−.116	−.073	−.085
	(.076)	(.079)	(.078)	(.080)
Bachelor's degree	−.204	−.393	−.265	−.333
	(.111)	(.115)	(.124)	(.126)
Black	.202	.168	.136	.132
	(.082)	(.084)	(.085)	(.086)
Hispanic	−.048	−.081	−.059	−.087
	(.092)	(.094)	(.093)	(.095)
South	−.024	.020	−.009	.022
	(.080)	(.082)	(.082)	(.083)
Industry dummy variables	no	yes	no	yes
Occupation dummy variables	no	no	yes	yes
Log-likelihood	−1,349	−1,282	−1,303	−1,267
Female supervisor = 1	930	930	930	930
Female supervisor = 0	1,050	1,050	1,050	1,050
N	1,980	1,980	1,980	1,980
DOF	22	33	37	48

Notes: Standard errors are in parentheses. Also included in equations are two additional regional dummy variables, two dummy variables for presence in a supplementary sample of the NLSY, three dummy variables for mother's education, a dummy variable for mother being a professional, a dummy variable for mother working for pay, a dummy variable for father not in household (at age 14), and a dummy variable for nonreporting of mother's characteristics.

Not surprisingly, tables 7.8 and 7.9 show that the strongest predictors of an individual working for a female supervisor are sector, industry, and occupation. This suggests that the female sector, industry, and occupation variables are highly correlated with the female supervisor variable. Thus, it is possible that the female supervisor variable is picking up the effects of

Table 7.9   Probit Estimates of the Probability of Working for a
            Female Supervisor (Men)

	(1)	(2)	(3)	(4)
Intercept	−1.425	−1.741	−1.007	−1.505
	(.169)	(.305)	(.242)	(.456)
Female sector	.708	.517	—	—
	(.092)	(.100)	—	—
Experience	−.010	−.032	−.027	−.045
	(.056)	(.059)	(.058)	(.060)
Experience squared	−.001	.002	.001	.004
	(.006)	(.006)	(.006)	(.007)
Tenure	−.143	−.274	−.224	−.333
	(.172)	(.182)	(.182)	(.189)
Tenure squared	.013	.053	.033	.069
	(.065)	(.069)	(.069)	(.071)
Less than high school	.066	.103	.097	.104
	(.102)	(.106)	(.108)	(.110)
Some college	.269	.192	.161	.135
	(.112)	(.119)	(.119)	(.124)
Bachelor's degree	.092	−.152	−.005	−.136
	(.166)	(.177)	(.182)	(.191)
Black	.216	.122	.122	.057
	(.106)	(.111)	(.112)	(.116)
Hispanic	.034	−.012	−.006	−.033
	(.119)	(.124)	(.123)	(.126)
South	−.195	−.150	−.140	−.116
	(.106)	(.112)	(.112)	(.115)
Industry dummy variables	no	yes	no	yes
Occupation dummy variables	no	no	yes	yes
Log-likelihood	−656	−608	−604	−580
Female supervisor = 1	212	212	212	212
Female supervisor = 0	2,107	2,107	2,107	2,107
N	2,319	2,319	2,319	2,319
DOF	22	33	36	47

Notes: Standard errors are in parentheses. Also included in equations are two additional regional dummy variables, two dummy variables for presence in a supplementary sample of the NLSY, three dummy variables for mother's education, a dummy variable for mother being a professional, a dummy variable for mother working for pay, a dummy variable for father not in household (at age 14), and a dummy variable for nonreporting of mother's characteristics.

job "type," even when these other variables are controlled for. It may be difficult, then, to separate the effect of supervisor gender, per se, from the effect of the sex-type of the job. Recall that this is what Ferber and Green (1991) hypothesize might have occurred in their analysis of the effect of supervisor gender, even though they included a control for percentage female in occupation in the earnings equations.

The results thus far suggest that working for a female supervisor has a negative effect on wages for both men and women. This finding is not consistent with the productivity effects theory described earlier, which predicts no supervisor gender wage differential. One possible interpretation of the finding is that the negative effect is due to employee discrimination. This implies that *both* male and female employees look upon a female supervisor as a "positive" job characteristic (and are willing to receive lower wages because of it); this does not seem very plausible, however.[18] As mentioned above, another possibility is that the female supervisor variable is picking up something about the "type" of job being held. Alternatively, the negative wage effect associated with working for a female supervisor may be due to on-the-job training that is occurring, which suggests that there will be a later payoff in the form of increased wages and possibly a promotion. The next two parts of this section, which look at perceived likelihood of promotion and wage profiles, will attempt to test whether this hypothesis is driving the supervisor gender effect.

PERCEIVED LIKELIHOOD OF PROMOTION

The human capital theory described in the second section suggests that individuals may earn less in the first period, owing to on-the-job training (systematically associated with a certain gender supervisor), but the payoff may come in the longer run in terms of a promotion and increased wages. The empirical analysis here looks at whether the perception of individuals on the likelihood of a future promotion (in 1982) is related to the gender of their supervisor. The NLSY survey asks individuals whether they believe that their chances for promotion are good; responses range from 1 (not true at all), to 4 (very true). To take into account the ordered nature of the question, an ordered probit was estimated.[19] The results are shown in tables 7.10 (for women) and 7.11 (for men).[20]

The results suggest that for female employees, supervisor gender does not have a statistically significant effect on the perceived likelihood of a promotion. The only variable that does seem to have an impact is tenure, with higher tenure associated with a higher perceived likelihood of promotion. In other specifications (not shown), industry and occupation also appear to matter. For men, the results are similar: supervisor gender and sector do not affect the perceived likelihood of a promotion. However, tenure does have an effect (as do occupation and industry in some specifications), as well as having a bachelor's degree or higher.

The results here do not lend support to the training story. However, on-the-job training may be associated only with increased wages (analyzed below) rather than promotions. In addition, information on whether an actual promotion occurs in the future would probably be more useful as a (more) direct test of the theory. This is not available for this time period in the data, however.

Table 7.10 Ordered Probit Estimates and Marginal Effects of Perceived Likelihood of Promotion (Women)

| | | Marginal Effects | | | |
		Choice = 1	Choice = 2	Choice = 3	Choice = 4
Intercept	.787	—	—	—	—
	(.104)				
Female supervisor	−.012	.003	.001	−.001	−.003
	(.049)				
Female sector	.047	−.013	−.006	.004	.015
	(.050)				
Experience	−.054	−.001	−.001	.000	.002
	(.036)				
Experience squared	.005	−.003	−.003	−.003	−.003
	(.004)				
Tenure	.209	−.055	−.027	.016	.066
	(.108)				
Tenure squared	−.066	.017	.008	−.005	−.021
	(.039)				
Less than high school	−.096	.024	.013	−.006	−.031
	(.076)				
Some college	.089	−.024	−.011	.008	.027
	(.063)				
Bachelor's degree	−.038	.010	.005	−.003	−.012
	(.090)				
Black	.012	−.003	−.002	.001	.004
	(.069)				
Hispanic	.059	−.016	−.007	.005	.018
	(.076)				
South	.149	−.042	−.017	.014	.045
	(.068)				
Log-likelihood	−2,690				
Choice = 1	361				
Choice = 2	496				
Choice = 3	627				
Choice = 4	496				
N	1,980				

Notes: Standard errors are in parentheses. Also included in equations are two additional regional dummy variables as well as two dummy variables for presence in a supplementary sample of the NLSY. Choices range from 1 (lowest) to 4 (highest).

WAGE PROFILE

Thus far the results suggest that for both men and women there is a negative wage effect associated with working for a female supervisor in 1982. This effect could be consistent with the training theory if it is found that wages are lower during the first period, but then rela-

Table 7.11   Ordered Probit Estimates and Marginal Effects of Perceived Likelihood of Promotion (Men)

		Marginal Effects			
		Choice = 1	Choice = 2	Choice = 3	Choice = 4
Intercept	1.003	—	—	—	—
	(.097)				
Female supervisor	−.063	.008	.006	−.001	−.013
	(.080)				
Female sector	−.078	.013	.010	−.001	−.022
	(.050)				
Experience	−.024	.005	.004	−.001	−.008
	(.033)				
Experience squared	−.001	.021[a]	.015[a]	−.002[a]	−.034[a]
	(.004)				
Tenure	.233	−.050	−.036	.006	.080
	(.100)				
Tenure squared	−.076	.016	.012	−.002	−.026
	(.037)				
Less than high school	.092	−.021	−.014	.004	.031
	(.058)				
Some college	.029	−.007	−.005	.001	.011
	(.070)				
Bachelor's degree	.207	−.049	−.029	.012	.066
	(.104)				
Black	−.038	.008	.006	−.001	−.013
	(.062)				
Hispanic	.114	−.026	−.017	.005	.038
	(.070)				
South	.212	−.050	−.030	.012	.068
	(.061)				
Log-likelihood	−3,062				
Choice = 1	309				
Choice = 2	512				
Choice = 3	806				
Choice = 4	692				
N	2,319				

Notes: Standard errors are in parentheses. Also included in equations are two additional regional dummy variables as well as two dummy variables for presence in a supplementary sample of the NLSY. Choices range from 1 (lowest) to 4 (highest).
[a] Marginal effect has been multiplied by 100.

tively higher in later periods. This section will look at the wage profile for the 1982–1984 period in order to investigate whether there is a positive wage effect in later periods as the training story would suggest (or, at the least, whether there is positive relative wage growth associated with having worked for a female supervisor early in individuals' careers).

Log of hourly wage equations over the 1982–1984 period were estimated as a seemingly unrelated regressions system.[21] Estimation was carried out using a balanced panel of data.[22] Estimation was undertaken in two ways. First, specifications used only 1982 "individual and job characteristics"; in a sense, this is like a reduced form estimation, treating the 1983 and 1984 characteristics as a function of the 1982 characteristics. Then, estimation was undertaken using the 1983 and 1984 "individual and job characteristics" in each respective wage equation.

Results are shown in tables 7.12 (for women) and 7.13 (for men); in the tables, the coefficients from the female supervisor variable are presented from a number of different specifications. Table 7.12 shows that under all of the different specifications, the effect of having a female supervisor becomes less negative in later periods (and not statistically different from zero) for women. Under some specifications, there is (very limited) evidence of some positive wage growth associated with working for a female supervisor.[23] However, the influence of early career supervisor gender on future wage levels does not show signs of becoming positive as the training theory would suggest. And looking out further on the wage trajectory does not alter this conclusion.[24] In other words, the female supervisor effect is found to go to zero over time.

For men, the results suggest that the female supervisor effect also becomes less negative in later periods (and statistically not significant in some specifications). As with women, there is some evidence of positive wage growth over time, although the wage trajectory associated with having an early career female supervisor does not surpass that associated with having a male supervisor. That is, the female supervisor variable, which negatively affects hourly earnings in 1982, does not positively affect earnings in 1983 or 1984. And looking further out on the wage trajectory does not show differently.

SPECIFIC VERSUS GENERAL TRAINING

Perhaps looking at some labor market outcomes that seek to differentiate between specific (useful within the firm) and general (portable between firms) training (Becker 1975) will help provide some further insights into whether any on-the-job training is occurring that is systematically associated with supervisor gender. The outcomes that will be looked at are perceived learning on the job and turnover.

The NLSY poses a question regarding perceived learning on the job; it asks individuals whether they believe that the skills that they are learning on the current job would enable them to be able to obtain a "better" job. Responses are ordered and range from 1 (not true at all) to 4 (very true). Parsons (1985) discusses this question with respect to the NLSY and the

Table 7.12   Seemingly Unrelated Regressions (SUR) System Estimates of Supervisor Gender Effects on Log of 1982–1984 Hourly Wages, by Specification (Women)

	Female Supervisor Coefficients by Year (γ)				
	γ_{82}	γ_{83}	γ_{84}	$\gamma_{83} - \gamma_{82}$	$\gamma_{84} - \gamma_{82}$
1982 Individual and job characteristics					
Female sector	−.033	−.010	−.005	.023	.028
	(.015)	(.017)	(.017)	(.014)	(.016)
Female sector and	−.041	−.019	−.015	.022	.026
industry dummy variables	(.015)	(.017)	(.018)	(.015)	(.016)
Occupation dummy	−.035	−.013	−.007	.022	.028
variables	(.015)	(.017)	(.017)	(.015)	(.016)
Occupation and industry	−.040	−.017	−.013	.023	.027
dummy variables	(.015)	(.017)	(.018)	(.015)	(.016)
All-year individual and job characteristics					
Female sector	−.032	−.013	−.011	.019	.021
	(.015)	(.016)	(.017)	(.015)	(.016)
Female sector and	−.039	−.021	−.020	.018	.019
industry dummy variables	(.015)	(.016)	(.017)	(.015)	(.016)
Occupation dummy	−.035	−.014	−.013	.021	.022
variables	(.015)	(.016)	(.017)	(.015)	(.016)
Occupation and industry	−.040	−.020	−.021	.020	.019
dummy variables	(.015)	(.016)	(.017)	(.015)	(.017)

Notes: Standard errors are in parentheses. γ is the coefficient on the supervisor gender dummy variable that equals 1 for female supervisor and 0 for male supervisor. Standard errors for $\gamma_{83} - \gamma_{82}$ and $\gamma_{84} - \gamma_{82}$ were obtained through a simple application of the delta method. $N = 1,454$ for each year. Also included in all specifications are variables for experience, tenure, education, race and ethnicity, and region, as well as two dummy variables for presence in a supplementary sample of the NLSY.

occurrence of on-the-job training. However, while Parsons has interpreted this measure as evidence of a "good" job, I have interpreted it as one regarding whether the job provides any general training.[25]

To take into account the ordered nature of the question on learning, an ordered probit was estimated; marginal effects were calculated in the manner described earlier. The empirical findings are shown in tables 7.14 (for women) and 7.15 (for men). The results suggest that for women, working for a female supervisor has a positive impact on the probability of stating that a high level of learning is occurring on the job. For men, the results appear to be just the opposite; that is, working for a female supervisor has a negative (although nonsignificant) impact on the probability of stating that a high level of learning is occurring on the job. Once controls are added for industry or occupation, the effect for women of working for a female supervisor becomes statistically insignificant. It is also interesting

Table 7.13 SUR System Estimates of Supervisor Gender Effects on Log of 1982–1984 Hourly Wages, by Specification (Men)

	Female Supervisor Coefficients by Year (γ)				
	γ_{82}	γ_{83}	γ_{84}	$\gamma_{83} - \gamma_{82}$	$\gamma_{84} - \gamma_{82}$
1982 Individual and job characteristics					
Female sector	−.119	−.050	−.055	.069	.064
	(.029)	(.031)	(.033)	(.027)	(.031)
Female sector and	−.101	−.036	−.047	.065	.054
industry dummy variables	(.028)	(.031)	(.033)	(.028)	(.031)
Occupation dummy	−.097	−.025	−.042	.072	.055
variables	(.029)	(.032)	(.033)	(.028)	(.032)
Occupation and industry	−.093	−.022	−.043	.071	.050
dummy variables	(.028)	(.032)	(.033)	(.029)	(.032)
All-year individual and job characteristics					
Female sector	−.127	−.062	−.059	.065	.068
	(.029)	(.030)	(.031)	(.027)	(.031)
Female sector and	−.111	−.050	−.051	.061	.060
industry dummy variables	(.028)	(.029)	(.031)	(.028)	(.031)
Occupation dummy	−.110	−.044	−.047	.066	.063
variables	(.029)	(.030)	(.031)	(.028)	(.032)
Occupation and industry	−.103	−.043	−.046	.060	.057
dummy variables	(.028)	(.029)	(.030)	(.029)	(.032)

Notes: Standard errors are in parentheses. γ is the coefficient on the supervisor gender dummy variable that equals 1 for female supervisor and 0 for male supervisor. Standard errors for $\gamma_{83} - \gamma_{82}$ and $\gamma_{84} - \gamma_{82}$ were obtained through a simple application of the delta method. $N = 1,852$ for each year. Also included in all specifications are variables for experience, tenure, education, race and ethnicity, and region, as well as two dummy variables for presence in a supplementary sample of the NLSY.

to note that for men, the female sector variable has a negative, statistically significant effect on the probability of being in a high learning job, while for women, the female sector variable has a positive, statistically significant effect. Thus, it appears that within gender, the directions of the supervisor and sector effects are identical. The results regarding learning on the job do not suggest that general training is systematically associated with a certain gender supervisor for either male or female employees.

A prediction of the human capital theory is that specific training is expected to be associated with lower levels of turnover (Becker 1975). Thus, one would expect lower likelihoods of voluntary quits, layoffs, and fires associated with specific training. In order to look at the influence of supervisor gender on turnover, multinomial logits were estimated on the probability of a job ending within the next year due to layoff, fire, or voluntary quit, relative to staying with the same employer.[26] The results are shown in tables 7.16 (for women) and 7.17 (for men). For women, it appears that working for a female supervisor decreases the probability of

Table 7.14 Ordered Probit Estimates and Marginal Effects of Perceived Learning on the Job (Women)

| | | Marginal Effects | | | |
		Choice = 1	Choice = 2	Choice = 3	Choice = 4
Intercept	.849	—	—	—	—
	(.109)				
Female supervisor	.101	−.015	−.015	−.009	.038
	(.051)				
Female sector	.305	−.051	−.044	−.018	.113
	(.053)				
Experience	.031	−.004	−.005	−.003	.012
	(.037)				
Experience squared	−.002	.021[a]	.022[a]	.016[a]	−.059[a]
	(.005)				
Tenure	.519	−.071	−.075	−.052	.197
	(.113)				
Tenure squared	−.166	.023	.024	.017	−.063
	(.041)				
Less than high school	−.353	.038	.048	.048	−.134
	(.077)				
Some college	.077	−.011	−.011	−.007	.029
	(.066)				
Bachelor's degree	.312	−.052	−.045	−.018	.115
	(.097)				
Black	−.102	.013	.014	.011	−.039
	(.072)				
Hispanic	.041	−.006	−.006	−.004	.016
	(.080)				
South	.168	−.026	−.024	−.013	.063
	(.070)				
Log-likelihood	−2,285				
Choice = 1	151				
Choice = 2	276				
Choice = 3	633				
Choice = 4	915				
N	1,975				

Notes: Standard errors are in parentheses. Also included in equations are two additional regional dummy variables as well as two dummy variables for presence in a supplementary sample of the NLSY. Choices range from 1 (lowest) to 4 (highest).
[a]Marginal effect has been multiplied by 100.

being laid off from a job; the female sector variable has a similar effect. For men, the results suggest that working for a female supervisor increases the probability of a job ending due to being fired. In addition, working in a female sector decreases the likelihood of being laid off, as with women, but increases the likelihood of a voluntary quit.

Table 7.15   Ordered Probit Estimates and Marginal Effects of
Perceived Learning on the Job (Men)

		Marginal Effects			
		Choice = 1	Choice = 2	Choice = 3	Choice = 4
Intercept	1.029	—	—	—	—
	(.101)				
Female	−.103	.013	.016	.011	−.040
supervisor	(.081)				
Female sector	−.166	.020	.025	.019	−.065
	(.069)				
Experience	.083	−.011	−.013	−.008	.032
	(.034)				
Experience	−.009	.001	.001	.001	−.003
squared	(.004)				
Tenure	.431	−.060	−.066	−.041	.167
	(.104)				
Tenure	−.161	.022	.025	.015	−.062
squared	(.039)				
Less than high	−.006	.001	.001	.001	−.002
school	(.060)				
Some college	.093	−.014	−.014	−.008	.036
	(.073)				
Bachelor's	.393	−.071	−.060	−.014	.144
degree	(.109)				
Black	−.189	.023	.028	.022	−.074
	(.064)				
Hispanic	−.013	.002	.002	.001	−.005
	(.073)				
South	.218	−.035	−.034	−.014	.082
	(.062)				
Log-likelihood	−2,747				
Choice = 1	173				
Choice = 2	342				
Choice = 3	778				
Choice = 4	1,020				
N	2,313				

Notes: Standard errors are in parentheses. Also included in equations are two additional regional dummy variables as well as two dummy variables for presence in a supplementary sample of the NLSY. Choices range from 1 (lowest) to 4 (highest).

DISCUSSION OF THE EMPIRICAL RESULTS

Empirical results regarding the effects of supervisor gender on current wages, perceived likelihood of promotion, wage paths, wage growth, perceived learning on the job, and turnover were presented in the earlier parts of this section. Tables 7.18 (for women) and 7.19 (for men) depict the direction of the supervisor gender effects on these labor market outcomes.

Table 7.16   Multinomial Logit Estimates of the Probability of a
Job Ending Within the Next Twelve Months of the
1982 Interview Date Due to Layoff, Fire, or Voluntary Quit
(Relative to Staying with the Same Employer) (Women)

	Layoff	Fire	Quit
Intercept	−1.356	−1.458	−.334
	(.437)	(.618)	(.278)
Female supervisor	−.576	.023	.039
	(.208)	(.310)	(.129)
Female sector	−.518	−.191	−.112
	(.203)	(.315)	(.134)
Experience	.084	−.128	−.015
	(.153)	(.236)	(.096)
Experience squared	−.015	−.012	−.008
	(.019)	(.032)	(.013)
Tenure	−.527	−1.658	−.993
	(.454)	(.700)	(.291)
Tenure squared	.023	.361	.153
	(.165)	(.262)	(.106)
Less than high school	.361	.676	.232
	(.308)	(.483)	(.225)
Some college	−.434	−1.380	−.078
	(.263)	(.547)	(.159)
Bachelor's degree	−1.410	−1.217	−.445
	(.495)	(.581)	(.222)
Black	.395	.208	−.278
	(.274)	(.401)	(.188)
Hispanic	−.236	—[a]	−.584
	(.311)		(.211)
South	.120	.477	.532
	(.309)	(.439)	(.189)
Log-likelihood	−1,311		
Stay	956		
Layoff	121		
Fire	47		
Quit	363		
N	1,487		

Notes: Standard errors are in parentheses. Also included in equations are two additional regional dummy variables as well as two dummy variables for presence in a supplementary sample of the NLSY.
[a]Cell has 0 Hispanic women.

The strongest empirical finding suggests that working for a female supervisor in 1982 had a negative impact on that period's wages for both men and women. This result rules out the productivity effects theory, which predicts no supervisor gender wage differential. One possible inter-

Table 7.17 **Multinomial Logit Estimates of the Probability of a Job Ending Within the Next Twelve Months of the 1982 Interview Date Due to Layoff, Fire, or Voluntary Quit (Relative to Staying with the Same Employer) (Men)**

	Layoff	Fire	Quit
Intercept	−.593	−2.381	−.386
	(.295)	(.566)	(.264)
Female supervisor	.030	.833	.038
	(.260)	(.360)	(.212)
Female sector	−.505	.014	.504
	(.255)	(.394)	(.169)
Experience	.073	.078	−.119
	(.103)	(.205)	(.087)
Experience	−.006	−.017	.006
squared	(.011)	(.022)	(.010)
Tenure	−1.187	−.823	−1.278
	(.310)	(.610)	(.286)
Tenure	.274	−.002	.196
squared	(.112)	(.253)	(.111)
Less than high	.346	1.401	.595
school	(.176)	(.307)	(.165)
Some college	−.424	−.779	.039
	(.234)	(.554)	(.183)
Bachelor's degree	−1.726	−.723	−.376
	(.532)	(.772)	(.256)
Black	.010	.621	−.028
	(.194)	(.336)	(.178)
Hispanic	−.073	.008	.174
	(.219)	(.401)	(.185)
South	−.151	−.269	.678
	(.184)	(.336)	(.185)
Log-likelihood	−1,781		
Stay	1,039		
Layoff	281		
Fire	71		
Quit	405		
N	1,796		

Notes: Standard errors are in parentheses. Also included in equations are two additional regional dummy variables as well as two dummy variables for presence in a supplementary sample of the NLSY.

pretation of the negative effect on current wages is that it is due to employee discrimination. However, this would suggest that both male and female employees have a preference for working for a female supervisor (and are willing to receive lower wages in return for this "positive" job attribute).

Table 7.18 Summary of Female Supervisor Effects (Women)

	Specification				
	1	2	3	4	5
Current wages	(–)*	(–)*	(–)*	(–)*	(–)*
Perceived likelihood of promotion	(–)	(–)	(–)	(–)	(–)
Wage growth					
1982 Individual and Job Characteristics	(+)*	(+)*	(+)	(+)*	(+)*
All-Year Individual and Job Characteristics	(+)	(+)	(+)	(+)	(+)
Perceived learning on the job	(+)*	(+)*	(–)	(+)	(+)
Job separation					
Layoff	(–)*	(–)*	(–)*	(–)*	(–)*
Fire	(+)	(+)	(+)	(+)	(+)
Quit	(+)	(+)	(+)	(+)	(+)

Notes: Specification 1 includes the following variables: female supervisor, experience, experience squared, tenure, tenure squared, three dummy variables for education level, black, Hispanic, three regional dummy variables, and two dummy variables for presence in a supplementary sample of the NLSY.

Specification 2 includes all of those variables in Specification 1 plus a dummy variable for working in a female sector.

Specification 3 includes all of those variables in Specification 1 plus a dummy variable for working in a female sector and industry dummy variables.

Specification 4 includes all of those variables in Specification 1 plus occupation dummy variables.

Specification 5 includes all of those variables in Specification 1 plus industry and occupation dummy variables.

*Statistically significant at least at the 10 percent significance level.

A second potential explanation for the negative wage effect associated with working for a female supervisor is that it may be due to on-the-job training that is occurring. This suggests that there would be a later payoff in the form of increased wages and possibly a promotion. The results from the estimation of the supervisor gender effect on employees' wage growth suggest that although there is a negative wage effect associated with working for a female supervisor in the first period, there does appear to be a small amount of relative positive wage growth associated with working for

Table 7.19	Summary of Female Supervisor Effects (Men)

	Specification				
	1	2	3	4	5
Current wages	(−)*	(−)*	(−)*	(−)*	(−)*
Perceived likelihood of promotion	(−)	(−)	(−)	(−)	(−)
Wage growth					
1982 Individual and Job Characteristics	(+)*	(+)*	(+)*	(+)*	(+)*
All-Year Individual and Job Characteristics	(+)*	(+)*	(+)*	(+)*	(+)*
Perceived learning on the job	(−)*	(−)	(−)	(−)	(−)
Job separation					
Layoff	(−)	(+)	(+)	(+)	(+)
Fire	(+)*	(+)*	(+)*	(+)*	(+)*
Quit	(+)	(+)	(+)	(−)	(−)

Notes: Specification 1 includes the following variables: female supervisor, experience, experience squared, tenure, tenure squared, three dummy variables for education level, black, Hispanic, three regional dummy variables, and two dummy variables for presence in a supplementary sample of the NLSY.

Specification 2 includes all of those variables in Specification 1 plus a dummy variable for working in a female sector.

Specification 3 includes all of those variables in Specification 1 plus a dummy variable for working in a female sector and industry dummy variables.

Specification 4 includes all of those variables in Specification 1 plus occupation dummy variables.

Specification 5 includes all of those variables in Specification 1 plus industry and occupation dummy variables.

*Statistically significant at least at the 10 percent significance level.

a female supervisor (and, in fact, this is much stronger for male employees).[27] However, the female supervisor variable does not show a positive effect on wage levels in later periods, as the on-the-job theory would suggest; looking further out on the wage path does not appear to alter this conclusion.[28] Thus, it should be noted that the supervisor gender effect essentially goes to zero over time for both men and women. In addition, results regarding learning on the job and turnover do not provide clear-cut support for the training theory.[29]

Before moving to the concluding section of this paper, a couple of other potential explanations for the supervisor gender effect on current wages that have been mentioned throughout the paper will be more fully explored. One alternative explanation is that the negative wage effect associated with working for a female supervisor may be picking up a "crowding" effect for women, in the sense that the female supervisor variable is proxying for the sex-type of a job. Indicators for sector, industry, and occupation attempted to control for this possibility. However, recall that it was observed that the female sector, industry, and occupation variables are the best predictors of working for a female supervisor. Reskin and Hartmann (1986) point out that even within a particular sector or occupation, more finer occupation levels, such as job titles, might be segregated by sex. In addition, Blau (1977) and Groshen (1990) point out the presence of sex segregation by establishment within occupational categories. Thus, even though attempts were made to control for the sex-type of the job, it is certainly conceivable that the sex segregation that appears to exist at finer job levels was captured through the supervisor gender variable.[30]

A sorting story might be more appropriate to explain the negative female supervisor effect for men. Again, supervisor gender may be proxying for sex-type of job (associated with certain job characteristics) and some men may have tastes such that they are willing to work in these jobs, despite the lower wages. However, when job characteristics (such as fringe benefits and job safety) were added the supervisor gender effect remained, which does not lend support to this sorting explanation.

A second alternative explanation for the effect on current wages associated with working for a female supervisor (that is closely tied to the first explanation) involves the supervisor's position in the hierarchy. That is, if female supervisors tend to be lower down in a firm hierarchy, one might expect their employees also to be on lower levels of their job ladders. This, too, might generate the finding of a negative effect on current wages associated with working for a female supervisor for both male and female employees.[31] Thus, what might have been found is the effect of working in a lower-level job, rather than the specific impact of working for a female supervisor.

CONCLUSION

Supervisors can potentially have more than just very short-term effects on their employees' labor market outcomes, and this may particularly be so early in employees' careers. For this reason, who supervises whom may be important. The paper presented here looks at both the short-term and longer-term influences of early career supervisor gender on young workers' labor market experiences. In order to untangle the various reasons why supervisor gender might matter, three simple theories regarding the possible influence of supervisor and employee gender matches were developed. These included employee preferences regarding gender of supervisor, differential productivity effects of supervisors on their employees, and the possible role of supervisors in providing on-the-job training and promotion opportunities that employees may receive. From these theories empirically testable implications regarding current wages, perceived likelihood of promotion, wage growth, and wage paths were obtained. They were then tested using a panel of data from the National Longitudinal Survey of Youth (NLSY).

The empirical results suggest that for both male and female employees there is a negative effect on current wages associated with working for a female supervisor; this effect persists when controls for industry, occupation, or whether the individual works in a female-dominated sector are added. The female supervisor variable is found to have no impact on individuals' perceived likelihood of promotion and minimal positive effects on employees' wage growth. In effect, the positive wage growth found suggests that the supervisor gender impact goes to zero over time. The empirical findings do not provide strong, clear-cut support for the discrimination, productivity effects, or on-the-job training theory.

It also cannot be ruled out that the female supervisor variable is picking up something about the sex-type of the job, although indicators for working in a job sector with a high percentage of women, industry, and occupation are included to try to control for this. It is possible that the sex-typing of a job goes beyond these aggregate measures, and that the sex segregation that may exist at finer job levels was captured through the supervisor gender variable. Similarly, if female supervisors tend to be in lower positions in a firm hierarchy, their employees might also be on lower levels of their job ladder; this, too, might generate a negative wage effect. Again, then, the empirical results might indicate not the effect of working for a female supervisor, per se, but rather the effect of working in a certain "type" of job.

In order to try to get at the impact of early career supervisor gender on employees' labor market experiences more directly, it would be ideal to have firm-level data. These data might include detailed job descriptions, information about on-the-job training, wages, and promotions over time for employees, and the supervisor's relative position in the job hierarchy. Alternatively, in the 1996 wave of the NLSY, the supervisor gender question will be asked again, along with a question on the gender composition of the other employees supervised by that supervisor. Questions regarding actual promotions and on-the-job training will also be included, as will questions pertaining to whether the individual is a supervisor, and, if so, what the gender composition of his or her employees is. This information allows the effect of supervisor gender on mid-career labor market experiences to be examined, as well as the impact of being in a supervisory role.

ACKNOWLEDGMENTS

I would like to thank Francine Blau, Ronald Ehrenberg, George Jakubson, Solomon Polachek, Cordelia Reimers, Michael Cooper, Debra Dwyer, and Daniel Hosken for their useful comments. Financial support for this research was provided by a doctoral dissertation grant from the National Science Foundation and by a grant from the National Center for the Workplace; I am grateful for their support. The views expressed are those of the author and do not reflect the policies of the Bureau of Labor Statistics or the views of other BLS staff members.

APPENDIX

In this appendix, three simple theories of the influence of supervisor gender are developed and their implications are discussed; a less detailed outline of the theories appears in the second section of this paper. The primary goal is to see whether there are empirically testable implications that differentiate the theories. Three different paths for the effect of supervisor gender on their employees are proposed in the theories; they are: (1) employee preferences—male (or female) employees prefer not to work for male (or female) supervisors;[32] (2) productivity effects—all male (or female) employees who are matched with male (or female) supervisors become less productive; and (3) training effectiveness—when male (or female) employees are matched with male (or female) supervisors training is more costly.

THEORY 1: EMPLOYEE DISCRIMINATION

Becker's classic theory of employee discrimination (1971) provides a natural place to begin in the development of a theory of employee preferences regarding supervisor gender. One particular case that Becker explores fits into a scenario in which all employees prefer not to work with a certain "type" (say female) of supervisor.[33] Baldwin, Butler, and Johnson (1993) expand upon Becker's work by allowing for two differentiated "types" in each labor grouping—that is, two types of employees (male and female) as well as two types of supervisors (male and female). In their paper, one type of employee (male) has a preference against being supervised by one type of supervisor (female). The analysis presented here takes the Baldwin, Butler, and Johnson structure as a starting point, but builds in a labor market equilibrium consideration that is more in the spirit of Becker's work.

The model begins as follows: Assume that a competitive firm determines that the optimal size for a work group consists of N employees and one supervisor. There are two types of employees, female and male, who are perfect substitutes (that is, equally well qualified and productive).[34]

There are also two types of supervisors, female and male, who are perfect substitutes, but complementary with employees. To summarize, one supervisor and N employees are required per work group, and female and male supervisors are equally good at performing their job, as are female and male employees.

Employee discrimination against a certain type of supervisor will now be added to the model. Suppose, for example, that all male employees do not like to work for female supervisors, but female employees are indifferent to their supervisor's type. In this situation, male employees demand a wage premium (Becker 1971) if they work for a female supervisor. Assume that a male employee requires a wage of $W_E^D(1 + \delta)$ when working with a female supervisor; $W_E^D \times \delta$ is the added monetary amount needed to compensate him for working with the disliked type of supervisor (female).

Thus, in order to minimize costs, all competitive firms will systematically match male employees with male supervisors. Female employees will be matched with male or female supervisors (as long as male employees are all matched with male supervisors). If, given demand, the proportion of male supervisors relative to male employees accommodates this matching situation, then no compensating wage differential will arise. That is, all employees will be paid the same wage, but there will be segregation in the form of male employees matched only with male supervisors.

On the other hand, if some male employees are matched with female supervisors in the labor market equilibrium under this discrimination scenario, it indicates that given demand and the supplies of female and male supervisors, female employees (relative to male employees) are in short supply. As noted above, male employees matched with female supervisors require a higher wage of $W_E^D(1 + \delta)$. The extra amount, $W_E^D \times \delta$, is the compensating wage differential male employees demand for working for a female supervisor. At the margin, the relative added value of one additional female employee is $W_E^D \times \delta$, which implies that under this discrimination scenario the equilibrium wage of all female employees will be $W_E^D(1 + \delta)$. Intuitively, this occurs because the wage of the relatively scarce female employees will be bid up to this level by competitive firms, owing to the compensating wage differential demanded by male employees. Appendix figure 7.1 outlines the wage for each type of employee, depending upon the supervisor match. Recall that under this discrimination scenario, male employees will be matched with male supervisors whenever possible. This suggests that the combination of male supervisors and female employees will not occur (since all available male supervisors will be matched with male employees).

Now, following Becker (1971), in order for both female and male supervisors to be employed *and* there to be any male employees being supervised by female supervisors in equilibrium, the cost to the competi-

Appendix Figure 7.1   Employee Wages

	Male Supervisor	Female Supervisor
Male Employees	W_E^D	$W_E^D(1+\delta)$
Female Employees	.....	$W_E^D(1+\delta)$

Appendix Figure 7.2   Work Group Costs (One Supervisor and N Employees)

	Male Supervisor	Female Supervisor
Male Employees	$W_S^M +$ $N \times W_E^D$	$W_S^F +$ $N \times W_E^D(1+\delta)$
Female Employees	.....	$W_S^F +$ $N \times W_E^D(1+\delta)$

Appendix Figure 7.3   Supervisor Wages

	Male Supervisor	Female Supervisor
Male Employees	$W_S^F +$ $N \times W_E^D \times \delta$	W_S^F
Female Employees	.....	W_S^F

tive firms of each type of work group must be equal. Recall that N employees are matched with one supervisor; the cost of each type of work group is in appendix figure 7.2. Setting costs equal, this suggests that $(W_S^M - W_S^F)$ = $N \times W_E^D \times \delta$. All male supervisors receive a higher wage than all female supervisors, since using the same argument as above the presence of male employees being supervised by female supervisors suggests that male supervisors are in relatively short supply. And, at the margin, the relative added value of one additional male supervisor is $N \times W_E^D \times \delta$.[35] Supervisor wages are depicted in appendix figure 7.3.

The model described above implies the following: (1) Male employees are expected to be supervised by male supervisors and (2) if there is a female supervising male employees, those male employees will receive a wage premium. If (2) holds, then (3) all female employees will receive a wage equal to that of the male employees who work for a female supervisor, (4) female employees will not be supervised by male supervisors, and (5) all male supervisors will have a higher wage than all female supervisors.

THEORY 2: PRODUCTIVITY

A second theory of the influence of supervisor gender points to the effect of supervisor gender on the productivity of employees. The framework that will be utilized in the development of a productivity effects model is the same as that described above. Suppose, for example, that working for a female supervisor decreases male employee productivity by a certain fixed amount (θ), but has no effect on the productivity of female employees.[36] In other words, the employee output from a male employee and female supervisor match is θ lower (say worth $Q - \theta$) than employee output (still Q) from the three other possible match combinations—male employee with a male supervisor, female employee with a female supervisor, and female employee with a male supervisor.

In this situation, all competitive firms will systematically match male employees with male supervisors. If any male employees are matched with female supervisors under the resulting "productivity effects" equilibrium, it indicates that given demand and the supplies of female and male supervisors, female employees (relative to male employees) are in short supply. Otherwise, we would never see male employees matched with a female supervisor because of this productivity loss.

As in theory 1, the matching of male employees with female supervisors in the labor market equilibrium also has implications for the wages of female employees. At the margin, the relative added value of one additional female employee is θ, which implies that the equilibrium wage of all female employees will be $W_E^P + \theta$, taking W_E^P as the male employee wage. This occurs because the wage of the relatively scarce female employees will be bid up to this level by competitive firms owing to the productivity loss associated with male employees (matched with female supervisors). Appendix figure 7.4 outlines the wages of employees based upon the supervisor match. Note that under this "productivity effects" equilibrium, if male employees are matched with female supervisors the combination of male supervisors and female employees will not occur (since all available male supervisors will be matched with male employees).

Thus, in order for both types of employees and supervisors to be employed, as well as there to be any male employees matched with female supervisors, the cost (for a given level of output) to the competitive firms of each type of work group must be equal. Recall that N employees are matched with one supervisor; these costs are shown in appendix figure 7.5. Setting costs equal, this suggests that ($W_S^M - W_S^F$) = $N \times \theta$. Again, all male supervisors receive a higher wage than female supervisors (see appendix figure 7.6). This follows from the same argument as above; the presence of male employees being supervised by female supervisors suggests that male supervisors are in relatively short supply. And, at the margin, the relative added value of an additional male supervisor is $N \times \theta$.

In summary, the model described above implies that (1) male employees are expected to be supervised by male supervisors. However, in the extreme case where some male employees are supervised by females the following occur: (2) All female employees will receive a higher wage than all male employees, (3) female employees will not be supervised by male supervisors, and (4) all male supervisors will receive a higher wage than all female supervisors. What should be noted at this point is that one major implication that is in the discrimination effects model does not occur here. Here, male employees do not receive a different wage when working with a female supervisor.

THEORY 3: HUMAN CAPITAL

The underlying idea in the third theory is that early career on-the-job training contributes to employees' future wage growth and promotion opportunities. If the cost of training depends upon the gender match between supervisors and employees, then certain gender matches might imply relatively more training opportunities for those employees, and thus a relatively higher likelihood of promotion and increased wage growth. The model begins as follows: To keep things simple, a two-period framework is utilized. Assume that within a job, there are two potential paths, or "tracks," on which an employee can be placed.[37] On the "training track" (fast track) the employee receives training from his or her supervisor in the first period.[38] Training will decrease an employee's productivity in period 1, but increase it in period 2. If an employee is trained in period 1, he or she will then be promoted to a higher position in period 2 (up one rung on the job ladder). On the "no-training track" the employee does not receive training.

The employee's contribution to output (marginal product) on each track for periods 1 and 2 is shown in appendix figure 7.7. Here t is greater than zero, and a_i is between zero and one. Note that a_i has an employee subscript (i); the lost output (cost) from training depends upon the employee who is being trained. However, t does not have any subscript; once an individual is trained, his or her productivity does not depend on his or her "trainability" (a_i).

Which employees should be placed on which track? An efficient promotion rule suggests that an employee will receive on-the-job training and a subsequent promotion (be placed on the training track) if the increased

Appendix Figure 7.4   Employee Wages

	Male Supervisor	Female Supervisor
Male Employees	W_E^P	W_E^P
Female Employees	.....	$W_E^P + \theta$

Appendix Figure 7.5   Work Group Costs (One Supervisor and N Employees)

	Male Supervisor	Female Supervisor
Male Employees	$W_S^M + N \times W_E^P$	$W_S^F + N \times W_E^P$
Female Employees	.....	$W_S^F + N \times (W_E^P + \theta)$

Appendix Figure 7.6   Supervisor Wages

	Male Supervisor	Female Supervisor
Male Employees	$W_S^F + N \times \theta$	W_S^F
Female Employees	.....	W_S^F

output post-training is greater than the lost output during training:[39]

$$(1-a*)+(1+t)=1+1$$
$$\Rightarrow a* = t; \tag{1}$$

$a*$ is the threshold below which training will result in a higher sum of output in periods 1 and 2 (recall this is a two-period model) compared with the no-training track. That is, it is efficient for employees whose trainability (a_i) is lower than t to be placed on the training track.

To keep things very simple, it is assumed that within the job applicant population there are individuals who can be trained at high cost (with training cost (a_i) equal to a_H) and individuals who can be trained at low cost (with training cost (a_i) equal to a_L). In addition, assume that $a_L < t = a^* < a_H$. Clearly, it is only efficient for those individuals with a low training cost (a_L) to be placed on the training track.

Given equation 1, and the knowledge of the two possible levels of trainability of job market applicants, it is assumed that a competitive firm determines that the optimal size for a work group consists of N employees and one supervisor. The competitive firm then hires a number of employees to fill work groups of size N. During the interview process, both the firm and the employee learn the individual employee's trainability (a_i). Thus, the employer will assign the low-training-cost employees to the training track and the high-training-cost employees to the no-training track.

What wage schedule will attract workers of each type to the efficient track? For those who do not receive training, the wages in periods 1 and 2 offered by the competitive firm are assumed to equal the employee's contribution to output (marginal product) each period, which is 1. Thus, $W_1^N = W_2^N = 1$. For those who will receive training, wages in both periods will be set so that the net contribution per training track employee is greater than or equal to zero over the two periods (as well as at least as great as the no-training track wage):

$$[(1 - a_L - W_1^T) + (1 + t - W_2^T)] \geq 0$$
$$\Rightarrow [(1 - a_L) + (1 + t)] \geq W_1^T + W_2^T (\geq W_1^N + W_2^N (= 1 + 1)). \qquad (2)$$

Since equation 2 is one equation with two unknowns, only the total wages paid over the two periods will be defined.[40] However, it is assumed here that a Becker (1975) type of framework for firm-specific (or general) training occurs; thus, the training track employee wage is less than what it would have been without training ($1 = W_1^N \geq W_1^T \geq 1 - a_L$) in period 1 and more than what it would have been without training ($1 = W_2^N \leq W_2^T \leq 1 + t$) in period 2.[41] This implies an increasing wage profile for employees on the training track. The wage profiles for individuals on both tracks are sketched in appendix figure 7.8.

Thus far supervisor type has not played a role. Suppose that the only time that supervisor type can have a differential effect is during training in period 1. Some supervisor-employee type matches may be more productive in training than others. The literature on mentoring provides one rationale why this might be so. This could also occur for a number of other reasons, including ease of information transfer (communications), networking, and so on.

Suppose that if a male employee on the training track is matched with a female supervisor, the lost output during training in period 1 is an additional fixed amount θ_M; the benefit from training in period 2 remains

**Appendix Figure 7.7   Employee Productivity
on the No-Training
Track and the
Training Track**

	No-Training Track	Training Track
Period 1	1	$1 - a_i$
Period 2	1	$1 + t$

unchanged. Now the cost of training this employee is $\theta_M + a_L$ (which in total is assumed to be less than t—so training will still occur). If a male employee is matched with a male supervisor (or a female employee is matched with either type of supervisor) the costs and benefits from training remain unchanged. This has implications for who is matched with whom on the training track; one would expect that male employees will be systematically matched with male supervisors owing to the lower training cost.

In summary, the labor market implications of the model are as follows: (1) Employees on the training track are expected to have steeper wage profiles than those on the no-training track (this involves a lower wage than otherwise in period 1 and a higher wage than otherwise in period 2), (2) individuals on the training track are expected to receive a promotion following the period of on-the-job training, and (3) male employees on the training track are expected to be systematically matched with male supervisors.[42] Putting (1) through (3) together, male employees who work with male supervisors are expected, on average (because they are more likely to be on the training track), to have higher wage growth as well as higher promotion probabilities than male employees with female supervisors. Note that if (firm-) specific training is occurring, then individuals on the training track would also be expected to have lower rates of turnover (Becker 1975). In addition, if the model were extended so that female employees' training costs were also affected by a certain type of supervisor, then additional systematic matching of employee and supervisor gender on the training track would occur with the types of implications listed above.

What should be noted is that some implications regarding supervisor gender here do not arise in the discrimination and productivity effects models described above. These involve wage paths and promotion probabilities.[43]

Appendix Figure 7.8   Employee Wage Profiles for the No-Training Track and the Training Track

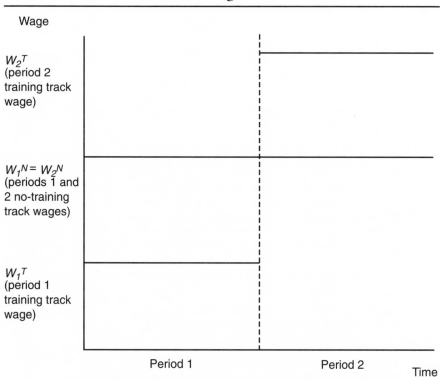

NOTES

1. However, Goldin (1986) notes, in her work on monitoring costs and occupational segregation in manufacturing industries at the turn of the century, that in female-intensive industries female supervisors were used to supervise female workers and male piece-rate workers.

2. Within an employee discrimination framework, Ferber and Green's results (1991) suggest that both men and women prefer to work for female supervisors and are willing to receive lower wages in return for this "positive" job attribute; this does not seem very plausible.

3. In addition, the causes could be different, given that Ragan and Tremblay's data (1988) consist of individuals who are very young (just beginning their careers), while individuals in Ferber and Green's data (1991) are older and have much longer labor market experience.

4. The 1980 Census of the Population data are used because they are closest to the year's data used most in the empirical analysis in this paper. A small number of occupations include separate three-digit codes that

identify both supervisors and employees; most of these are shown in table 7.1.

5. The 1990 Census of Population data depict an increase in the proportion of female supervisors (from 1980), particularly in the first three occupations listed in table 7.1.

6. Recall that (5) is not testable with the NLSY data set because it does not contain supervisory wages.

7. "At the margin" refers to the "value" of the last female employee hired by firms (note that this employee will be placed with a female supervisor).

8. For simplicity, a two-period model is assumed.

9. See appendix figure 7.8 for a sketch of the wage profiles for each track.

10. In the extreme case that a male employee on the training track is matched with a female supervisor, then the types of wage implications of the "productivity effects" model occur. That is, all male training track employees earn a relatively lower wage than all female training track employees. However, given that the wage difference that matters in this model is between the training track and the no-training track employees (and male employees on the training track will be matched whenever possible with male supervisors) this case has not been emphasized.

11. As will be noted later in the paper, the conclusions do not change much when the wage trajectory is extended out further in time.

12. Tenure in 1982 has been restricted to three years or less because one objective of this paper is to test for the impact of early career supervisor-provided on-the-job training, which is assumed to happen within the first few years on the job. The only constraints placed on the 1983 and 1984 interview data are that the wages are between $2 and $50 (and individuals are not in the military), since supervisor gender may have an effect on (for example) hours worked per week. Note that the wage used in the analysis is for the "CPS job" for each interview year; this is defined as the "current/most recent job since the last interview," so that individuals are not necessarily employed at the time of each year's interview. Lynch (1992) uses this same definition in her analysis of private sector training using the NLSY.

13. Note that a direct measure of supervisor-provided on-the-job training is not provided in the NLSY during this time period; thus, information about learning, promotions, and wage profiles are used as an indirect test of this occurrence.

14. Sorensen (1989) follows this type of procedure.

15. Note that the number of individuals in the 1983 and 1984 samples fell. For women, 197 of the 308 missing wage observations in 1983 and 241 of the 390 in 1984 were due to individuals not working. For men, 112 of the 267 missing wage observations in 1983 and 108 of the 326 in 1984 were due to individuals not working.

16. Note that $-.034 = [\exp(-.035) - 1]$. When the female sector variable is treated as a continuous variable, the impact of the female supervisor variable remains virtually the same; recall that the female sector variable is defined in table 7.3.

17. Probits are often used in cases with a dichotomous dependent variable to estimate the probability of an event occurring (for example, the probability of a supervisor being female versus male). See Maddala (1983) for a further description of this technique.

18. The finding that the magnitudes of the female supervisor wage effects are not equal for male and female employees further argues against the discrimination theory.

19. Ordered probits are often used in cases with an ordered (or ranked) polychotomous dependent variable to estimate jointly the probability of an event occurring (for example, the probability that an individual states the likelihood he or she will receive a promotion is very high versus high versus low versus very low). See Greene (1993) for a further description of this technique.

20. Marginal effects for continuous variables were calculated by taking the derivative of the probability of the particular event (for example, the response is "not true at all"), obtaining the predicted value for each individual in the sample, and then averaging over the sample. For dichotomous variables (such as supervisor gender), the difference in the probabilities of the particular event (again, for example, the response is "not true at all") defined when the dichotomous variable equals 1 and equals 0 was calculated for each individual, and then averaged over the sample. (See Greene 1993 for a further description of this calculation.) This all corresponds to the sample analog of the expected marginal effect for a random individual in the population.

21. The seemingly unrelated regressions system consists of stacked wage equations (by year), estimated by generalized least squares (which allows the disturbance terms across time periods to be correlated). One benefit of this technique is that it allows the covariance between all coefficient estimates to be obtained easily, which is useful for hypothesis testing (to test, for example, whether the female supervisor coefficients in 1982 and 1983 are equal).

22. In a balanced panel the number of observations is constant across each year (thus, here individuals must be present in the sample for the years 1982–1984). Probit estimations of the probability of being in the 1983 and 1984 samples do not suggest that supervisor gender systematically influences the probability of being present in the later samples.

23. Although, at best a Wald test rejects the null hypothesis that the difference in coefficients is zero at the 10 percent significance level.

24. That is, looking at 1987 and 1990 data.

25. Reed and Dahlquist (1994) also interpret this question as providing a measure of general on-the-job training. Also note that Parson's empirical analysis (1985) focuses on males in the NLSY.

26. Multinomial logits are often used in cases with an unordered poly-chotomous dependent variable to estimate jointly the probability of an event occurring (for example, the probability of an individual being laid off versus being fired versus quitting, as opposed to staying with the employer). See Maddala (1983) for a further description of this technique. The NLSY Work History data file was used for this. Those individuals who had stopped working at their job prior to the time of their 1982 interview (429 women and 435 men) were excluded from the analysis. The other exclusions are due to incomplete data as well as a different reason for leaving the job than the cells described above. Blau and Kahn (1981) look at the probability of a voluntary quit using NLS data; Farber (1994) looks at the hazard of a job ending using the NLSY, but does not explore why the job ended.

27. In other words, wages associated with working for a female supervisor may be lower in period one owing to training (as the empirical results suggest), but then there may be positive wage growth in later periods when the benefits of training are reaped.

28. In addition, since supervisor gender information is not available for later periods, it cannot be ruled out that the change in the variable's effect over time is possibly picking up the effect of that later period's supervisor gender. To get a sense of how much change might be occurring, some use of the 1980 data might be useful. Selecting the 1980 sample with the same criteria as that for the 1982 sample used in this paper, and requiring presence in the 1982 sample, results in a much smaller subsample of 665 women and 849 men. Of the 304 women with female supervisors in 1980, 109 changed to a male supervisor in 1982; of the 361 women with male supervisors in 1980, 106 changed to a female supervisor. Of the 56 men with female supervisors in 1980, 43 changed to a male supervisor in 1982; of the 793 men with male supervisors in 1980, 59 changed to a female supervisor.

29. Note that wage effects, promotion, turnover, and learning on the job are indirect ways to try to capture the occurrence of supervisor-provided on-the-job training; thus, it may not be very surprising that clear support for the training theory has not been found.

30. In this regard, it is also interesting to note that in the analyses the female sector and female supervisor variables nearly always have empirical impacts that move in the same direction.

31. An interesting finding is that for both male and female employees, supervisor gender has no impact on perceived competence of supervisor.

32. Recall that Ragan and Tremblay (1988) test for this, although they do not work out in detail a formal model (with all of its implications) as is done in this paper.

33. Arrow (1985) presents a similar model, in which the preferences of the discriminating labor group (say employees) are a function of the (racial) composition of the other labor group (say supervisors).

34. In the interest of "readability," I have used gender rather than a more general language of "types" of workers (for example, types X and Y).

35. In the Baldwin, Butler, and Johnson (1993) model, male employees receive a compensating wage differential for working for a female supervisor, as here. In addition, only those female supervisors who supervise male employees receive a wage cut. However, the question arises as to why some female supervisors would be willing to take the wage cut and why female supervisors' wages do not get bid down (relative to male supervisors' wages) in general.

36. θ is the monetary value of the productivity decrease.

37. Baker, Gibbs, and Holmstrom (1994), for example, observe that there are different career paths (tracks) within firms.

38. See Parsons (1990) for a discussion and review of the literature regarding the provision of on-the-job training by firms.

39. For example, see Lazear and Rosen (1990). Discounting is ignored here, for simplicity.

40. In equation 2 the best alternative wage is assumed to be the no-training wage. One could also imagine a scenario where those individuals with low training costs (a_L) have a higher alternative wage. If it is assumed that all of the rent (return from training) goes to the employees, then the net benefit to the firm in equation 2 is set equal to zero.

41. Hashimoto (1981) develops a model for firm-specific training where a rule for employee-firm sharing of the costs of firm-specific investment is derived. Note that if the training cost (a_H) for the high-training-cost people was placed in the first line of equation 2—in other words, equation 2 was rewritten for the high-training-cost individuals—then the total wages on the training track would be lower than those on the no-training track. Thus, the high-training-cost individuals will receive higher wages in the no-training track job.

42. In the extreme case that a male employee on the training track is matched with a female supervisor, then the types of wage implications of the "productivity effects" model occur. That is, all male training-track employees earn a relatively lower wage than all female training-track employees. However, given that the wage difference that matters in this model is between the training track and the no-training track employees (and male employees on the training track will be matched whenever possible with male supervisors) this case has not been emphasized.

43. Table 7.2 provides a summary of the labor market implications of the three theories presented above.

Commentary on Chapter 7

Solomon W. Polachek

In many ways current empirical analyses of individual labor market success lag behind recent theoretical models of personnel practices. Failing to get at the role one's supervisor plays in the earnings process is one illustration. (Exceptions include Laband and Lentz 1995 and Johnson and Scandura 1994.) One's supervisor may enhance productivity so sufficiently as to benefit not only the firm, but workers as well. This mentoring process has ramifications regarding both corporate behavior and governmental policy. Thus, understanding mentoring is important, and for this reason the Rothstein paper is a valuable addition to the labor economics literature.

The author's approach is to test several discrimination models using observations on 1,980 women and 2,319 men employed at least thirty hours per week who are not in the military, not in school, and not self-employed taken from the 1982–1984 National Longitudinal Survey of Youth (NLSY). Rather than immediately discuss the discrimination models, I look at the empirical work first, and then determine which models best fit the data.

Her empirical work (summarized in comment table 7.1) concentrates on estimating the impact of having a female supervisor on seven dependent variables: (1) current wage level, (2) wage gain, (3) perceived promotion likelihood, (4) perceived learning on the job, (5) probability of being laid off, (6) probability of being fired, and, finally, (7) probability of quitting. Two results are noteworthy. First, having a female supervisor decreases men's current wages more than women's (row 1). Second, having a female supervisor creates greater wage growth for men than for women (row 2). The only other statistically significant results are that women perceive greater learning from female supervisors and have a lower layoff probability; but men have a greater probability of being fired. However, gender differences of these latter results are statistically insignificant (denoted as NS in the table).

Rothstein examines essentially three theories: (1) an employee discrimination model in which the workers do not like working for supervisors of the opposite gender, (2) a productivity model in which workers find their output diminished when working with a supervisor of the opposite gender, and (3) a human capital model in which workers receive training from supervisors of the same gender. She concludes that "the empirical results do not provide strong, clear-cut support for any of the three theories." While I agree with these results,

Commentary Table 7.1   Summary of Rothstein Results

Impact of Female Supervisor on	Impact[a]		Rothstein Source Tables[b]	Statistical Approach
	Female	Male		
Wage level	$\vdash\dashv$	<	$\vdash\dashv$	7.12, 7.13, 7.6, 7.7	OLS
Wage growth	+	<	+	7.12, 7.13	Seemingly unrelated regression with panel data
Perceived promotion likelihood	$\vdash\dashv^{NS}$	<	$\vdash\dashv^{NS}$	7.10, 7.11	Ordered probit
Perceived learning on job	+		$-^{NS}$	7.14, 7.15	Ordered probit
Job separation: layoff	−		$+^{NS}$	7.16, 7.17	Logit
Job separation: fire	$+^{NS}$		$+^{NS}$	7.16, 7.17	Logit
Job separation: quit	$+^{NS}$		$+^{NS}$	7.16, 7.17	Logit

[a] The impact of a female supervisor on each of the seven labor market variables is denoted by the indicated sign. When relevant, an inequality sign indicates gender differences in magnitude. The sign for absolute value is | |. NS signifies magnitudes that are generally statistically insignificant.

[b] The numbers refer to the specific Rothstein tables that generated the specified result.

I suspect that the discrimination and productivity theories probably could have been ruled out on *a priori* grounds, that the evidence for the human capital on-the-job training model might be stronger than the paper suggests, and that rather than being an independent variable the supervisor variable might be proxying occupational segregation. After justifying these assertions, I make several suggestions to possibly enhance future empirical work.

I begin with the discrimination theory (commentary figure 7.1). Two variations are presented: one in which males need a wage premium to work for a female supervisor (upper panel), and one in which females need a premium to work for a male supervisor (lower panel). As Rothstein shows, efficiency dictates pairing male workers with male supervisors (the first case) and female workers with female supervisors (the second case). The extent to which male workers are paired with female supervisors in the first case (and female workers with male supervisors in the second) is indicative

Commentary Figure 7.1   Employee Discrimination Model

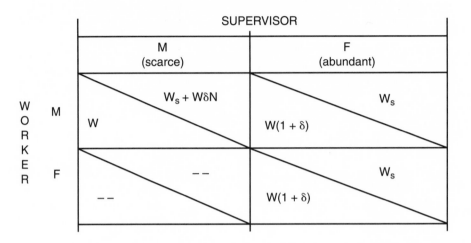

Male Workers Need Premium to Work with Female Supervisors

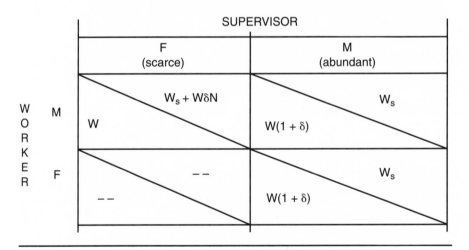

Female Workers Need Premium to Work with Male Supervisors

of a male supervisor scarcity coupled with an abundance of female supervisors. As Rothstein shows, this male supervisor scarcity causes firms to pay workers (independent of gender) a wage premium to work for women ($w(1 + \delta)$) and to pay male supervisors a premium over female supervisors. As a by-product *no* women work for men supervisors at all. Paying male supervisors more than female supervisors (($w_s + w \delta N$) vs. w_s) is not implausible, but assuming both women managers to be abundant and women workers to receive greater wages than men is unrealistic. Similarly, in the second case, predicting female supervisors to be paid better than male supervisors (even though female workers get less than male workers) is far-fetched. Thus, these discrimination theories can easily be dismissed, though Rothstein's empirical work nicely confirms this.

Rothstein's second theory assumes a worker's productivity to depend upon supervisor gender (commentary figure 7.2). Scenario one (upper panels) is that men working for women lowers male productivity, and scenario two (lower panels) is that women working for men lowers female productivity. Similar to the discrimination model above, efficient behavior implies pairing men to male supervisors (scenario one) and women to female supervisors (scenario two). Similar to the discrimination models, wages of workers and supervisors under both scenarios can be predicted. But here, too, unrealistic predictions emerge. For example, scenario one predicts higher female worker wages than male worker wages, and scenario two predicts female supervisors to be paid more than male supervisors. Thus, as before, one would be surprised were the empirical work to support these models, and no doubt it does not. Indeed, Rothstein rightly rules out these discrimination models before going on to the human capital approach.

While I suspect Rothstein is correct to move on, I believe many discrimination advocates would be more comfortable were she to test other discrimination models. And clearly there are many. For example, suppose that firms simply perceived women's output to be lower than men's (statistical discrimination). This means that female supervisors might be assigned to less productive lines (ones with older equipment), thus implying lower relative wages for both female supervisors and anyone (male or female) working in the less capital-intensive line. Since relatively more female workers are assigned to the weaker lines their wages are depressed less relative to males under the aegis of a female supervisor.

Of course, the problem with these discrimination models is that they are static in nature, dealing only with current wages, while having no life-cycle implications particularly regarding wage growth through human capital investments including job mobility. I am sure there are many wage growth scenarios, but I will go on to the human capital model whose purpose is precisely to look at just such implications.

Rothstein assumes larger training costs when men are paired with female rather than male supervisors. Based on this assumption, she concludes that men receive less training from female supervisors than male supervisors, and that women receive more training from female supervisors. As such, she predicts a positive female supervisor impact on wages for men (commentary table 7.2, row 1, column 3) and a negative sign for women (row 5, column 3). Less investment for men leads to smaller wage growth

Commentary Figure 7.2   Productivity Model

Female Supervisors Lower Male Workers' Productivity

		SUPERVISOR	
		M	F
WORKER	M	Q	$Q - \theta$
	F	Q	Q

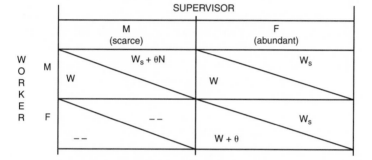

Male Supervisors Lower Female Workers' Productivity

		SUPERVISOR	
		F	M
WORKER	F	Q	$Q - \theta$
	M	Q	Q

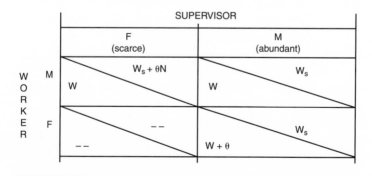

Commentary Table 7.2 Implications of the Three Models Assuming that Same-Gender Matches Are "More Productive" and the Empirical Findings

| | Implications of the Three Models | | | |
	Discrimination	Productivity	Human Capital	Empirical Findings
Example 1: Female Supervisor and Male Employee				
Employee wage in period 1	positive	no effect	positive[a] negative[b]	negative
Employee wage profile	no prediction	no prediction	negative[a] positive[b]	positive
Employee wage growth	no prediction	no prediction	negative[a] positive[b]	positive or no effect
Promotion probability	no prediction	no prediction	negative[a] positive[b]	no effect
Example 2: Female Supervisor and Female Employee				
Employee wage in period 1	negative	no effect	negative	negative
Employee wage profile	no prediction	no prediction	positive	positive
Employee wage growth	no prediction	no prediction	positive	positive or no effect
Promotion probability	no prediction	no prediction	positive	no effect

Note: If opposite-gender matches are assumed to be "more productive," then the signs in columns 1–3 of the table are reversed.

This is a modified version of table 14 in Rothstein's original paper presented at the Gender and Family Issues in the Workplace Conference. It is essentially her table 7.2 (in this volume) augmented by column 4 containing her empirical findings.

[a] Assumes males receive less training with female supervisor.

[b] Assumes compensation effects of tables 7.12 and 7.13.

(negative signs in rows 2 and 3 of column 3) and a lower promotion probability (negative sign in row 4) for men and opposite positive signs for women (rows 6–7). Data weakly bear out the predictions for women (column 4) yielding a negative coefficient in row 5 and a positive coefficient in row 6, but not for men (column 4) since one obtains a negative sign in row 1. However, taking the negative sign at face value, namely, that men obtain *more* (not less) training from female supervisors as implied by tables 7.12 and 7.13, the remaining signs (a positive effect on wages and wage growth) are consistent, thus supporting the human capital model.

Given my own work on wages I tend to agree with this interpretation. However, an alternative immediately comes to mind. Suppose that a supervisor's gender simply proxies an occupation's gender composition.[1] Female occupations most likely have female supervisors, so that having a female supervisor merely implies that one is in a female occupation. Were this the case one finds that female occupations pay less than male occupations, that being in a female occupation is a greater wage depressant for men than for women, and that wages are rising more quickly in female than in male occupations—all findings adequately documented in current literature (see Polachek 1987; Katz and Murphy 1992). Attributing supervisor's gender to reflect occupational segregation need not negate human capital since gender differences in occupational segregation can be attributed to life-cycle labor supply (see Polachek 1981).

One might argue that Rothstein tries to get at this possibility by modeling supervisor gender. However, she abandons this approach because models with supervisor gender yield poor results. Perhaps these poor results emerge from model misspecification. Rothstein uses "family characteristics:" that is, whether mother worked for pay, whether mother was a professional, mother's education, and whether a father figure was present in the household. Clearly, these variables are exogenous and predetermined, but it is not obvious that they predict supervisor gender.

Perhaps one could better get at the role of a supervisor's gender by exploiting the NLSY data more fully. Rothstein uses only 1982 data on supervisor gender. However, 1980 data are also available. Maybe more information on the role of supervisor gender can be gleaned by distinguishing labor market success for those with a female supervisor in *both* 1980 *and* 1982 compared with having a female supervisor in only one of the years.[2] One might also be able to interact supervisor gender with occupation, industry, and education to test for differential effects of one's supervisor.

Finally, one can question whether Rothstein's results generalize. The NLSY concentrates on workers in their teens and 20s, ages characterized by typically higher than normal job turnover. It is not obvious what impact supervisors have on this age group, so replicating this study for older workers would probably be valuable.

I close by reemphasizing my earlier statement that Rothstein's study is a valuable addition to the labor economics literature, especially given the dearth of empirically oriented work ascertaining the role that one's supervisor plays in one's earning potential. Understanding supervisor roles clearly has implications regarding corporate hiring policies, worker job choice, and government affirmative action policies. I look forward to seeing additional research on this important topic.

NOTES

1. Rothstein's table 7.1 supports this notion since female occupations tend to have female supervisors.

2. All this of course assumes that workers have one supervisor and the supervisor is either a male or female supervisor. Multiple supervisors would lead to a more complicated dummy variable structure.

Commentary on Chapter 7

Cordelia W. Reimers

This paper tackles an interesting and important question that elicits strong opinions, often based on stereotypes—for example, that women are more sensitive and nurturing, men are more authoritarian, and both are likely to favor their own gender—but without much systematic evidence. Young workers need to know whether their supervisor's gender will affect their pay and career path and, if so, why. Is it because their productivity and training will be affected, because of discrimination, or because supervisor gender is associated with high-status versus low-status departments or fast-track versus slow-track jobs? Employers need to know whether their workers' productivity will be affected by whether their supervisors are male or female. The answers bear on whether the "glass ceiling" is simply the residue of past custom and lingering discrimination or whether it is rooted in productivity considerations—in which case it will be much more resistant to change.

Rothstein proposes three theories of why supervisor gender might influence labor market outcomes of young workers. All of them rely on gender "mismatches" between supervisors and employees. They implicitly assume frictionless labor markets with perfectly elastic supplies of each type and gender of labor to the firm, but fixed supplies to the market. Theory 1 posits employee discrimination against supervisors of the "wrong" gender. According to theory 2, current productivity is affected by the supervisor-employee gender combination. Theory 3, on the other hand, says that training quality, and therefore future productivity, is affected by the supervisor-employee gender combination.

Thus, all of Rothstein's theoretical models rely on negative effects of certain supervisor-employee gender combinations. However, it is important to keep in mind that, in the world imagined here, one type of mismatch will never occur in market equilibrium. If the only "bad" matches were ones between the relatively scarce types of supervisor (female) and employee (male), such mismatches would never actually take place. To see this, suppose that female supervisors are bad for male employees' utility, productivity, or training. Since the share of supervisors who are male is larger than the share of employees who are male (see table 7.1), the market would assign all male employees to male supervisors, and female employees to both male and female supervisors, with no "mismatches" occurring.

Thus, if female supervisors are assumed to have a negative effect on young male workers, we need a richer theory to explain why men would be assigned to them in market equilibrium. Such mismatches must be an equilibrium outcome in order to have an impact on wages. If the mismatches are just optimization errors (that is, "accidents"), then there would be no systematic market pressures causing wages to adjust.

What about other types of gender mismatch? Suppose that female supervisors are bad for female employees, but not for male employees. Then women would be assigned to male supervisors insofar as possible. Only in occupations where women constitute a larger proportion of supervisors than men do of employees (for example, food preparation and financial records processing) would it be necessary for women to supervise women, with the hypothesized negative consequences. Alternatively, suppose that male supervisors are bad for male employees. Such a mismatch could be avoided in the above-mentioned occupations, but not in others, where there are not enough female supervisors to match all the male employees. On the other hand, if male supervisors are bad for female employees, mismatches will be unavoidable, given the current relative numbers of male and female supervisors and employees.

Unfortunately, the empirical results of this study are inconsistent with the implications of all three theoretical models. Rothstein's main findings are that having a female supervisor has a significant negative effect on the current wage of both male and female young workers, but no significant effect on their future wages or perceived chances of promotion. Thus, the data fail to support the hypothesis that supervisor gender affects training costs or effectiveness. If training were affected, we would expect to see a positive impact on future wages as well as the negative impact on current wages. The finding of greater subsequent wage growth of young workers after having a female supervisor is to be expected, as their wages approach the average for all workers after having been depressed. Since their wages do not become higher than average, there is no basis for interpreting the wage growth as a payoff to training provided by the supervisor.

The empirical results also fail to support the hypothesis that having a female supervisor reduces a worker's utility or productivity. We saw above that if female supervisors adversely affect only male employees, such mismatches would not occur (except by accident, without affecting wage rates). If female supervisors are disliked by female as well as male employees, then the predicted compensating differential for working for a woman would be *positive*, not negative. If female supervisors hurt the productivity of both women and men, Rothstein's theory shows that there would be no impact on employees' wages; rather, female *supervisors'* wages would be reduced.

Nor does this study find empirical support for the hypothesis that male supervisors impair productivity of either female or male workers. If male supervisors hurt female (but not male) employees' productivity, then both male employees and female supervisors should get a wage premium, as the relatively scarce inputs; but there would be no wage differential among employees due to supervisor gender. If male supervisors hurt males' (but not females') productivity, then both female employees and supervisors should receive a wage premium, but again there would be no employee wage differences based on supervisor gender. If male supervisors reduce both males' and females' productivity, their own wages would be reduced, but there would be no effect on employees' wages.

Within Rothstein's theoretical framework, the only case in which all types of gender combinations would exist in equilibrium and a female supervisor would depress both male and female workers' current (but not future) wages is if both men and women prefer working for a woman; that is, if there is employee discrimination against male supervisors. In this case both men and women will pay for the privilege of working for a woman via a wage reduction, and all types of work groups will be observed.

If women (but not men) prefer a female supervisor, then women will be matched with women insofar as possible, while all male employees will be assigned to male supervisors. Since there are not enough female supervisors to go around, some female employees will be assigned to male supervisors and will require a compensating wage differential since this reduces their utility. Male employees, being the relatively scarce input, will get the compensating differential, too, as a rent, even though they do not care about their supervisor's gender. No matches between female supervisors and male employees will occur in equilibrium.

Alternatively, suppose that men (but not women) prefer to be supervised by a woman. Then male employees will be assigned to female supervisors insofar as possible. In most occupations there are not enough female supervisors to go around. In these occupations, some of the men and all of the women will have male supervisors. Male employees who are assigned to a male supervisor will require a compensating differential. At the margin, this raises the value of an additional female employee, and female employees' wages will be bid up to match. Thus, male employees' wages will be higher if they have a male supervisor, and now it is the women who receive a rent. No female-female matches will exist in equilibrium. On the other hand, in the few occupations where there are enough female supervisors for all the male employees, men will not work for men in equilibrium, and supervisor gender will not affect wages.

So far, it would seem that we have a hypothesis—employee discrimination by both men and women against male supervisors—that is consistent with the empirical evidence. But in this scenario, Rothstein's theory predicts that female supervisors would get a higher wage than male supervisors, as a rent to the relatively scarce resource. Since employees of female supervisors get a lower wage, cost equalization across work groups supervised by men and women requires a higher wage for female supervisors. While Rothstein's data do not include supervisors' wages, I strongly doubt that this prediction would be confirmed by any data! So we need to look further for a theory that can explain her empirical results.

One common supposition not mentioned by Rothstein is that supervisors play favorites; employees of their own gender get better performance ratings, raises, and access to training than equally (or even less) productive or trainable employees of the opposite gender. However, supervisor discrimination (that is, favoritism) does not predict that both men and women would be paid more when they have a male supervisor. Moreover, if male supervisors favor male employees, men would never work for women in market equilibrium.

The explanation of the empirical results that seems most plausible to me is one suggested by Rothstein after finding that the results do not support any of her theoretical models. It is that female supervisors tend to be in "female" sex-typed jobs, in which wages are depressed by "crowding," and in the lower-status, lower-wage, slow-track departments in a firm's hierarchy. Their supervisees, therefore, have lower wages; but this is because of their job and departmental assignment, no matter what their supervisor's gender. Insofar as occupational variables do not adequately capture within-firm job hierarchies and the sex-typing of jobs, the supervisor-gender coefficient is subject to omitted variable bias. In other words, female supervisors appear to depress their workers' current wages because of the kinds of jobs they supervise, not because they have any direct negative effect.

Chapter 8

Three Perspectives on Policy

1. Work and Family Benefits
Olivia Mitchell

2. Work-Family Policies and Equality Between Women and Men
Barbara Bergmann

3. The Role of Child Care and Parental Leave Policies in Supporting Family and Work Activities
H. Elizabeth Peters

This chapter offers three perspectives on the policy implications of the papers included in this volume. In the first section, Olivia S. Mitchell summarizes recent trends in the availability of "family-friendly" policies. The following sections by Barbara R. Bergmann and H. Elizabeth Peters consider some of the larger issues which are raised as these policies evolve. Bergmann particularly emphasizes the impact of family-friendly policies on gender equality, while Peters focuses on potential conflicts among the various goals which family and workplace policies are designed to address.

Work and Family Benefits

Olivia S. Mitchell

This paper examines recent developments in a particular type of employee benefits, namely, those commonly termed "work and family benefits." It is my goal to describe briefly what these benefits are and what they are evolving into as employers seek to shape their benefit offerings to meet new American patterns of work and family.

Over the past decade, this complex and somewhat broad group of employee benefit offerings has become a topic earning much public comment. Many consulting and research groups publish listings of the most "family-friendly" companies in America catching the eye of national news reporters. Numerous business magazines spotlight companies that go the extra mile to help attract and retain young family-minded employees. Many large companies today include information about corporate-sponsored child care in their recruitment brochures, others tout medical coverage for same-sex partners, and still others proudly point to national elder care referral networks to help employees check up on their elderly parents who live a good distance away.

What is common to this diverse set of benefit offerings? In what sense can they be defined as "family" or, more broadly, "work and family" benefits? Is there any evidence that they are increasing in scope, as the news media would have us believe? And should we interpret evidence of an upward trend in these benefits as proof that American companies are more family-friendly than ever before? As I will show, there is very little quantitative evidence on many of these questions, and hence there is scope and need for much new research. In particular there is no representative survey evidence indicating what companies and their workers spend each year on work and family benefits, much less how these patterns changed over the last several years. What evidence there is suggests some movement toward the types of benefits likely to be preferred by workers with dependents. I also show, however, that companies venturing into these new benefit arenas have found them fraught with difficulties.

DEFINING WORK AND FAMILY BENEFITS

Nonspecialists might be surprised to learn that there is no single definition of what is, or is not, a work and family benefit. If one casts an eye over the range of employee benefit plans most frequently offered, such as income replacement plans (for example, disability/life/medical insurance, pensions), time off with pay (for example, vacation/personal/sick leave), and in-kind benefits (for example, free or low-cost merchandise, free or subsidized child or elder care), it seems that most of these should be included in a family-friendly catchall list. That is, insurance plans offer both the worker and his/her dependents peace of mind against the threat of high medical bills, or loss of income due to inability to work (or lack of desire to remain on the job beyond a certain age). Time off opportunities can be and often are used to tend to oneself or one's dependents when ill or on vacation, or when children's school is out. In-kind benefits help subsidize consumption costs for workers and their dependents—for instance, lowering food or travel costs, or helping employees find and pay for care for children and/or elderly parents. Employers offering these forms of compensation can and sometimes do cast them as family-friendly benefits, even though this often results in relabeling old benefit plans rather than radically restructuring nonsalary benefits.

How then can we judge whether U.S. companies have truly become more family-friendly? Finding benefit offerings that do not simply involve a relabeling of old benefits is made possible by turning to published data from the Employee Benefit Survey (EBS), a nationwide inventory of employee benefit plan features and provisions collected periodically by the Bureau of Labor Statistics (BLS) of the U.S. Department of Labor. Here we report a short time-series for a handful of benefits provided by medium-sized and large firms—the only arguably "clear-cut" set of family benefits for which comparable statistics are available over time.[1]

Available information is displayed in three figures derived from the BLS surveys. Figure 8.1 indicates the proportion of employees working in medium-sized and large firms that offered *unpaid* maternity and paternity benefits in 1988, 1989, 1991 and 1993, which were the years the EBS was fielded for this set of companies. The evidence shows that there was a sharp rise in maternity leave provisions for women, from 33 percent in 1988 to 60 percent just five years later. Even larger proportional increases apply to paternity leave provisions.

This sharp increase in benefit coverage is a direct consequence of the 1993 Family and Medical Leave Act, which mandated companies with fifty workers or more to offer up to twelve weeks of unpaid leave on the birth of a child (and including adoption and foster care). Because the Act went into effect in August 1993, and the EBS data collection process occurred partway through

**Figure 8.1   Family Time Off Benefits: Proportion of Employees
Offered Coverage**

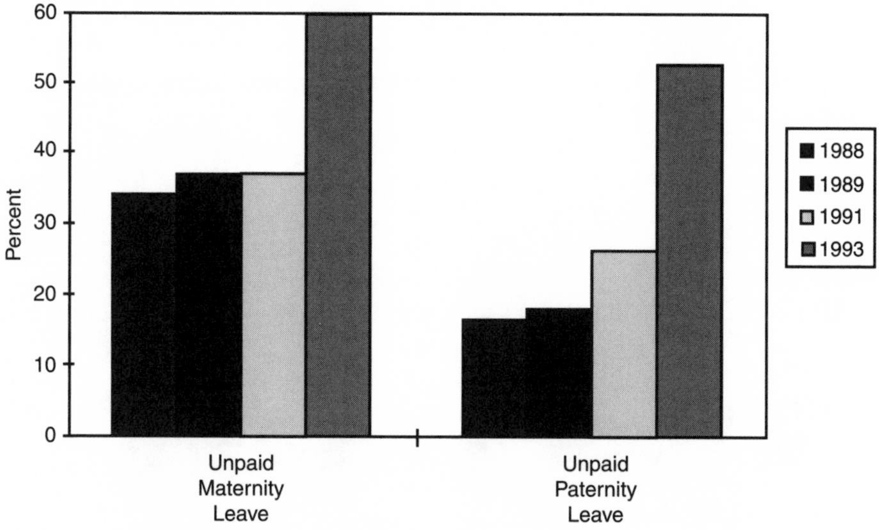

Source: U.S. Department of Labor (various years).

the law's implementation period, the 1993 data include a mix of plans before and after the Act's taking effect. As a result, it should be expected that as companies move into compliance, coverage rates will rise over time.

In support of the view that the 1993 legislation in fact did bring about a rapid rise in parental leave time are other statistics on *paid* parental leave (not shown in figure 8.1). The 1993 Act did not require that *paid* leave be offered, and the evidence suggests that most employers do not provide it now, nor have they for years. There is no upward time trend of family-friendly benefits here: The proportion of employees offered paid maternity leave stood at about 3 percent in 1993 compared with 2 percent in 1988 when the first EBS collected these data (in both cases 1 percent of the plans offered paid paternity leave).[2] On a related matter, the data reveal no upswing trend in *paid personal leave*, a benefit likely to be particularly appealing to parents: In 1988, 24 percent of the workers were offered personal leave (most such arrangements provide three days per year or less), and by 1993 the figure had dropped slightly to 21 percent. So on the one hand, unpaid leave is now more accessible to both mothers and fathers on the arrival of a child, but on the other hand, this movement seems to be mainly attributable to mandates rather than a comprehensive effort on the part of benefit designers.

Figure 8.2   Family Benefits: Proportion of Employees with Coverage

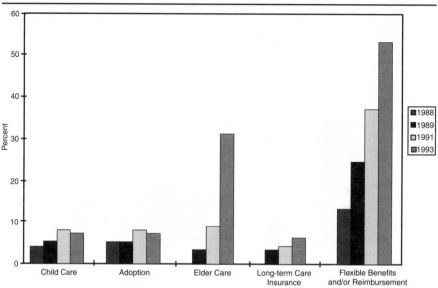

Source: U.S. Department of Labor (various years).

Another question that one might ask is whether employers have become more accommodating in helping employees pay for costs associated with dependent care, either by subsidizing these payments directly or by offering employees access to group insurance pools.

Figure 8.2 summarizes available information on this point. There has been little growth since the late 1980s along several important dimensions: Only 7 percent of employees in this sample who needed adoption help or child care were offered direct financial support in 1993. While this figure is higher than the 4 or 5 percent in 1988, it is nowhere near the coverage rates that readers of the popular press might expect given frequent news stories on child care offerings in corporate America. Lack of growth also characterizes long-term care plans, probably because nursing home insurance is still a relatively new product and because many employees do not perceive an immediate need to obtain coverage for themselves (and their dependents).

Before concluding that medium-sized and large firms are not becoming more family-friendly, however, two dramatic changes in the benefits environment must be noted in figure 8.2. One is that elder care is one of the fastest-growing benefits in the marketplace, initially provided by only a handful of firms but now offered to more than one third of all EBS employees surveyed. Unfortunately, the EBS questionnaire provides no additional insight into what types of elder care benefits are provided, nor what their cost might be to companies or workers. Recent discussion of these plans in the business press suggests that they are usually "resource and referral" programs, offering employees guidance on finding day care or nursing services for elderly parents, counseling services for dependent elderly relatives, and the like. Those interested in family benefits will find this a prime area for further research.

The second rapidly growing corporate plan that can be considered a family-friendly benefit is the flexible benefits and/or reimbursement account. As figure 8.2 shows, coverage for this option has grown more rapidly than the others listed, and in 1993 53 percent of employees were offered these benefits, up from 13 percent in 1988. The essence of these plans is that they permit certain expenses to be paid for out of pretax income—in particular, dependent care costs (and some health care costs). Such plans are most useful to those using relatively high-cost providers, since the tax code allowing workers to set aside up to $5,000 pretax per year is limited to expenses paid for licensed providers. Dependent care accounts are clearly helpful to employees in family settings where they bear a substantial portion of the cost of taking care of children or dependent elderly parents.

A final area in which progress can be judged on the family benefits front is medical insurance plans. Figure 8.3 summarizes two key family-friendly features of such health insurance programs: whether the medical plan offers well-baby care and whether the plan provides immunization and inoculation coverage. Coverage increases are apparent for both benefits, but the growth in well-baby care is particularly marked, rising from 31 to 48 percent among the employees in the medium-sized and large firms surveyed. Certainly this trend is in part attributable to the rapid spread of health maintenance organizations (HMOs) and other prepaid plans, since these tend to emphasize prevention more than the traditional indemnity plans of the past. It is probable that changes in the national medical insurance market produced some of these new corporate medical plans appealing to families, though some innovative approaches to plan design were no doubt sought by employers.

THE GROWING COMPLEXITIES OF DEFINING "FAMILY"

A significant problem that companies confront when defining which benefits are family-friendly is that it is becoming difficult to define exactly what a family is. In the past, families could usually be defined by residential unit, but now complex marriage and divorce patterns often result in split custody arrangements. For example, employer-provided health care plans offer family coverage to children who spend a substantial part of the year living with a different parent, perhaps one not even living in the same city. This creates difficulties for many HMO and man-

Figure 8.3   Medical Benefits: Proportion of Employees Offered Coverage

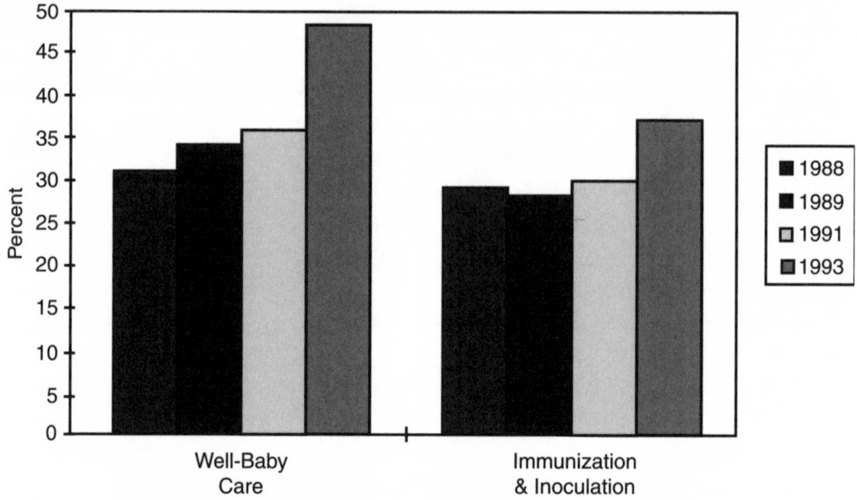

Source: U.S. Department of Labor (various years).

aged care health plans. Employee benefit designers are also having to cope head-on with defining who is eligible for family benefit coverage when their employees have "blended" families with stepchildren from several different unions or when benefit plans cover older children who have returned home after completing schooling. Defining which spouse's parents can be covered under elder care arrangements can be likewise treacherous.

A related issue is the fact that some larger companies have recently begun to provide health insurance benefit coverage for unmarried same-sex partners, requiring that benefit designers take a careful look at how eligibility is defined and what benefits are offered. This stance has not always proven to be politically popular. Recent news reports revealed that Texas politicians reneged on tax provisions designed to attract an Apple computer manufacturing plant to their community when it was discovered that Apple makes health care insurance available to same-sex partners. While this controversy was settled in the employer's favor, it demonstrates that defining "family" has become sensitive beyond many benefit designers' initial expectations, and not all of these family-friendly benefits necessarily generate positive publicity.

How should employers think about defining family relationships for benefits purposes? A step was taken in the 1993 Family and Medical Leave Act, where legislators offered a relatively broad view of family relationships. A recent legislative analysis points out that "[t]he bill recognizes that fewer Americans live in families with two parents, one of whom stays home to care for the children. Often both parents work and a child might be a stepchild rather than a biological child of the employee requesting leave. Therefore, the definition of 'child' includes not only biological and adopted children, but also stepchildren, foster children, legal wards, and children of people acting 'in loco parentis' (that is, in place of parents—grandparents, for example)" (Foster Higgins, *Spotlight*, February 17, 1993, p. 3). Thus far, the interpretation of the "elder parent" relationship has been limited to the traditional cases, but it can be presumed that the definitions will be challenged in the near term (for example, can a divorced woman receive elder care benefits for her ex-husband's widowed mother?). If much money is behind these benefits, incentives will immediately arise to redefine family structure in still new ways.

THE NEAR-TERM OUTLOOK

In assembling these tantalizingly few bits of evidence on company policy toward family benefits in the United States, it becomes clear that several trends are making the workplace more family-friendly. However, these movements are slow, in part because the definition of what a family is appears to have changed of late, and along with this definition, family needs have changed. These needs are to some extent being met in the workplace:

(1) Employers examined here are offering more time off to working people, particularly more leave for maternity and paternity, mainly attributable to the 1993 Family and Medical Leave Act. There is no parallel rise in paid time off, however.

(2) Many employees are covered by tax-qualified reimbursement accounts that allow them to use pretax earnings to cover dependent care and out-of-pocket medical expenses. These accounts certainly represent important and valuable family-friendly changes.

(3) Many employees at medium-sized and large firms receive medical care plans with family-friendly aspects such as well-baby care and immunization.

What is not yet well known is how much these new work and family benefits cost and how the burden is borne. For example, the costs of mandated employee benefits are generally thought to be imposed on employees in the form of lower pay and other benefits (and/or lower labor demand), implying that the additional benefits legislated under the 1993 Act described above may have cost covered employees in other ways. Sometimes employers have found that offering family benefits is useful in gaining public attention, but few have been willing to attach both cost and benefit price tags to these plans. The danger in this latter approach is that after the novelty of a plan has worn off and the plan's expenses mount up, a corporation's commitment to such a benefit may wear thin. Only if the benefit plan design is subject to careful testing will the plan's essential features be made internally consistent and the plan warrant continuation, in this increasingly challenging world for benefits specialists.

ACKNOWLEDGMENTS

Tricia Quarmby provided capable research assistance, Fran Blau offered useful comments, and research support is acknowledged from the Wharton School. Opinions are the author's alone.

NOTES

1. Somewhat different versions of the EBS study have been administered to public-sector (state and local) employers and also to small employers in the recent past. However, the questionnaires were not identical to those on the medium-sized and large firms discussed here, and published data on work and family benefits are not available in this format. See U.S. Department of Labor (various years).

2. Many states' workers' compensation plans offer women paid time off after the birth of a child, a policy that can substitute for paid maternity leave to some extent. In addition, the Pregnancy Discrimination Act of 1978 requires that companies offering medical disability leave plans must cover pregnancy like any other disability (firms without such programs are not required to institute them).

Work-Family Policies and Equality Between Women and Men

Barbara R. Bergmann

Workplace policies designed to enable employees to carry on comfortably the activities of their private lives can have an important effect on the degree of equality between women and men. The desirability and importance of such equality is under contention, and workplace policies are one of the fields of battle. I would argue that there is a tendency for "family-friendly" policies to be formulated in such a way as to promote greater inequality. For those of us who put a high value on equality between the sexes, it is thus particularly important that we pay close attention to the effects of these policies on equality. The usual target of such policies is the legally married heterosexual couple with children. But the problems of single parents—even more acute—also deserve attention, as do those of homosexual couples.

In the traditional work arrangements of urban married people in this century only the husband had paid employment and, with minor exceptions, the wife did all of the unpaid "family work."[1] This radical difference in activities was both a source and an expression of gender inequality. The entry of married women into paid employment has considerably reduced gender inequality, but has made surprisingly little change in the allocation of unpaid family work between spouses. (See Hood 1993; Hochschild and Machung 1989.) Husbands have benefited from the increased cash income from the paid work that wives have come to do, but they have not had to put out additional effort to any great extent. Wives have also benefited, but to a lesser extent. The benefit to them of the increased income (and in some cases the increase in interesting activities and opportunities) has been partly counterbalanced by their greater workload.

One reason that husbands of employed women have continued to withhold their labor from the tasks of running the household has been the strength and persistence of the ideology that declares each task as appropriate for a person of a particular sex. Another is the low status associated with family work. Still another has been the lack of ability of wives to enforce or motivate changes in husbands' duties. Still another is the lack of

277

public discussion about what the norm should be and the shame that should be visited on those violating it.

Of course, one result has been greatly increased strain on the wife, as the time she has devoted to the performance of work has increased and her opportunities for leisure and sleep-time have decreased. This increased burdening of the wife has been the major source of demands for workplace policies that accommodate family life. A second source has been the abandonment by some wives of certain activities, which have been felt to be particularly valuable, such as the care for very young children at home by a parent. Workplace policies that simply allow the resumption by the wife of those abandoned duties, or facilitate her doing them, can be viewed as a partial return to the traditional arrangements.

Policies that provide the opportunity for part-time work are of this type, particularly if the part-time status means low pay and benefits, routine duties, and low promotion opportunities. Husbands are unlikely to take this kind of work, and the wives who do take it are cementing the inequality of their status. Maternity leaves that extend significantly beyond the time necessary to overcome the disability caused the mother by the child's birth and that are designed to allow the mother (but not the father) to engage herself in childrearing are also of this type. When the wife takes care of children, it is very common for her also to do at the same time all of the cleaning, cooking, and laundry. (This apparently happens less often when the husband shares care of children while the wife is at work.)

Workplace policies that promote greater equality can take several forms. They can allow for or encourage greater participation in family duties by the male partner. They can promote the purchase of substitutes for unpaid family labor. Reductions in work time can be given as reduced daily hours rather than as additional days of vacation. If both spouses work full time, a shorter standard working day is probably more conducive to the sharing of family duties by both partners. More days of vacation may be used by the husband to go off fishing with male companions, or the family may spend more time at a summer home, where the wife continues to do all the domestic tasks. Workplace subsidization of child care, or the siting of child care facilities at the workplace probably have an effect of promoting equality, because they relieve the family of a function usually carried on by the wife.

The requirement that leave associated with a birth (or an adoption) be shared by both spouses is potentially an important way of encouraging equality. The form usually adopted—which requires the father to take only a small part of the leave on pain of losing it—probably has little if any positive effect. In Sweden, for example, such leave is commonly used to lengthen a man's vacation (Haas 1987). However, a series of leaves in which the mother and father alternated spells that lasted several months each could provide within-family care for very young infants in a way that would promote similar duties for both parents. Financial arrangements that provided for the receipt by the couple of a constant proportion of their usual joint income, regardless of which parent was staying home at any particular moment, possibly subsidized by the state, would help to establish this pattern.

The discussion thus far has pertained largely to heterosexual couples with children. An additional concern about family-friendly policies that must be attended to is their effect on the absolute and relative status of single people, with and without children and those not in jobs, all of whom are more likely to be women than men. A reduction in hours, matched by a proportional drop in pay, may make life more difficult for lower-income female single parents. The provision by employers of health insurance and other benefits to spouses may have the effect of reducing the rewards to those without officially recognized spouses. Employer-provided benefits that cost the employer money and that require relative affluence if they are to be taken advantage of (such as subsidized holiday packages or the matching of employee pension contributions by the employer) may also penalize the relatively hard-up single mother.

In the United States, benefits to families such as health insurance, vacations, sick pay, and the like have been provided by some employers to some of their workers. The trend now is for employers to provide such benefits to a smaller proportion of their workers (those designated full time, nontemporary). In Europe, on the other hand, such benefits have tended to be provided under government auspices. The latter type of arrangement is probably in most cases preferable in promoting equality of the sexes, since those left out in the United States tend to be predominantly women.

In general, family-friendly policies, like "family values," can push us in a retrograde direction. They cannot be assumed to be benign. Policies that may help one group may hurt others. Policies that appear to make life easier for women, and that may even be welcomed by a majority of women, may cement women's inequality. The equity of such policies deserves close scrutiny.

NOTE

1. In African American families, and those of recent immigrants, in which the husband did not have good access to employment at the rate of pay standard for white men, wives did take employment.

The Role of Child Care and Parental Leave Policies in Supporting Family and Work Activities

H. Elizabeth Peters

As a society we espouse a number of goals and values that family and workplace policies are designed to address: (1) equality of opportunity, (2) supporting a viable and productive labor force, (3) a concern for the well-being of children, (4) the importance of the family, and (5) help for the deserving poor. The weight that any individual puts on each of these goals will vary, but the philosophies of both major political parties in the United States incorporate all of these goals to some degree. Because of the prevailing gender role stereotypes, workplace and family issues are closely linked for women. An important objective of a number of recent policies is to facilitate women's participation in both work and family activities. One problem in designing social policy is that a specific policy intended to address one of the goals may conflict with another of the goals. In the following pages I will describe several types of family and work policies that have been implemented in the United States or in other developed countries and assess the degree to which the policies can and do achieve the goals listed above. In particular, I will contrast child care subsidies—the primary family and work policy in the United States—with policies that allow maternity and paternity leave.

CHILD CARE POLICIES

One way for women to combine work and family responsibilities is to have child care provided by someone other than the mother. In the United States in 1991 child care expenditures for employed mothers who paid for care averaged $63 per week, or 7 percent of income. Poor families spent 27 percent of income on child care. Twenty-three percent of employed mothers with children under age 5 used a day care center as their primary mode of child care, 31 percent used family day care (that is, care in another home), 20 percent report the child's father as the primary child care provider, and 16 percent had other care provided in the child's own home

(Casper, Hawkins, and O'Connell, 1994).[1] Day care centers are regulated, although regulations regarding child-adult ratios, group size, and caregiver training vary widely across states. Only some states require that family day care providers be licensed, and there is no regulation of in-home care at all. Most European countries offer near universal child care for preschoolers (ages 3–5), but child care for younger children is less readily available.

Government child care programs can subsidize child care in a number of ways: (1) direct provision of child care services (for example, Head Start), (2) subsidies to private suppliers of child care (for example, tax exclusions for employer-provided child care), or (3) subsidies to the purchasers of child care. An example of the last category is the Child Care Tax Credit (CCTC), the largest federal child care program in the United States. For families with one child, the CCTC offers a tax credit equal to 20–30 percent of child care expenses up to $2,400 ($4,800 for families with two children or more). The credit is available, however, only to families who pay income taxes, and Robins (1989) reports that less than 1 percent of the benefits go to poor families. One notable feature of the CCTC is that it puts no restrictions on the quality of child care that is purchased, whereas child care providers who receive subsidies usually must certify that they meet at least a minimum level of quality.

Annual child care expenditures for all families in the United States with children under age 15 in 1984—net out-of-pocket family expenditures plus the cost of federal child care programs—totaled $14.9 billion (in 1988 dollars); a little more than one third of that total came from the federal government. By 1988 total expenditures had grown to $23.7 billion. Although federal child care expenditures increased by 23 percent, parental expenditures increased by much more—almost 80 percent (Family and Child Well-Being Research Network, 1995).

MATERNITY AND PARENTAL LEAVE

Most western countries provide some type of maternity leave, but the generosity of these policies ranges from one-year paid leave at a 90 percent replacement rate in Sweden[2] to twelve weeks unpaid leave in the United States. Another important difference is that some countries cover only mothers who were previously employed for a period of time (for example, Canada and Great Britain), whereas other countries provide the benefits to all mothers regardless of prior labor market status (for example, Germany and Sweden). Maternity leave for a specified number of weeks following childbirth is mandatory in a several countries including France, Sweden, and Austria. Sweden allows women to work part-time for pay and receive part-time maternity leave (Phipps 1993). The availability of paid leave for fathers is another aspect of family leave policies that differs across countries. While most assume that for health reasons the mother will leave her job for at least a few weeks, in many countries (for example, Sweden and Germany) either the mother or the father is eligible for additional paid leave. In general, however, fathers are less likely to take parental leave than are mothers. In 1987 in Sweden only 25 percent of eligible fathers took any leave (Kamerman 1991). The differing structure of family leave policies—paid versus nonpaid leave, maternity or parental, duration and generosity of benefits, eligibility requirements, and part-time availability—will affect the utilization of the program and the ability of the program to achieve the various family and work goals outlined above.

EMPLOYMENT EFFECTS

Subsidies to nonparental child care are likely to increase the participation of women with young children. Averett, Peters, and Waldman (1997) estimated the elasticity of married women's labor supply with respect to child care costs to be −.88. In contrast, paid maternity leave should decrease the employment of mothers, at least for the period during which the benefits are available. The effects of unpaid maternity leave on women's employment are still unclear.

What is the relationship between employment and equality of opportunity? Temporary replacements for women in skilled jobs may be costly and difficult to find. Therefore, employers are likely to value continuity of employment and short leaves of absence. Reliable child care available at a low cost could enable women to reenter the workplace more quickly. If the availability of paid maternity benefits caused longer absences from work, employers might be more reluctant to hire or promote women of childbearing age.

On the other hand, given the age structure of the population in most industrialized countries, employers are beginning to be faced with a shortage of younger workers. The benefits to the employer from discriminating against qualified women because of the expected cost of maternity leave will have to be balanced against the cost of having a pool of less qualified men to choose from due to increasing labor shortages. Employers who have invested in the skills of their employees have an interest in retaining the workers, even when employment is interrupted for a short period owing to childbirth. Although some women will prefer to stay at home with their children for a longer period of time—even with no pay and job search costs when they return—others will be willing to return to their jobs more quickly. Because of declining marginal productivity (or marginal utility) of spending time at home with the children, the availability of part-time work could speed up a mother's return to the workforce.

FAMILY AND CHILDREN

A concern for the health of mothers and infants underlies most pregnancy and maternity leave policies, but that motivation alone would dictate fairly short leaves, on the order of twelve weeks. An additional implicit motivation for a more extensive leave policy is the idea that parental care is "better" than nonparental care and that allowing mothers to stay home with their children would strengthen the family. Another argument is that family leave would increase a mother's choice set: She would be able to choose whether to work in the market or provide care for her children. Most research has found no evidence that a mother's employment is harmful to children over age 1. For infants the evidence is mixed; some studies have found negative effects on children when the mother works full time during the first year, while other studies have found no effects of mother's employment. In addition, it is possible that high-quality child care may have beneficial effects on the development of children who come from economically disadvantaged families.

Welfare programs were originally designed to allow poor mothers of young children to be able to stay home and care for those children. As employment of mothers in the general population increased dramatically over time, the American public's tolerance for subsidizing welfare mothers to stay home diminished. The welfare reform bill passed by the United States Congress in 1996 requires that the recipient be in a job-training program or have a job after a certain duration of welfare receipt. The bill also recognizes the need for low-cost child care to enable mothers to enter and remain in the labor force.

WHO SHOULD PAY?

Children are a national resource, and a highly educated and civically responsible population provides many positive externalities. This argument has been explicitly recognized in policies that provide universal and free public education to children aged 5–18. In the United States the argument has been largely ignored when it comes to the cost of child care for younger children. Families, and especially women, have borne the primary cost of the rearing of their young children. The cost is paid in the form of lower earnings, a shorter work life, and reduced access to high-powered jobs.

NOTES

1. The remainder cared for their child at work or the child was already in school.

2. An additional three months of paid leave is available with a smaller benefit. Note that this leave may be taken anytime before the child's eighth birthday.

References

Addison, John T., and Pedro Portugal. 1992. "Advance Notice and Unemployment: New Evidence from the 1988 Displaced Worker Survey." Industrial and Labor Relations Review 45(4): 645–664.

Addison, John T., and W. Stanley Siebert. 1993. Social Engineering in the European Community. The Social Charter, Maastricht and Beyond. Current Controversies, no. 6. London: Institute of Economic Affairs.

Aghion, Phillipe, and Benjamin Hermalin. 1990. "Legal Restrictions on Private Contracts Can Enhance Efficiency." Journal of Law, Economics, and Organization 6(2): 381–409.

Akerlof, George. 1976. "The Economics of Caste and of the Rat Race and Other Woeful Tales." Quarterly Journal of Economics 90: 599–617.

Akerlof, George A., and William T. Dickens. 1982. "The Economic Consequences of Cognitive Dissonance." American Economic Review 72(3): 307–319.

American Bar Association, Young Lawyers Division. 1990. The State of the Legal Profession. Chicago: American Bar Association.

Arrow, Kenneth J. 1985. "Some Mathematical Models of Race Discrimination in the Labor Market." In Collected Papers of Kenneth J. Arrow, vol. 6. Cambridge, MA: Belknap Press.

Averett, Susan L., H. Elizabeth Peters, and Donald M. Waldman. 1997. "Tax Credits, Labor Supply and Child Care." Review of Economics and Statistics 79(1).

Babbitt, Kathleen. 1995. "Producers and Consumers: Women of the Countryside and Cooperative Extension Service Home Economists, New York State, 1870–1935." Ph.D. diss., State University of New York, Binghamton.

Baker, George, Michael Gibbs, and Bengt Holmstrom. 1994. "The Internal Economics of the Firm: Evidence from Personnel Data." Quarterly Journal of Economics 91(4): 881–919.

Baldwin, Marjorie L., Richard J. Butler, and William G. Johnson. 1993. "A Hierarchical Theory of Occupational Segregation and Wage Discrimination." East Carolina University. Mimeo.

Becker, Gary S. 1971. The Economics of Discrimination. 2nd ed. Chicago: University of Chicago Press.

———. 1975. Human Capital. 2nd ed. Chicago: University of Chicago Press.

Belsky, J. 1988. "The Effects of Infant Day Care Reconsidered." Early Childhood Research Quarterly 3: 235–272.

Benham, Lee. 1974. "Benefits of Women's Education within Marriage." Journal of Political Economy 82(2, part II): S57–S72.

Bergmann, Barbara R. 1974. "Occupational Segregation, Wages and Profits When Employers Discriminate by Race or Sex." Eastern Economic Journal 1(1–2): 103–110.

———. 1986. The Economic Emergence of Women. New York: Basic Books.

Blank, Rebecca, and Richard Freeman. 1994. "Evaluating the Connection Between Social Protection and Economic Flexibility." In Social Protection Vs. Economic Flexibility, edited by Rebecca Blank. Chicago: University of Chicago Press.

Blau, Francine D. 1977. Equal Pay in the Office. Lexington, MA: Heath.

Blau, Francine D., and Marianne A. Ferber. 1992. The Economics of Women, Men, and Work. 2nd ed. Englewood Cliffs, NJ: Prentice-Hall.

Blau, Francine D., Marianne A. Ferber, and Anne E. Winkler. Forthcoming. The Economics of Women, Men, and Work. 3rd ed. Englewood Cliffs, NJ: Prentice-Hall.

Blau, Francine D., and Lawrence M. Kahn. 1981. "Race and Sex Differences in Quits by Young Workers." Industrial and Labor Relations Review 34(4): 563–577.

———. 1992. "The Gender Earnings Gap: Learning from Some International Comparisons." American Economic Review 82 (May): 533–538.

———. 1994. "Rising Wage Inequality and the U.S. Gender Gap." American Economic Review 84(May): 23–28.

———. 1996. "Gender and Youth Employment Outcomes: The U.S. and West Germany, 1984–91." Working Paper. Cornell University, September.

Bookman, Ann. 1991. "Parenting Without Poverty: The Case for Funded Parental Leave." In Parental Leave and Child Care, edited by Janet Hyde and Marilyn Essex. Philadelphia: Temple University Press.

Bravo, Ellen. 1991. "Family Leave: The Need for a New Minimum Standard." In Parental Leave and Child Care, edited by Janet Hyde and Marilyn Essex. Philadelphia: Temple University Press.

Brazelton, T. Berry. 1986. "Issues for Working Parents." American Journal of Orthopsychiatry 56(1): 14–25.

Bretz, Robert D., Jr., George T. Milkovich, and Walter Read. 1990. "Comparing the Performance Appraisal Practices in Large Firms with the Directions in Research Literature: Learning More and More about Less and Less." Working Paper No. 89-17. Center for Advanced Human Resource Studies, Cornell University, Ithaca, NY.

Brocas, Anne-Marie, Anne-Marie Cailloux, and Virginie Oget. 1990. Women and Social Security: Progress Towards Equality of Treatment. Geneva: International Labour Office.

Cannings, Kathy, and Claude Montmarquette. 1991. "The Attitudes of Subordinates to the Gender of Superiors in a Managerial Hierarchy." Journal of Economic Psychology 12(4): 707–724.

Card, David. 1992. "Using Regional Variation in Wages to Measure the Effects of the Federal Minimum Wage." Industrial and Labor Relations Review 46(1): 22–37.

Carnegie Task Force on Meeting the Needs of Young Children. 1994. Starting Points: Meeting the Needs of Young Children. New York: Carnegie Corporation of New York.

Casper, Lynne M., Mary Hawkins, and Martin O'Connell. 1994. "Who's Minding the Kids? Child Care Arrangements: Fall 1991." Current Population Reports, series P70-36. Washington, DC: U.S. Government Printing Office.

Caughy, Margaret, J. DiPietro, and D. Strobino. 1994. "Day-Care Participation as a Protective Factor in the Cognitive Development of Low-Income Children." Child Development 65: 457–471.

Clarke-Stewart, K. A. 1991. "A Home Is Not a School: The Effects of Child Care on Children's Development." Journal of Social Issues 47(2): 105–123.

Coleman Mary T., and John Pencavel. 1993a. "Trends in the Market Work Behavior of Women Since 1940." Industrial and Labor Relations Review 46(4): 653–676.

———. 1993b. "Changes in the Work Hours of Male Employees Since 1940." Industrial and Labor Relations Review 46(2): 653–676.

Commission of the European Communities. 1990. Employment in Europe 1990. Belgium: Office for Official Publications of the European Communities.

Cookingham, Mary E. 1984. "Bluestockings, Spinsters and Pedagogues: Women College Graduates, 1865–1910." Population Studies 38: 349–364.

Corcoran, Mary, and Greg J. Duncan. 1979. "Work History, Labor Force Attachment, and Earnings Differences Between Races and Sexes." Journal of Human Resources 14: 3–20.

Dalto, Guy C. 1989. "A Structural Approach to Women's Hometime and Experience-Earnings Profiles: Maternity Leave and Public Policy." Population Research and Policy Review 8(3): 247–266.

Decker, Linda. 1991. "Keeping Mum." Pensions and Employee Benefits 13(6): 17–19.

Ehrenberg, Ronald, and George Jakubson. 1988. Advance Notice Provisions in Plant Closing Legislation. Kalamazoo, MI: W.E. Upjohn Institute for Employment Research.

Employee Benefits Research Institute. 1995. EBRI Databook on Employee Benefits. 3rd ed. Washington, DC: Employee Benefits Research Institute.

England, Paula, and Barbara Kilbourne. 1989. "Markets, Marriages, and Other Mates: The Problem of Power." In Beyond the Marketplace: Rethinking Economy and Society, edited by Roger Friedland and A. F. Robertson. New York: Aldine de Gruyter.

Family and Child Well-Being Research Network. 1995. New Social Indicators of Child Well-Being. Vienna, Austria: European Centre.

Farber, Henry S. 1994. "The Analysis of Interfirm Worker Mobility." Journal of Labor Economics 12(4): 554–593.

Farrell, Joseph, and Suzanne Scotchmer. 1988. "Partnerships." Quarterly Journal of Economics 103(2): 279–298.

Ferber, Marianne A., and Carole A. Green. 1991. "Occupational Segregation and the Earnings Gap: Further Evidence." In Essays on the Economics of Discrimination, edited by Emily P. Hoffman. Kalamazoo, MI: W.E. Upjohn Institute for Employment Research.

Ferber, Marianne A., Carole A. Green, and Joe L. Spaeth. 1986. "Work Power and Earnings of Women and Men." American Economic Review 76(2): 53–56.

Ferber, Marianne A., Joan Huber, and Glenna Spitze. 1979. "Preference for Men as Bosses and Professionals." Social Forces 58(2): 466–476.

Ferber, Marianne A., and Joe L. Spaeth. 1984. "Work Characteristics and the Male-Female Earnings Gap." American Economic Review 74(2): 260–264.

Fiske, Susan T., and Shelley E. Taylor. 1991. Social Cognition. 2nd ed. New York: McGraw-Hill.

Foster Higgins. 1993. *Spotlight*. February 17.

Frank, Meryl, and Robyn Lipner. 1988. "History of Maternity Leave in Europe and the United States." In The Parental Leave Crisis Toward a National Policy, edited by Edward F. Zigler and Meryl Frank. New Haven: Yale University Press.

Frank, Robert H. 1985. Choosing the Right Pond: Human Behavior and the Quest for Status. New York: Oxford University Press.

Freeman, Richard B. 1977. The Overeducated American. New York: Academic Press.

French, Howard W. 1989. "In Overhaul of Hospital Rules New York Slashes Intern Hours." New York Times, July 3, 1989, p. 1, col. 3.

Friedan, Betty. 1963. The Feminine Mystique. New York: Norton.

Galanter, Marc, and Thomas Palay. 1991. Tournament of Lawyers: The Transformation of the Big Law Firm. Chicago: University of Chicago Press.

Garrett, Patricia, Sally Lubeck, and DeeAnn Wenk. 1991. "Childbirth and Maternal Employment: Data from a National Longitudinal Survey." In Parental Leave and Child Care, edited by Janet Hyde and Marilyn Essex. Philadelphia: Temple University Press.

Gill, Richard T. 1991. "Day Care or Parental Care." Public Interest, pp. 3–16.

Gilliand, Pierre. 1989. "Evolution of Family Policy in the Light of Demographic Development in West European Countries." International Social Security Review 42(4): 395–426.

Gilson, Ronald, and Robert Mnookin. 1985. "Sharing Among the Human Capitalists: An Economic Inquiry into the Corporate Law Firm and How Partners Split Profits." Stanford Law Review 37: 313–392.

———. 1989. "Coming of Age in a Corporate Law Firm: The Economics of Associate Career Paths." Stanford Law Review 41: 567–595.

Glass Ceiling Commission. 1995. "A Solid Investment: Making Full Use of the Nation's Human Capital." Recommendations of the Glass Ceiling Commission. Washington, DC: U.S. Government Printing Office, November.

Goldin, Claudia. 1986. "Monitoring Costs and Occupational Segregation by Sex: A Historical Analysis." Journal of Labor Economics 4(1): 1–27.

———. 1989. "Coming of Age in a Corporate Law Firm: The Economics of Associate Career Paths." Stanford Law Review 41: 567–595.

———. 1990. Understanding the Gender Gap: An Economic History of American Women. New York: Oxford University Press.

———. 1991. "Marriage Bars: Discrimination Against Married Women Workers, 1920 to 1950." In Favorites of Fortune: Technology, Growth, and Economic Development Since the Industrial Revolution, edited by H. Rosovsky, D. Landes, and P. Higgonet. Cambridge, MA: Harvard University Press.

———. 1992. "The Meaning of College in the Lives of American Women: The Past Hundred Years." National Bureau of Economic Research Working Paper No. 4099.

———. 1994. "How America Graduated from High School: 1910 to 1960." National Bureau of Economic Research Working Paper No. 4762.

Greene, William H. 1993. Econometric Analysis. 2nd ed. New York: Macmillan.

Groshen, Erica L. 1990. "The Structure of the Female/Male Wage Differential: Is It Who You Are, What You Do, or Where You Work?" Journal of Human Resources 26(3): 457–472.

Groshen, Erica L., and Alan B. Krueger. 1990. "The Structure of Supervision and Pay in Hospitals." Industrial and Labor Relations Review 43(3): 134-S–146-S.

Gruber, Jonathan. 1994. "The Incidence of Mandated Maternity Benefits: Evidence from Health Insurance Benefits for Maternity." American Economic Review 84(3): 622–641.

Gruber, Jonathan, and Alan Krueger. 1991. "The Incidence of Mandated Employer-Provided Insurance: Lessons from Workers' Compensation Insurance." In Tax Policy and the Economy, edited by David Bradford. Cambridge, MA: Massachusetts Institute of Technology Press.

Haas, Linda. 1987. "Fathers' Participation in Parental Leave." Social Change in Sweden. No 37.

Hashimoto, Masanori. 1981. "Firm-Specific Human Capital as a Shared Investment." American Economic Review 71(3): 475–482.

Hayes, Cheryl D., John L. Palmer, and Martha Zaslow. 1990. Who Cares for America's Children? Child Care Policy for the 1990's. National Research Council. Washington, DC: National Academy Press.

Helitzer, Jack B. 1990. "State Developments in Employee Benefits: Parental Leave." Benefits Law Journal 3: 121–130.

Hill, Anne, and June O'Neill. 1994. "Family Endowments and the Achievement of Young Children with Special Reference to the Underclass." Journal of Human Resources 29(4): 1064–100.

Hochschild, Arlie Russell and Anne Machung. 1989. The Second Shift: Working Parents and the Revolution at Home. New York: Viking.

Hood, Jane C., ed. 1993. Men, Work, and Family. Newbury Park, CA: Sage.

Hunt, David Marshall, and Carol Michael. 1983. "Mentorship: A Career Training and Development Tool." Academy of Management Review 8(3): 475–485.

Hyland, Stephanie. 1990. "Helping Employees with Family Care." Monthly Labor Review 113 (September): 22–26.

International Labour Office. 1984. "Protection of Working Mothers: An ILO Global Survey (1964–84)." Women at Work 2. Geneva: International Labour Office Publications.

———. Various years. Legislative Series. Geneva: International Labour Office Publications.

Jacobsen, Joyce, and Laurence Levin. 1992. "The Effects of Intermittent Labor Force Attachment on Women's Earnings." Monthly Labor Review 118 (September): 14–19.

Johnson, Nancy Brown, and Terri A. Scandura. 1994. "The Effect of Mentorship and Sex-Role Style on Male-Female Earnings." Industrial Relations 33(2): 263–274.

Joshi, Heather, Pierella Paci, and Jane Waldfogel. 1996. "The Wages of Motherhood: Better or Worse?" Discussion Paper, Suntory and Toyota International Centres for Economics and Related Disciplines, London School of Economics.

Juster, Thomas F., and Frank P. Stafford. 1991. "The Allocation of Time: Empirical Findings, Behavioral Models, and the Problems of Measurement." Journal of Economic Literature 29(2): 471–522.

Kahn, Shulamit, and Kevin Lang. 1991. "The Effects of Hours Constraints on Labor Supply Estimates." Review of Economics and Statistics 73(4): 605–611.

Kamerman, Sheila B. 1988. "Maternity and Parenting Benefits: An International Overview." In The Parental Leave Crisis: Toward a National Policy, edited by Edward F. Zigler and Meryl Frank. New Haven: Yale University Press.

———. 1991a. "Child Care Policies and Programs: An International Overview." Journal of Social Issues 47(2): 179–196.

———. 1991b. "Parental Leave and Infant Care: U.S. and International Trends and Issues, 1978–1988." In Parental Leave and Child Care, edited by Janet Hyde and Marilyn Essex. Philadelphia: Temple University Press.

Kamerman, Sheila B., and Alfred Kahn, eds. 1991. Child Care and the Under-3s: Policy Innovation in Europe. Westport, CT: Auburn House.

Kamerman, Sheila B., and Alfred Kahn. 1995. Starting Right: How America Neglects Its Youngest Children and What We Can Do About It. New York: Oxford University Press.

Kamerman, Sheila, B., Alfred Kahn, and Paul Kingston. 1983. Maternity Policies and Working Women. New York: Columbia University Press.

Kaplan, Gisela. 1992. Contemporary Western European Feminism. New York: New York University Press.

Katz, L., and K. M. Murphy. 1992. "Changes in Relative Wages, 1963–1987: Supply and Demand Factors." Quarterly Journal of Economics 107(1): 35–78.

Klerman, Jacob Alex. 1995. "Characterizing Leave for Maternity." Labor and Population Program Working Paper No. 93-34, Santa Monica, CA: RAND.

Klerman, Jacob Alex, and Arleen Leibowitz. 1994. "The Work-Employment Distinction Among New Mothers." Journal of Human Resources 29(2): 277–303.

———. 1995. "Labor Supply Effects of State Maternity Leave Legislation." Mimeo.

Korenman, Sanders, and David Neumark. 1991. "Does Marriage Really Make Men More Productive?" Journal of Human Resources 26(Spring): 282–307.

———. 1992. "Marriage, Motherhood, and Wages." Journal of Human Resources 27(Spring): 233–235.

Krueger, Alan B. 1994. "Observations on Employment-Based Government Mandates, with Particular Reference to Health Insurance." Working Paper No. 323. Industrial Relations Section, Princeton University.

Kuhn, Peter. 1992. "Mandatory Notice." Journal of Labor Economics 10(2): 117–137.

Laband, David, and Bernard Lentz. 1995. "Workplace Mentoring in the Legal Profession." Southern Economic Journal 61(3): 783–802.

Landers, Renee M., James B. Rebitzer, and Lowell J. Taylor. 1996. "Rat Race Redux: Adverse Selection in the Determination of Work Hours." American Economic Review 86(3).

———. Forthcoming. "Human Resource Practices and the Demographic Transformation of Professional Labor Markets." In Broken Ladders: Managerial Careers in the New Economy, edited by Paul Osterman. New York: Oxford University Press.

Lang, Kevin. 1986. "A Language Theory of Discrimination." Quarterly Journal of Economics 101: 363–382.

Lang, Kevin, and Peter-John Gordon. 1995. "Partnerships as Insurance Devices: Theory and Evidence." Rand Journal of Economics 26(4): 614–29.

Lazear, Edward P. 1990. "Job Security Provisions and Employment." Quarterly Journal of Economics 55(3): 699–726.

Lazear, Edward P., and Sherwin Rosen. 1990. "Male-Female Wage Differentials in Job Ladders." Journal of Labor Economics 8(1): S106–S123.

Leete-Guy, Laura, and Juliet Schor. 1994. "Assessing the Time Squeeze Hypothesis: Estimates of Market and Non-Market Hours in the United States, 1969–1987." Industrial Relations 33(1): 25–44.

Leibowitz, Arleen, and Jacob Alex Klerman. 1995. "Explaining Changes in Married Mothers' Employment Over Time." Demography 32(3): 365–378.

Leonard, Jonathan. 1987. "Carrots and Sticks: Pay, Supervision, and Turnover." Journal of Labor Economics 5(4): S136–S152.

Levine, David I. 1991. "Just-Cause Employment Policies in the Presence of Worker Adverse Selection." Journal of Labor Economics 9(3): 294–305.

Lynch, Lisa M. 1992. "Private-Sector Training and the Earnings of Young Workers." American Economic Review 82(1): 299–312.

Machung, Anne. 1989. "Talking Career, Thinking Job: Gender Differences in Career and Family Expectations of Berkeley Seniors." Feminist Studies 15(1).

Maddala, G. S. 1983. Limited-Dependent and Qualitative Variables in Econometrics. New York: Cambridge University Press.

McGuire, Thomas G., and Christopher J. Ruhm. 1993. "Workplace Drug Abuse Policy." Journal of Health Economics 12(1): 19–38.

Mitchell, Olivia. 1990. "The Effect of Mandatory Benefit Packages." In Research in Labor Economics, vol. 11, edited by L. Bassi, D. Crawford, and R. Ehrenberg. Greenwich, CT: JAI Press.

Moeller, Robert G. 1993. Protecting Motherhood: Women and the Family in the Politics of Postwar West Germany. Berkeley, CA: University of California Press.

Moffitt, Robert. 1990. "The Effect of the U.S. Welfare System on Marital Status." Journal of Public Economics 41: 101–124.

Moffitt, Robert, and Peter Gottschalk. 1993. "Trends in the Covariance Structure of Earnings in the U.S.: 1969–1987." Unpublished paper.

Neumark, David, and Sanders Korenman. 1994. "Sources of Bias in Women's Wage Equations: Results Using Sibling Data." Journal of Human Resources 29(Spring): 379–405.

Newcomer, Mabel. 1959. A Century of Higher Education for American Women. New York: Harper.

Nickell, Stephen. 1981. "Biases in Dynamic Models with Fixed-Effects." Econometrica 49(6): 1417–426.

O'Connell, Martin. 1990. "Maternity Leave Arrangements: 1961–1985," Work and Family Patterns of American Women. Current Population Reports, P–23 No. 165. Washington, DC: U.S. Government Printing Office for U.S. Bureau of the Census.

O'Neill, June, and Solomon Polachek. 1993. "An Analysis of Recent Trends in the Male-Female Wage Gap." Journal of Labor Economics 11(January): 205–228.

Organization for Economic Cooperation and Development. 1989. Main Aggregates 1960–1987. National Accounts, vol. 1. Paris: OECD Department of Economics and Statistics.

———. 1995. "Long-Term Leave for Parents in OECD Countries." Mimeo.

———. Various years. Labour Force Statistics: 1957–1968, 1960–1971, 1962–1982, 1966–1986, 1968–1988. Paris: OECD, Department of Economics and Statistics.

Parsons, Donald O. 1985. Wage Determination in the Post-Schooling Period: The Market for On-the-Job Training. Pathways to the Future, vol. 6, edited by

R. D'Amico et al. Columbus: Center for Human Resource Research, Ohio State University.

———. 1990. "The Firm's Decision to Train." In Research in Labor Economics, vol. 11, edited by L. Bassi, D. Crawford, and R. Ehrenberg. Greenwich, CT: JAI Press.

Pencavel, John. 1986. "Labor Supply of Men: A Survey." In Handbook of Labor Economics, edited by Orley Ashenfelter and Richard Layard. Amsterdam: North-Holland.

Phipps, Shelley A. 1993. "International Perspectives on Income Support for Families with Children." Luxembourg Income Study Working Paper Series No. 103.

Pleck, Joseph. 1990. "Family Supportive Employee Policies and Men's Participation." Paper presented to the Panel on Employer Policies and Working Families, Committee on Women's Employment and Related Social Issues, Commission on Behavioral and Social Sciences and Education, National Research Council, Washington, DC.

Polachek, S. 1981. "Occupational Self-Selection: A Human Capital Approach to Sex Differences in Occupational Structure." Review of Economics and Statistics 63: 60–69.

———. 1987. "Occupational Segregation and the Gender Gap." Population Research and Policy Review 47–67.

President's Task Force of Women's Rights and Responsibilities. 1970. A Matter of Simple Justice. Task Force Report. Washington, DC: U.S. Government Printing Office, April.

Ragan, James F., Jr., and Carol Horton Tremblay. 1988. "Testing for Employee Discrimination by Race and Sex." Journal of Human Resources 23(1): 123–137.

Rebitzer, James B., and Lowell J. Taylor. 1995a. "Do Labor Markets Provide Enough Short-Hour Jobs? An Analysis of Work Hours and Work Incentives." Economic Inquiry 32(2): 257–273.

———. 1995b. "Efficiency Wages and Employment Rents: The Employer Size Wage Effect in the Job Market for Lawyers." Journal of Labor Economics 13(4): 678–708.

———. 1996. "When Knowledge Is an Asset: An Economic Analysis of the Organization of Large Law Firms." M.I.T Working Paper.

Reed, W. Robert, and Julie Dahlquist. 1994. "Do Women Prefer Women's Work?" Applied Economics 26: 1133–144.

Reskin, Barbara F., and Heidi Hartmann. 1986. Women's Work, Men's Work: Sex Segregation on the Job. Washington, DC: National Academy Press.

Reskin, Barbara F., and Patricia A. Roos. 1990. "Explaining the Changing Sex Composition of Occupations." In Explaining Job Queues, Gender Queues: Explaining Women's Inroads into Male Occupations, edited by Barbara F. Reskin and Patricia A. Roos. Philadelphia: Temple University Press.

Robins, Philip K. 1989. "Federal Financing of Child Care: Alternative Approaches and Economic Implications." Institute for Research on Poverty Discussion Paper No. 890-89.

Rosen, Sherwin. 1992. "The Market for Lawyers." Journal of Law and Economics 35(2): 215–246.

Rossiter, Margaret. 1982. Women Scientists in America: Struggle and Strategies to 1940. Baltimore: Johns Hopkins University Press.

Rothschild, M., and J. Stiglitz. 1976. "Equilibrium in Competitive Insurance Markets: An Essay on the Economics of Imperfect Information." Quarterly Journal of Economics 80: 629–649.

Ruhm, Christopher J. 1992. "Advance Notice and Postdisplacement Joblessness." Journal of Labor Economics 10(1): 1–32.

———. 1994. "Advance Notice, Job Search, and Postdisplacement Earnings." Journal of Labor Economics 12(1): 1–28.

Shapiro, David, and Frank Mott. 1994. "Long-Term Employment and Earnings of Women in Relation to Employment Behavior Surrounding the First Birth." Journal of Human Resources 29(2): 248–275.

Shinn, Millicent Washburn. 1895. "The Marriage Rate of College Women." Century Magazine 50 (October): 946–948.

Sims, Christopher A. 1972. "Money, Income, and Causality." American Economic Review 62(4): 540–552.

Singell, Larry D., Jr., Jane H. Lillydahl, and Larry D. Singell, Sr. Forthcoming. "Will Changing Times Change the Allocation of Faculty Time?" Journal of Human Resources.

Smith, Ralph E. 1979. "The Movement of Women into the Labor Force." In The Subtle Revolution: Women at Work, edited by Ralph E. Smith. Washington, DC: The Urban Institute.

Social Security Administration. Social Security Programs Throughout the World. Various years. Washington, DC: U.S. Government Printing Office.

Solomon, Barbara Miller. 1985. In the Company of Educated Women. New Haven: Yale University Press.

Sorensen, Elaine. 1989. "Measuring the Pay Disparity Between Typically Female Occupations and Other Jobs: A Bivariate Selectivity Approach." Industrial and Labor Relations Review 42(4): 624–639.

Spalter-Roth, Roberta M., and Heidi I. Hartmann. 1990. Unnecessary Losses: Costs to Americans of the Lack of Family and Medical Leave. Washington, DC: Institute for Women's Policy Research.

Statistics Canada. 1985. "The Survey on Work Reduction: Microdata Documentation and Users Guide." Ontario, Canada: Statistics Canada.

Stoiber, Susanne A. 1990. "Family Leave Entitlements in Europe: Lessons for the United States." Compensation and Benefits Management 6(2): 111–116.

Strober, Myra H., and Agnes Miling Kaneko Chan. 1996. "The Road Winds Uphill All the Way: Gender, Income, and Income Aspirations for the Graduates of Stanford University and Todai University, Classes of 1981." Paper prepared for the annual meetings of the American Economic Association, San Francisco, January 3–5.

Strumberg, Robert, Janice Steinschneider, and George Elser. N.D. "State Legislative Source Book on Family and Medical Leave." Washington, DC: Center for Policy Alternatives.

Summers, Lawrence. 1989. "Some Simple Economics of Mandated Benefits." American Economic Review 79(2): 177–183.

Swaim, Paul, and Michael Podgursky. 1990. "Advance Notice and Job Search: The Value of an Early Start." Journal of Human Resources 25(2): 147–178.

Tannen, Deborah. 1994. Talking from 9 to 5: How Women's and Men's Conversational Styles Affect Who Gets Heard, Who Gets Credit, and What Gets Done at Work. New York: Morrow.

Trzcinski, Eileen. 1991. "Employers' Parental Leave Policies: Does the Labor Market Provide Parental Leave?" In Parental Leave and Child Care, edited by Janet Hyde and Marilyn Essex. Philadelphia: Temple University Press.

Trzcinski, Eileen, and William T. Alpert. 1994. "Pregnancy and Parental Leave in the United States and Canada." Journal of Human Resources 29(2): 535–554.

U.S. Bureau of the Census. 1953. Census of Population: 1950, vol. 4, Special Reports, part 5, chapter B, Education. Washington, DC: U.S. Government Printing Office.

———. 1955. Census of Population: 1950, vol. 4, Special Reports, part 5, chapter C, Fertility. Washington, DC: U.S. Government Printing Office.

———. 1964. Census of Population: 1960. Subject Reports. Women by Number of Children Ever Born. Final Report PC(2)-3A. Washington, DC: U.S. Government Printing Office.

———. 1966. Census of Population: 1960. Subject Reports. Age at First Marriage. Final Report PC(2)-4. Washington, DC: U.S. Government Printing Office.

———. 1972. Census of Population: 1970. Subject Reports. Marital Status. Final Report PC(2)-4C. Washington, DC: U.S. Government Printing Office.

———. 1973. Census of Population: 1970. Subject Reports. Women by Number of Children Ever Born. Final Report PC(2)-3A. Washington, DC: U.S. Government Printing Office.

———. 1983. 1980 Census of Population. "Detailed Occupation and Years of School Completed by Age for the Civilian Labor Force by Sex, Race, and Spanish Origin: 1980." Series PC80-S1-8. Washington, DC: U.S. Government Printing Office.

———. 1985. Census of Population: 1980. Subject Reports. Marital Characteristics. Final Report PC80-2-4C. Washington, DC: U.S. Government Printing Office.

———. 1989. "The Relationship Between the 1970 and 1980 Industry and Occupation Classification Systems." Technical Paper No. 59. Washington, DC: U.S. Government Printing Office.

———. 1992. Current Population Reports, series P-20 no. 470. "Fertility of American Women: June 1992." Washington, DC: U.S. Government Printing Office.

———. Various years. Current Population Reports, series P-20, various numbers. "Educational Attainment in the United States." Washington, DC: U.S. Government Printing Office.

———. Various years. Current Population Reports, series P-20, various numbers. "Fertility of American Women." Washington, DC: U.S. Government Printing Office.

U.S. Bureau of Education. Various years. Biennial Survey of Education. Washington, DC: U.S. Government Printing Office.

U.S. Department of Education. Various years. Biennial Survey of Education. Washington, DC: U.S. Government Printing Office.

U.S. Department of Health, Education, and Welfare, Office of Education. 1960. Higher Education Planning and Management Data, 1959–60. Circular No. 614. Washington, DC: U.S. Government Printing Office.

———. Various years. Biennial Survey of Education. Washington, DC: U.S. Government Printing Office.

U.S. Department of Health, Education, and Welfare, and U.S. Department of Education. Various years. OFE. Opening (Fall) Enrollment in Higher Education. Washington, DC: U.S. Government Printing Office.

———. Various years, Digest: Digest of Education Statistics, Washington, DC: U.S. Government Printing Office.

U.S. Department of Labor, Bureau of Labor Statistics. 1988. Employee Benefits in Medium and Large Firms. Bulletin No. 2336. Washington, DC: U.S. Government Printing Office.

———. 1989. Employee Benefits in Medium and Large Firms. Bulletin No. 2363. Washington, DC: U.S. Government Printing Office.

———. 1991. Employee Benefits in Medium and Large Private Establishments. Bulletin No. 2422. Washington, DC: U.S. Government Printing Office.

———. 1993. Employee Benefits in Medium and Large Firms. Bulletin No. 2456. Washington, DC: U.S. Government Printing Office.

———. 1993. Employee Benefits in Medium and Large Private Establishments. Bulletin No. 2422. Washington, DC: U.S. Government Printing Office.

———. 1993. "Work and Family: Changes in Wages and Benefits Among Young Adults." U.S. Department of Labor Report No. 849.

———. 1994. Employee Benefits in Small Private Establishments. Bulletin No. 2441. Washington, DC: U.S. Government Printing Office.

Van Kleeck, Mary. 1918. "A Census of College Women." Journal of the Association of Collegiate Alumnae 11(9): 557–591.

Waldfogel, Jane. 1994a. "Women Working for Less: Family Status and Women's Pay in the US and UK." Malcolm Wiener Center for Social Policy, Working Paper No. D-94-1. Harvard University.

———. 1995. "The Price of Motherhood: Family Status and Women's Pay in a Young British Cohort." Oxford Economic Papers 47(October): 584–610.

———. 1996. "Impacts of the Family and Medical Leave Act." Columbia University. Mimeo.

———. 1997. "The Effect of Children on Women's Wages." American Sociological Review 62:209–217.

———. Forthcoming. "The Family Gap for Young Women in the U.S. and Britain: Can Maternity Leave Make a Difference?" Journal of Labor Economics.

Wellington, Allison J. 1994. "Accounting for the Male/Female Wage Gap Among Whites: 1976 and 1985." American Sociological Review 59: 839–848.

Women's Legal Defense Fund. 1992. "Family and Medical Leave Legislation in the States." Memo "as of July 1."

Woo, Junda. 1992. "Climb to Top Is Steeper at Big Law Firms." Wall Street Journal. June 15, p. B8.

Wood, Robert, Mary Corcoran, and Paul Courant. 1993. "Pay Differentials Among the Highly-Paid: The Male-Female Earnings Gap in Lawyers' Salaries." Journal of Labor Economics 11(July): 417–441.

Woody, Thomas. 1929. A History of Women's Education in the United States. Vol. 2. New York: The Science Press.

Worton, Barbara. 1996. "Women at Work." Fortune, March 4.

Zigler, Edward F., Meryl Frank, and Barbara Emmel. 1988. "Introduction." In The Parental Leave Crisis: Toward a National Policy, edited by Edward F. Zigler, and Meryl Frank. New Haven: Yale University Press.

Index